EDUCATION FOR SUSTAINABLE DEVELOPMENT

How to Integrate in School Education

JUBILEE PADMANABHAN

ATLANTIC
PUBLISHERS & DISTRIBUTORS (P) LTD

ATLANTIC
PUBLISHERS & DISTRIBUTORS (P) LTD
7/22, Ansari Road, Darya Ganj, New Delhi
Tel.: +91-11-4077 5252, 2327 3880
E-mail: orders@atlanticbooks.com
Web: www.atlanticbooks.com

Reprint 2021, 2026

Published by Atlantic Publishers & Distributors (P) Ltd.

Printed & bound in India by Atlantic Print Services

Preface

Sustainable development is one of the most discussed issues nowadays, which is gaining priority day by day due to the exploitation of nature in a drastic way. It is from this apprehension that 'education for sustainable development' (ESD) emerged with an immediate urge to preserve and conserve our nature and natural resources. The concept of education for sustainable development entangles different nations and the world as a whole for a sustainable society, which merges the environment, and economic and social dimensions.

The present book entitled *Education for Sustainable Development: How to Integrate in School Education* contains the materials and modules developed as a part of my research work for doctoral degree. It is an attempt to integrate the concepts of ESD into the existing curriculum followed by adopting various strategies and activities to transact the same in the course of study. A curriculum was developed by integrating the concepts of sustainable development into science and social science of VII standard of NCERT syllabus and designing various pedagogical strategies. The contents and activities developed were validated with the help of experts as well as piloted before conducting the real study. The study was conducted for a period of one year whereby the experimental group was taught using the integrated ESD approach and the control group followed a traditional approach. The findings revealed that the integrated approach to ESD has helped in increasing awareness, critical thinking, problem-solving and participatory behaviour towards sustainable development (SD). It was found that the integrated approach to education for SD was effective in improving the knowledge, critical thinking and problem-solving on sustainable development among upper primary school students. There was no significant difference in knowledge, critical thinking, problem-solving and value preference on SD among upper primary male and female students. There was no significant difference between the value preference on SD of students in the experimental and control group. There was a significant difference in critical thinking and problem-solving of high, average and low knowledge students of experimental group. It was found that majority of the students in the experimental group had a good participation and performance skills to do activities that lead towards SD. Hence, the contents and strategies given in the book are practiced in real classroom situations and the effectiveness was also studied.

The book will be useful for all those concerned with the framing of curriculum on SD at upper primary level.

Jubilee Padmanabhan

Acknowledgements

I acknowledge my profound gratitude to my guide Dr. Manjula P. Rao, Professor in Education, Regional Institute of Education (NCERT), Mysore for her constant guidance, inspiring encouragement, involvement and support, compounded with her typical interest in every aspect of the study, without which this research could not have been possible. I am thankful to Dr. M.J. Ravindranath, CEE, Bengaluru, for his support and timely help in completing this study. My heartfelt thanks go to Dr. Ganapathy Bhatt, Mrs. Mohini, retired teachers of DMS, Mysore, Dr. Asha Kamath, Assistant Professor in Education, RIE, Mysore, Dr. Stephen T.A., Assistant Professor in Education, PKM College of Education, Mr. Rajendran, Assistant Professor in Education, CIE, Delhi, Dr. V.P. Smitha, Assistant Professor in Education, Centre for Teacher Education, Calicut University, Mr. Biju, Mr. Sharad Sure, Mr. Remith George Carri, Ms. Dhanya Krishnan, Mr. Rajesh and Mr. Jabbar, Research Scholars, RIE, Mysore for their scholarly feedback. I am especially thankful to Mr. Madhusoodananan, Principal, Chinmaya Vidyalaya, Taliparamba and Mrs. Vimala R., Principal, Chinmaya Vidyalaya, Payyanur for permitting me to do data collection. I am equally thankful to the students of VII standard of both the schools for their cooperation during data collection. Thanks are also due to the teachers and students of Kendriya Vidyalaya, Keltron Nagar, Kannur and Demonstration Multi-purpose School, Mysore, for permitting me to conduct the tryout of tools and materials.

I am grateful to Dr. Shireesh Pal Singh, Assistant Professor at Central University of Punjab for guiding me in publishing the book. Many people have helped me in completing this work. I express my gratitude to all of them, and to all my teachers and friends for supporting me during the study.

Jubilee Padmanabhan

Contents

Chapter 1

Introduction and Conceptual Framework

"Earth provides enough to satisfy every man's need, but not every man's greed."

—*Mahatma Gandhi*

The above quote by Mahatma Gandhi rightly mentions the nature of earth which has sufficient resources to meet the human needs, but not to satisfy the greed. It has great relevance in the modern world where people are exploiting the natural resources in an uncontrollable manner. Environment which is a combination of living and non-living things is very important for life to exist on the earth.

Man started the exploitation of the environment ever since he came into existence on earth. The exploitation of nature can be seen when he started to live in caves, led a nomadic life and settled and practiced agriculture. For the satisfaction of his basic needs and greed, he started to exploit the environment by cutting trees, destroying forests, destroying patches of land, constructing buildings, depleting of resources, using various modes of transportation, development in technology, etc. This exploitation reached its zenith when the population increased drastically.

The consequence of this devastation can be seen in many places in the form of deforestation, different types of pollution, ozone layer depletion, greenhouse effect, acid rain, various natural calamities, etc. A number of plants and animal species have started to become extinct. A large number of incurable diseases both for plants and animals have started to rule the earth. Even man fails to find suitable preventive measures to fight diseases.

Pollution, deforestation, loss of biodiversity, ozone hole, global warming are some of the environmental problems that are faced by the world today. Where did they come from? All the basic resources required for living come from the environment. It is the environment that provides raw materials to industries, food for people, fuel for transport, etc. The environment also absorbs the waste that developmental activity creates, which means that the environment is both a source and a sink for developmental activity. The ways people interact with the environment influence their health and well-being. Overusing environmental resources causes environmental degradation.

India has made considerable strides in slowing down its population growth rate. But with all the efforts, the current estimate is that our population will only stabilize somewhere in the middle of the century, by which time India will have become the most populous country of the world. Till then India adds a population of approximately one Australia to India every year. With about 16% of the world's population and a little over 2% of its land, there is already enormous pressure on the resources. But while the population increase puts pressure on the resources, the pressure of "development" is perhaps even greater. Unless development needs and those of poverty in particular, are dealt with simultaneously, there could be neither protection of the environment nor success in the programmes to achieve development (Sarabhai V. Kartikeya, 2000). Development is an important facet of the present world, which is essential for the societal well-being. But these developments should not exert much pressure on the resources which can deteriorate the environment. The environmental, social and economic wellness is the need of the hour, which amalgamates together in the concept of sustainable development.

A core principle behind sustainable development is a combination of economic, social and environmental conditions. Without a proper ecosystem, it is impossible to maintain a better society and economic development for our own and future generation. Thus, environmental dimension can be regarded as the ultimate boundary for sustainable development. The social dimension is to meet the basic needs of all people without exceeding the boundaries of the ecosystem. The economic dimension is a means to realize the goal within the limits of a socially and environmentally sustainable manner. Education for Sustainable Development is intended to educate all the stakeholders including the students, community, corporate, etc. about the importance and need for sustainable development in the present world. So Education for Sustainable Development (ESD) cannot be considered as having link only with environment but with development of social and economic aspects. The tripolar relationship of sustainable development is represented in Fig. 1.1.

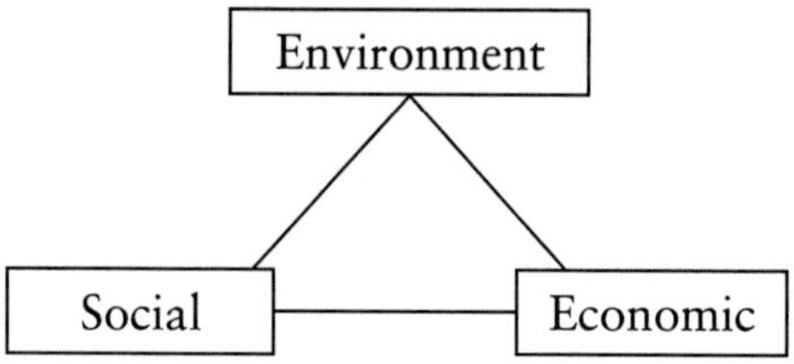

Fig. 1.1: Triangle of Sustainable Development.

These 'three pillars' of Sustainable Development are called as 'triple bottomline' or 'triad' of sustainable development. ESD aims at building up ones knowledge, skills, attitudes and values towards sustainable development which are some of the objectives of ESD.

Eduction for Sustainable Development

A useful way of thinking about the constituent parts of sustainable development is the WEHAB Agenda adopted at WSSD (World Summit on Sustainable Development) in 2002. WEHAB stands for Water, Energy, Health, Agriculture and Biodiversity. While the DESD (Decade of Education for Sustainable Development) discourse clearly recognizes the importance and validity of various fields of transformative education as forerunners of ESD, it vacillates widely on its commentary about topics and themes to be addressed by ESD. Although the finalized DESD International Implementation Scheme (IIS) (UNESCO, 2005b) does not emphasize the topic or theme-based approach to ESD, draft schemes (UNESCO, 2004, 2005a) listed 15 topics to be considered in promoting ESD. These 15 strategic perspectives categorized under socio-cultural, environmental and economic perspectives in the draft IIS of January 2005 (UNESCO, 2005a) were reorganized into 'sustainability issues' under 'three spheres of sustainable development' and the intersectional sphere in the final IIS (UNESCO, 2005b). The major topics to be addressed by ESD that are highlighted in draft and final DESD IIS (UNESCO, 2005a, 2005b) are given in Table 1.1.

Table 1.1: Major topics to be addressed by ESD as identified by UNESCO

"15 Strategic Perspectives" in Draft IIS		**"Sustainability Issues" in Final IIS**	
Socio-cultural perspective	• Human rights • Peace and human security • Gender equality • Cultural diversity and intercultural understanding • Health • HIV/AIDS • Governance	Social sphere	• Employment • Human rights • Gender equity • Peace and human security
Environmental perspective	• Natural resources (water, energy, agriculture, biodiversity) • Climate change • Rural transformation • Sustainable urbanization • Disaster prevention and mitigation	Environmental sphere	• Water • Waste
Economic perspective	• Poverty reduction • Corporate responsibility and accountability • Market economy	Economic sphere	• Poverty reduction • Corporate responsibility and accountability
		Cross-sectional sphere	• HIV/AIDS • Migration • Climate change • Urbanization

Sources: (i) UNESCO, 2005a, pp. 19-22 and (ii) UNESCO, 2005b, Annex I, p. 3, paragraph B.

In order to build knowledge on sustainable development. The United Nations Division for Sustainable Development has listed the areas or topics as coming within the scope of sustainable development. These areas to be addressed while addressing sustainable development are: Agriculture, Atmosphere, Biodiversity, Biotechnology, Capacity-building, Climate Change, Consumption and Production Patterns, Demographics, Desertification and Drought, Disaster Reduction and Management, Education and Awareness, Energy, Finance, Forests, Freshwater, Health, Human Settlements, Indicators, Industry, Information for Decision-making and Participation, Integrated Decision-making, International Law, International Cooperation for Enabling Environment, Institutional Arrangements, Land Management, Major Groups, Mountains, National Sustainable Development Strategies, Oceans and Seas, Poverty, Sanitation, Science, SIDS, Sustainable Tourism, Technology, Toxic Chemicals, Trade and Environment, Transport, Waste (Hazardous), Waste (Radioactive) and Waste (Solid) and water.

Education for Sustainable Development as an Integrated Part of School Curriculum

The national system of education, as defined in the National Policy on Education, 1986, visualizes a national curricular framework which contains a common core including several elements having a direct bearing on the natural and social environment of the pupils. The National Policy on Education, 1986 (NPE) states that the "protection of the environment" is a value which along with certain other values must form an integral part of the curriculum at all stages of education. The policy states: "There is a paramount need to create a consciousness of the environment. It must permeate all ages and all sections of society, beginning with the child. Environmental consciousness should inform teaching in schools and colleges. This aspect will be integrated in the entire educational process." There has been special emphasis on the need to give importance to environmental education, and this has been kept in view while designing curricula, framing the syllabi and developing textbooks. The philosophy behind the curricula is that environmental education could be infused into the curricula especially at the primary level.

It is accepted that Environmental Education (EE) should be a lifelong process beginning at the pre-school level and continuing through all formal and non-formal stages. Thus, children become the first and most important target group, and a strategy of EE which addresses itself to this group becomes imperative in the overall scheme of things. EE is not just a subject to teach, rather is an opportunity to let children use their own environment, of which the school is a part, as a source of information, a ground for learning, and a storehouse of experience which will last a lifetime. Thus, EE to be effective, should ideally utilize diverse learning situations and a broad array of approaches to teaching and learning about and from the environment, with due stress on practical activities and first-hand experience. The institutional framework includes space, organization and special environment which can be used for effective transaction of environmental education in schools. The main actors that interact within the framework are students, teachers, curriculum or instructional material and methods. Programmes and materials that attempt to address all these are essential to the realization of the goals of EE.

Today, EE in the formal educational system in India is handled at three levels. It is a composite subject called Environment at the primary school level; it is infused into environment in regular school subjects at the middle and secondary school level, and is a separate subject at the college level (Pandya, 2000). Environmental studies aims at educating the young child to be better equipped to face the ever changing environment in his future life.

The objective of environmental studies is the development of necessary attitudes, skills and concepts for the study of other environments (Nasrin, 2007).

Within the school system, it is the teachers who are communicators of knowledge as well as architects of attitudes, play the greatest role in ordering learning conditions and guiding or inspiring students' thinking and action in a desired direction. EE is not merely passing out facts and rules to be memorized by the students. Teachers need appropriate curricula, and material for communicating ideas effectively. Above all, the teacher also needs to adopt innovative methodologies and approaches to this process.

In the existing educational system, teachers are beset by a number of problems related to lack of resources, and physical or academic constraints. While the content for teaching is provided in the form of textbooks, the methodology, skills and support materials for the effective use of the instructional material are often not provided. Moreover, most teachers do not have time, resources and confidence to undertake the task of active teaching-learning which are the key to effective EE. Teacher's role in EE should be to assist learners in acquiring positive attitudes, recognizing, analysing, clarifying personal values concerning the environment, and developing skills to solve problems in order to live more harmoniously with the environment. Teachers need a great deal of support and encouragement towards an approach which promotes thinking, problem-solving and active participation of teachers and learners alike and this also helps teaching to move away from a dully repetition of facts. This support would need a two-fold approach—(a) the development of instructional and resource material, and methods that combine worthwhile content with an enjoyable process; and (b) the orientation and training of teachers in the optimum use of the same (Pandya Mamata, 2004). Figure 1.2 shows the different aspects being given emphasis in the EE from 1960 to 2000. It was seen that in 1960s nature studies were given emphasis. Later the emphasis was on environmental studies, rural studies, outdoor education, etc. It followed a transition from environmental studies to education for sustainable development.

In Fig. 1.2, nature studies, rural studies, field work, environmental studies, outdoor education and adventure education are almost self-explanatory, being a group of approaches to education that share a focus on 'in' the environment experiences. In the early days of 'nature' and 'rural' studies, emphasis was very much on teacher-directed 'show and tell' techniques. In recent years, fieldwork and environmental studies have encompassed more of what might be described as participatory, problem-solving techniques, but with a strong emphasis on scientific approaches involving detailed observations, measurements, and the gaining of empirically derived knowledge. 'Outdoor' and 'adventure' education are broader in scope and encompass outdoor activities in which students engage with the environment, such as mountaineering, walking, etc. They aim to provide opportunities that encourage enjoyment, appreciation and awareness of the environment. Those who work in the outdoor and adventure education fields strive to help change attitudes by exposing young people to new and relevant experiences which will lead to better understanding of themselves as well as their environment. Such activities often operate from centres or specialist bases, rather than schools.

Fig. 1.2: Map of the development of different aspects of environmental education.

Source: Joy A. Palmer (1998), *Environmental Education in the 21st Century: Theory, Practice, Progress and Promise.*

Urban studies promote the understanding of the social, physical and natural characteristics of the urban environment and their interrelationships. Aims of urban studies include fostering concern about the built environment, improving understanding of the conservation of nature in urban areas, developing wasteland as an education resource and providing city children with experiences of the 'natural' world. Urban studies are closely linked to heritage education, which focuses particular concern on the educational use of historic buildings and estates, and the study of our historic heritage. Both of these movements involve close links between educators and other professionals—architects, planners and other local government professionals.

Development education grew out of the increasing concern in the 1960s and 1970s of the United Nations, the churches and charitable organizations about 'Third World' poverty. Originally, development education focused on the plight of certain developing countries. In recent years, it has concerned with, understanding the level of development in a particular country; necessitating a study of global economic and political systems; understanding development processes within and between all countries, rich and poor; showing that what is appropriate development in one context is not necessarily appropriate in another; showing that the 'West' has much to learn from non-Western perspectives on development; and showing that the 'Third World' is not just a term to describe economically poor nations, but also encompasses areas and groups that have been marginalised by the workings of economic and political systems (e.g. women, the aged, the homeless, the unemployed, ethnic minorities, indigenous peoples, and poor, remote or un-influential parts of wealthy countries).

Peace education originated in the post-Second World War era. It aims to help students to create positive attitudes towards people of other nations and foster international understanding. In more recent years, its focus has broadened to include not only 'negative peace' (i.e. absence of war) but also 'positive peace' (i.e. ways of creating more just structures in and between societies). It concerns itself with questions of violence/non-violence, poverty/economic welfare and injustice/justice. It also embraces the study of conflict, conflict avoidance and resolution between individuals, groups and nations, and explores the question of humanity's relationship with the environment.

Human or human rights education also had a fairly limited original focus—on civil and political rights (e.g. freedom of speech, freedom of movement of individuals). Recent approaches have broadened to include social and economic rights (e.g. those that ensure material and bodily well-being such as the right to food and shelter) and non-Western concepts of rights and 'new rights' issues such as racism, sexism, the right to development, etc.

Global education developed out of the proliferation of 'educations' (i.e. development education, environmental education, human rights education, peace education) should attempt to cluster them all under an inclusive title. It was recognized that while these separate educations had their own distinctive features and starting points, their concerns are actually complementary and interdependent.

Earth education is an approach to environmental education that has been developed for the protection of Earth. The overall goal is "the process of helping people of all ages to live more harmoniously and joyously with the natural world". A range of structured programmes aims to "break down barriers in the natural world, encourage an understanding of how ecosystems work, and develop positive caring attitudes to the Earth".

Humane education is a broad field, ranging from the humane treatment of animals to world peace. It aims to "provide the basis for responsible planetary citizenship" and to "achieve compassionate change which challenges the selfish and anthropocentric attitudes that have encouraged exploitation of each other, animals and the world to the point where we are now threatening our very survival on this planet". Core concepts and attitudes addressed include a reverence for life, respect for animals as living creatures, and an understanding of and concern for keeping the environment safe and natural for all life.

Futures education aims to provide a more 'future-orientated' approach to the curriculum, and bridges the gap between environmental education and 'future studies'. Two interlinked questions relevant to this field are "What sort of images do people hold of a probable future?" and "What are people's ideas of preferable futures?" In other words, it is concerned with individuals' ideas about the future, how their ideas influence the way they act in the present, and how their present actions influence the future.

Education for sustainable development or sustainability aims to help people understand the inter-dependence of life on Earth, the effects of actions and decision relating to resource use, and factors which foster or impede sustainable development. It is concerned with developing people's awareness, values and attitudes, thus enabling them to be involved effectively in sustainable development (Palmer, 1998).

ESD has five major components: Knowledge, skills, perspectives, values and teaching issues which are to be addressed in a formal curriculum for sustainable development. The linkage of these five components is given in Fig. 1.3.

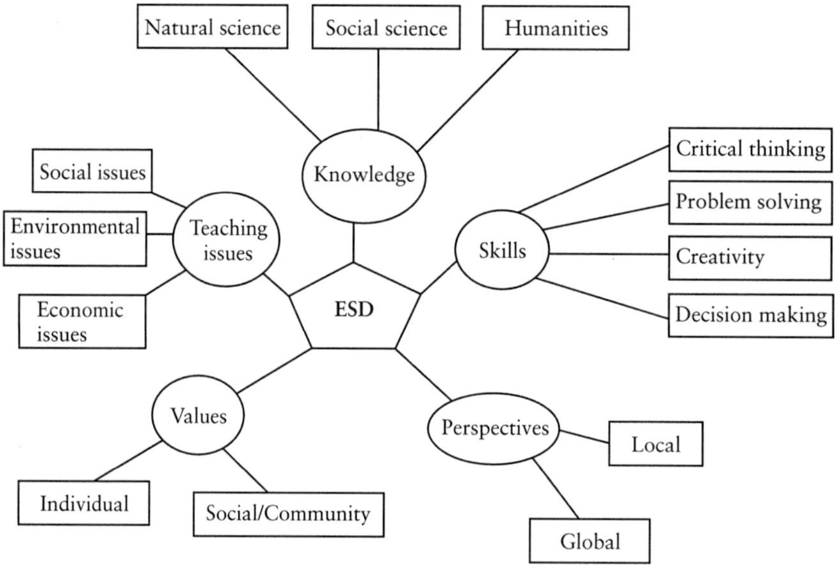

Fig. 1.3: Components of ESD.

Sustainable development encompasses the dimensions of environment, society and economy. But education for sustainable development includes the attainment of objectives such as knowledge, skills, perspectives, values and teaching issues towards sustainable development. People need basic knowledge from the natural sciences, social sciences, and humanities to understand, the principles of sustainable development, how these can be implemented, the values involved, and ramifications of their implementation. Knowledge about the different aspects of sustainable development should be given importance. It includes the knowledge or awareness about the different aspects of ESD such as agriculture, atmosphere, biodiversity, etc. which are listed in the United Nations Division for Sustainable Development.

ESD focuses largely on the major social, economic, and environmental issues that threaten the sustainability of the planet. Understanding and addressing these issues are the heart of ESD, and locally relevant issues should be included in any programme related to educating for sustainability. To be successful, ESD must go beyond teaching about these global issues. The issues involved in ESD include addressing locally relevant issues, which has to be considered in teaching. Reflecting on these issues is very essential while addressing sustainability. The best way to adopt this is by preparing an issue-based curriculum at all levels of education.

ESD must give people practical skills that will enable them to continue learning after they leave school and to have a sustainable livelihood. These skills will differ with community conditions which fall into one or more of the three realms of sustainable development—environmental, economic, and social. These skills include critical thinking, decision-making, problem-solving or creative skills which are essential for solving global and local issues that hinder sustainable development.

ESD carries with it perspectives that are important for understanding global issues as well as local issues in a global context. Every issue has a history and a future. Looking at the roots of an issue and forecasting possible futures based on different scenarios are part of ESD, which should also help in finding out the origin of any local or global issues and help in finding out the cause and solution for solving the same.

Values are also an integral part of ESD. Understanding one's own values, the values of the society one live in, and the values of others around the world are the central part of educating for a sustainable future. The values to be developed as a result of ESD have been described by UNESCO which include respect and care for the community of life, ecological integrity, social and economic justice, democracy, tolerance, non-violence and peace. Two common techniques—value clarification and value analysis—are useful to the value component of ESD. Value clarification has three approaches—Choosing, Prizing and Acting. Choosing include choosing freely from alternatives after thoughtful consideration of the consequences of each alternative. Prizing include cherishing and being happy with the choice, willing to affirm the choice publicly. Acting includes doing something with a choice repeatedly in some pattern of life (Raths et al., 1930, p. 30). Value analysis is a method based on a technique which makes possible to evaluate and measure customer/user satisfaction in order to explicit or implicit requirements of the entity under consideration with reference to the global costs.

Integrating the objectives, concepts and learning experiences of education for a sustainable development into syllabuses and teaching programmes are an important part of reform ."A basic premise of education for sustainability is that just as there is a wholeness and interdependence to life in all its forms, so must there be a unity and wholeness to efforts to understand it and ensure its continuation. This calls for both interdisciplinary inquiry and action. It does not, of course, imply an end to work within traditional disciplines. A disciplinary focus is often helpful, even necessary, in allowing the depth of inquiry needed for major breakthroughs and discoveries."

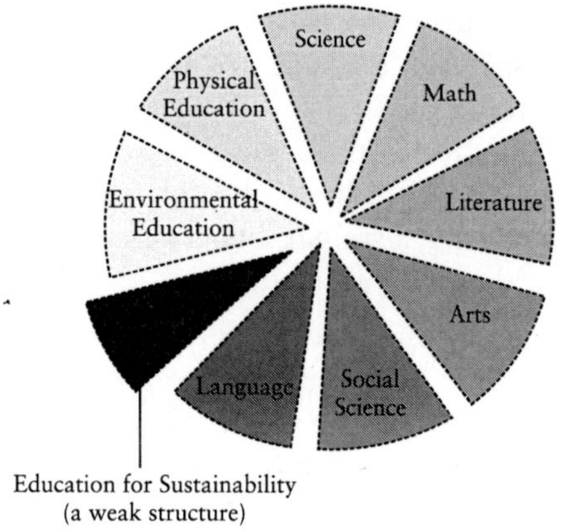

Fig. 1.4: Education for sustainability as an individual discipline.

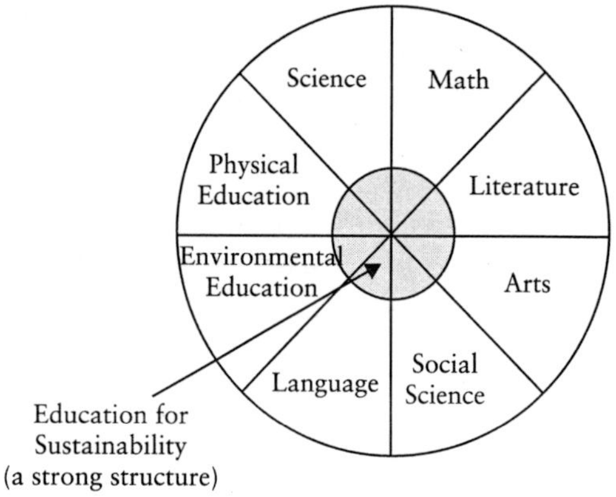

Fig. 1.5: Education for sustainability as a multidisciplinary subject.

Source: UNESCO (1997) Educating for a Sustainable Future: A Transdisciplinary Vision for Concerted Action, paragraph 89.

The figures 1.4 and 1.5 designate the importance of integrating ESD into the whole school curriculum.

Chapter 2

Researches on Education for Sustainable Development

Introduction

This chapter discusses about the review of related literature and researches carried out in the area. Literatures from various sources were reviewed to study the trend in the area. The reviewed literature and researches are categorized into (i) studies on Environmental Education (EE)—one of the components of ESD, (ii) studies related to issues on ESD, (iii) studies on sustainable development, (iv) studies on ESD and curriculum, and (v) studies on the effect of pedagogical approaches over education for sustainable development.

Studies on Environmental Education—One of the Components of ESD

Most of the researches in the past have been carried out in the area of Environmental Education which is one of the dimensions of ESD at present. Gupta et al. (1981) studied the awareness of environment among rural and urban schools and non-formal education centres and found that school going rural children did better than the urban samples and the non-formal centre students were more aware of environment than urban students. Padmini (2007) also stressed the importance of environmental awareness for sustainable development. Pande (2007) in her study on environmental awareness among rural and urban children found out that majority of the students did not appear to have much knowledge of the environment-related issues and problems and they were not aware of the importance of the content and the environmental issues. Results showed that children from urban habitation had a fair idea about the problems related to the environment than their rural counterparts. The reason given for this is, the classroom teaching and the media exposure; the rural children are deprived of these facilities for improving their mental horizon. Deopuria (1984) also compared the traditional and environmental approach and found that primary students did better than middle and secondary level students and both male and female teachers showed a positive attitude towards the environmental approach to learning. Subramaniam and Prabha (2008) found out that there was a significant difference in the awareness about environment between boys and girls and urban and rural areas, but no difference was found among schools of different types, namely matriculation, aided and government schools. Joshi (1981) also found that environment outside the class is potent enough to initiate learning and hence environmental education should be considered essential at least at primary level. Unfortunately, teachers and syllabus were found responsible for limiting the growth of this approach. Kumar and Patil (2007) found that students with EE background has better environmental attitude. It was also found that there is no significant difference between male and female students in their attitude towards environmental pollution and related issues. The higher secondary students improved their achievement on environmental pollution after viewing the video programme. Veliappan et al. (2008) studied the awareness about environmental pollution among higher secondary school students and found out that about two-third of the students had moderate awareness level on environmental pollution, and there were significant difference with reference to gender, age and geographical location of the school.

While preparing a curriçulum in environmental studies at college level, Pai (1981) also found that the experimental group gained more awareness than the control group in environmental activities. Vipindernagara and Dhillon (2007) observed a significant variation in the awareness on environmental education of secondary and elementary school teachers with the former scoring higher. No significant difference was noted in the EE awareness of male and female school teachers. But the interaction effects of level and sex showed significant difference upon EE awareness. Asha (2008) found out that the environmental awareness for promoting human health and quality of life of teacher educators was higher in females and urban teacher educators than male and rural teachers. But the awareness level did not differ significantly between science and arts teacher educators. Indu and Suryalatha (2008) conducted a study to find the awareness and attitude of the student teachers towards environmental issues and found out that majority of the student teachers had moderate attitude and the physical science student teachers were found to have a favourable attitude towards environmental protection in comparison to their life science counterparts. Locality, educational qualification and subject specialization did not contribute significantly towards the knowledge scores on environmental awareness of the student teachers. Rajeswari (2008) conducted a study on environmental awareness among adolescent students and found out that they have only average knowledge about environment. The level of awareness about environment does not differ significantly between male and female B.Ed. and D.T.Ed. students, Science students have better understanding of the concepts of environment than Arts students. Pande (2007) found that both urban and rural teachers are aware of the environment and know all about its protection and preservation. Jubilee and Manjula (2008) found out that majority of the Maldivian secondary school teachers have a moderate awareness of environmental problems, issues and other related aspects. They also have a positive attitude towards conserving the environment. The study revealed that there was a relationship between environmental awareness and environmental attitude and there was no significant difference between male and female teachers in their awareness and attitude towards environmental education. It was also found out that the environmental awareness do predict the environmental attitude of Maldivian secondary school teachers. Lakshmi and Sailaja (2008) found out that there were differences in the level of attitude towards environmental science and science among the women prospective secondary school teachers. The subject of methodology of B.Ed. level influenced the environmental attitude of the women prospective teachers and students of science subjects had higher attitude than that of other subjects. Attitude towards environmental science and science were significantly correlated. Ravikiran (2008) found out that there is a significant difference between male and female elementary teachers in their awareness towards ESD and there was no significant difference in awareness towards ESD between rural and urban teachers, government and private school teachers and teachers with different years of experience. It was also found that there was no significant difference in their attitude towards ESD between males and females, rural and urban, government and private school teachers and teachers with different years of experience.

Since attitudinal change is related to awareness, most of the studies reviewed were of these types. Studies on the attitude rewards EE were conducted by Mallika (1984), Sharma (1996), Sharma (1998), Radha (2005) shows that awareness of students and teachers are high. Sharma (1986), Indubala (1999) have also studied on teacher's attitude and awareness towards EE and found that there is high awareness and attitude about EE, but the pre-service teachers were not provided with suitable training experiences.

It is observed that studies are carried out in Environmental Education among students with different subject backgrounds. Kumar and Ram (2006) while studying about the awareness of environmental education among students, found out that in science stream, postgraduate students were more aware towards EE than the students of arts and commerce stream. The study also revealed that the female students of science and commerce stream were more aware than male students. In arts stream male students were more aware than female students towards EE, and no interaction between sex and subjects were found towards EE among postgraduate students. Suresh and Kadhirvanan (2007) conducted a study on the influence of personality on the environmental awareness ability of college students and found out that it is affected by demographic variables like subject specialization, residential area, parental income and parent's level of education. But gender does not affect them. The Delhi Chief Minister Dixit (2006) in an article stated that children are environment ambassadors, and youth should come forward in protection of environment which is facing a great challenge due to rapid urbanization. It is emphasized that one should be able to make a cleaner and greener Delhi only with constructive contribution of the younger generation who would also become role model for the entire society. Due to the efforts of various agencies and a massive involvement of the eco-club students and teachers, Delhi's green cover increased from 26 sq km in 1997 to 268 sq km in 2003 which has further gone up to more than 320 sq km.

Holden and Linnerud (2010) analyzed the relationship between environmental attitudes and energy use in the home and for transport by Norwegian household. Quantitative surveys were used to find statistical correlations, and qualitative analysis to reveal mechanisms that influences the ability to behave in an environmentally friendly way. Three theses about attitude, mechanisms and household consumption were presented. Firstly, a desire to project an environmentally friendly image has little influence on energy use in the home and for transport. Secondly, a sense of powerlessness prevents people from translating positive environmental attitudes into low energy use in the home and for everyday transport. Thirdly, a desire to self-indulge prevents people from translating possible environmental attitudes into low energy use for long distance leisure travel. These results have found to be important in implications for environmental policy. It is found that the public information and awareness campaigns could give consumers information on how to behave in an environmentally responsible manner, but tend only to influence categories of consumption with little environmental impact.

Dash, Mishra and Satapathy (2008), conducted a study on the attitude of secondary school teachers from Odisha towards Sustainable development and found that both pre-and in-service teachers had a positive attitude for sustainable development. Except low, middle and high socio-economic categories of Arts female in-service teachers, all categories had favourable attitude for sustainable development. Since teachers were more favourable than females and there was increase in attitude score with increase in socio-economic condition. Pre-service teachers irrespective of their years of training showed positive attitude. Two years programme teachers were more favourable than one-year and four-year pre-service teachers.

From the studies reviewed, one may conclude that, there are innumerable studies related to awareness and attitude on EE at school level. There were no gender difference in the environmental awareness and attitude of students, but majority of the studies showed that rural students had better awareness than their urban counterparts. It means that the rural children are naturally inclined to protecting environment, due to their close proximity to nature since their childhood when compared to urban. From the studies reviewed, it was observed that the variables other than awareness and attitude have not been explored and sustainable development has also not been the focus.

Studies Related to Issues on ESD

Studies were reviewed pertaining to various issues related to ESD. The social, economic and environmental issues falling under the scope of ESD are reviewed in this section. David (2007) conducted a research project on climate capabilities: an ethical analysis of anthropogenic climate change (2008-2010) which highlights the theoretical and practical conceivable need for universal climate change values versus the phenomenon of contextual moral outlooks. The paper contributes to further knowledge on the nature of intrinsic values threatened by climate change and also contributes to a critical debate on foundational ethical climate change values for global and local climate change justice in political practice. Silby and Kagawa (2010) is of view that ESD is the latest manifestation of the 'closing circle' of policy driven environmental education. Characterized by definition haziness, a tendency to blur rather than lay bare inconsistencies and incompatibilities and a cozy but ill considered association with the globalization agenda, the field has allowed the neoliberal marketplace worldview into the circle so that mainstream ESD facility embraces economic growth and an instrumentalist and managerial view of nature that goes hand in glove with an emphasis on the technical and the tangible rather than the axiological and intangible. Runaway climate change is imminent but there is widespread climate change denial including within mainstream ESD. A transformative educational agenda in response to climate change is offered. Recent calls for the integration of Climate Change Education (CCE) within the mainstream of ESD should be resisted unless the field breaks fire of the 'closing circle'. Robertson et al. (2004) opined that Environmental research in agriculture is largely reactive, focused on problems at small scales and conducted within narrow disciplinary boundaries. This approach has worked to abate a number of environmental problems created by agriculture, but it has not provided effective solutions for many of the most recalcitrant ones. Furthermore, the approach fails to position agriculture to deliver new environmental benefits that the public and policymakers increasingly demand. They are of the opinion that new vision is needed for environmental research in agriculture-one that is anticipatory; promotes long-term, systems-level research at multiple scales; better incorporates important interactions between the biophysical and social sciences; and provides for the proper evaluation of deployed solutions. Achieving this vision will require major changes in funding strategies, in institutional reward structures, and in policies that presently inhibit collaborations across disciplinary and institutional boundaries.

Tapas and Sunanda (2007) suggest that the climate issue dealt with in the textbooks of Bangladesh briefly compare to the present requirements. The Social Development Research Centre (SDRC) and Action Aid Bangladesh have developed a board game as part of a co-curricular activity for the secondary level. School awareness programmes can be used to promote and enable a culture of climate resilience at the community level. The learning kit when utilized by communities can play an effective role as an entry point into the raising of awareness on climate challenges in general, and in demonstrating how risks can be addressed and managed in community specific contexts. To achieve effective results, such co-curricular activity may be a useful tool. Introducing climate change issues in the textbook is a must for the country considering the present circumstances. Hyogo Framework for Action (HFA) has also suggested the introduction of the issue in the community in a non-formal way.

Constantina and Maria (2007) is of the view that environmental refugees and climate exiles are people who can no longer gain a secure livelihood in their homelands because of drought, soil erosion, desertification, deforestation and other environmental problems, together with the associated problems of population pressures and poverty. According to them, sustainability represents a sound way to deal with the environmental refugee issue, through greater policy emphasis on environmental protection, together with efforts to address associated problems of population growth, poverty, landlessness, and basic human needs. The key to this difficult prospect is education. Education for sustainable development is particularly important to ensure a clear understanding of sustainability among the local decision-makers, stakeholders and the general population, and it would prove a pay off and long run investment in fostering sustainable development in developing or developed countries.

Anjali and Chaman (2007), conducted a study on the pollution caused by various festivals in India, like Deepavali, Holi, Lohri, Ganesh chaturthi, Navratri, etc. Various natural resources are used (wood, flowers, water) for celebrating them. Many harmful resources are utilized (chemicals, poisonous colours) which have strong effects on the environment. The major agenda at this point of time is to create awareness among the people about safeguarding our environment from the harmful effects of our celebrations through "Environment Education" while also reiterating the importance of celebrating our rituals and customs which will help us to be rooted in our culture for years to come. Hence, various strategies was suggested for celebrating our festivals in an extensively eco-friendly manner. Further, the author stress on the recommendations for various religious groups/bodies to promote these new suggestions and alternatives for our festival celebrations.

Efrat et al. (2007) presents the result from a multinational EE project that took place throughout the year of 2004. The project relied on a theoretical model of combining together best practices in the field of EE and implementing them in a multinational setting which allows for multinational culture interactions and inquiries into a common environmental problem. By doing so, it was expected that social aspects of sustainable development and Education for Sustainability would evolve naturally and be addressed as a natural inherent part of the learning process rather than a topic addressed externally. The project involved 10th grade students from Israel, Cyprus and Greece. The 210 students were divided into working teams of six students each, with members of mixed nationalities—two students from each country. The project's core topic was bio-invasions to the Mediterranean Sea, in particular Lessepsian migration—the migration of species from Red Sea to the Mediterranean Sea through the Suez Canal. Students in the three participating countries simultaneously collected data along the Lessepsian migration route. The data was analyzed by each team in accordance with the teams' specific research questions. Thirty-five multinational teams presented their final results. The project's implementation model included an internet site which was constructed for communications among academic supporters from the fields of education and marine ecology, high school teachers from three Mediterranean countries, high school students from the three countries, and a facilitator who coordinated the multi pathways communications and interactions. Results showed a high acquisition of scientific skills and environmental knowledge among the students.

Sharma and Goel (2010) are of the view that there is a huge gap in energy/power production, supply and demand in India. A large section of the country's population suffers from power cut throughout the day or no power supply at all. Major portion of the energy production in India is being fulfilled by thermal and hydro power plants currently, which is not sufficient for the total energy demand of the country. It is therefore important to consider an alternative source of energy production, which is environment friendly as well as economically feasible for the Indian people. Wind and solar energy are the most environmentally sustainable sources of power generation which have been harnessed successfully in several countries, but they require high initial investment. Nuclear power would be an alternative to fulfill the energy demands of the country. India has been successful in making nuclear agreement recently with nuclear fuel producing countries to get uninterrupted supply of nuclear fuel (i.e. Uranium) to solve power shortage in the country. Before installing any nuclear power generation plants in India, it is important to implement stringent regulations for the health and safety of the people and for protection of the environment, soil and water from the nuclear and hazardous waste produced in the power plants. Although some initiatives have been taken for radioactive waste disposal in India, the current hazardous and nuclear waste storage/disposal regulations are still too soft and not being implemented properly in the country. There are several examples of improper handling of hazardous waste by industries in India and elsewhere, which ultimately pollutes the surface water and groundwater continuously.

Baker (2002) did an analysis of the structural and institutional contexts in which poverty exists with an understanding of the everyday livelihood strategies used by households who are poor. The study goes beyond conventional income poverty measures by bringing together a sustainable livelihoods framework and participatory poverty assessment methods. Participatory method was used to study the poverty of those living in difficult circumstances to participate in an analysis of their own livelihood situation. A participatory poverty assessment has been facilitated with a small group of women who are members of the food co-op at Project SHARE. The participatory poverty assessment explores issues of well-being, assets, and the role of institutions, coping strategies and a community action plan. The contribution of both the exploration of assets and the participatory poverty assessment are brought together in a discussion of livelihoods including issues of well-being, gender, social solidarity, capabilities and functioning and the power of institutions. The combination of a sustainable livelihoods framework and a participatory poverty assessment has demonstrated the importance of non-material needs, uncovered unmet needs, demonstrated the importance of social relationships in sustaining livelihoods, added to an understanding of poverty as an inseparable interaction between means and ends, and demonstrated how the institution of welfare administration shapes and constrains the possibilities for livelihood well-being.

Corvalan, Kjellstrom and Smith (1999) in their paper discuss the links among health, environment, and sustainable development and present a framework that extends from the epidemiological domain to the policy domain and include the driving forces that generate environmental pressures, creating changes in the state of the environment and eventually contributing to human exposures. Health effects are the end result of this complex net of events. Environmental health interventions should not be limited to treatment of cases and directly reducing human exposures. The paper discusses the need for integrated action at all levels and, in particular, on the need to focus on long-term action directed at reducing the driving forces that generate the environmental health threats. Only this approach can achieve sustained health benefits and environmental protection in accord with the principles of sustainable development.

McCurdy et al. (2004) are of view that Pediatric medical and nursing education currently lacks the environmental health content necessary to appropriately prepare pediatric health care professionals to prevent, recognize, manage, and treat environmental-exposure-related disease. Leading health institutions have recognized the need for improvements in health professionals' environmental health education. Given the biologic, psychological, and social differences between children and adults, there is a need for environmental health education specific to children. The National Environmental Education and Training Foundation, in partnership with the Children's Environmental Health Network, created two working groups, one with expertise in medical education and one with expertise in nursing education. The working groups reviewed the transition from undergraduate student to professional to assess wherein those processes pediatric environmental health could be emphasized. The medical education working group recommended increasing education about children's environmental health in the medical school curricula, in residency training, and in continuing medical education. Similarly, the nursing working group recommended increasing children's environmental health content at the undergraduate, graduate, and continuing nursing education levels. Working groups also identified the key medical and nursing organizations that would be important in leveraging these changes.

Fien and Maclean (2000), opined that our schools and educators face a compelling responsibility to serve society by fostering the transformations needed to set up on a path to sustainable development in the 21st century. Mortensen (2000) focus on the need to have science embedded at the core of the education for sustainability and the need to increase and enhance teacher education to develop the necessary interdisciplinary thinking and transformative learning for the new millennium.

Sunitha (2007), conducted a review on the disaster management system in Tamil Nadu, India and the capacity of local community to respond to natural disasters, and to propose a strategy using audio-visual media for the dissemination of tsunami knowledge while raising public awareness of tsunami and other coastal disasters with respect to the 'two step flow' model of media influence. Natural disaster takes a huge toll of human lives and property which severely hampers development. It may not be possible to prevent natural disasters totally, but an effective pre-disaster planning and preparedness through audio visual tools could be done in order to reduce the adverse effects of the hazards and the consequent economic loss.

Dinah and Cecily (2001) opined that within their value chains of suppliers through customers, many businesses are becoming more aware of the environmental aspects and impacts of their organizations. Viewed as a continuum of behaviour, business environmentalism can range from simply complying with the law to accepting and pursuing a goal of sustainable development. The point on the continuum at which an organization chooses to operate is reflected in its environmental mission, policies, and actions. They have examined attributes of the various levels of behaviour and classification of some organizational mission statements. David (2007) conducted a research project on climate capabilities: an ethical analysis of anthropogenic climate change (2008-2010) which highlights the theoretical and practical conceivable need for universal climate change values versus the phenomenon of contextual moral outlooks which contributes to knowledge on the nature of intrinsic values threatened by climate change and also contributes to a critical debate on foundational ethical climate change values for global and local climate change justice in political practice. Ding and Shen (2010) presents a model of the Sustainable Development Value (SDV) which integrates sustainability assessment into the building process. SDV measures the significance of the concerned project to the attainment of Sustainable Development Value at different stages of a building life cycle and the SDV at each stage will be amalgamated into the model of SD ability (SDA). SDA is used as a prototype to demonstrate the extent of sustainable performance to aid decision-making. They present a methodological framework of SDV and SDA and the implementation was demonstrated using a case study.

The exercise of review revealed that there have been studies undertaken on sustainable development in the areas of Energy (production, demand and supply), poverty alleviation, agriculture, drought, soil erosion, deforestation, desertification, pollution etc. The studies give emphasis to specific areas that hinder sustainability or help in attaining sustainability. Many areas that need sustainability are yet to be explored and researched upon in order to solve issues related to sustainable development.

Studies on Sustainable Development

Tasaki et al. (2010) have surveyed Sustainable Development Indicators (SDIs) adopted by 28 National governments, regions and international organizations and compiled them into database. The aims of the study were to understand the elements of Sustainable Development (SD), examine SDIs developed in certain fields and countries and determine future tasks to improve SDI development. A total of 1,790 indicators were surveyed and classified into 77 sub-categories in four categories. Most of the indicators measure various SD elements and the indicators reflected each country's developmental stage and specific concerns. Several advanced or unique indicators were also identified. Five major tasks in the future development of SDIs identified were: (a) Creating time conscious indicators, (b) Measuring interactions between elements of a system, (c) Dealing with trans-boundary issues in a national SDI systems, (d)Measuring SD quality (including subjective elements), and (e) Including ordinary citizens by showing the relationship between SDI and everyday life. The indicators identified were: (i) Social—social aggregated indicator; poverty and dependence; economic inequality; gender inequality; generation inequality; regional inequality; race/immigrant inequality; social exclusion (including the disabled); work; working conditions; national status; food safety; mortality, life expectancy and health; sanitation and drinking water; alcohol; child care; education; literacy and numeracy; culture, leisure and time; family; social relationship and participation; international cooperation; housing; child living conditions; services and public facilities; information; crime; social security; population change; peace/conflict; spiritual; (ii) Environmental—environmental aggregated indicator; climate change; ozone layer depletion; air quality; agriculture and livestock; soil; chemicals; land-use; landscape; forests; desertification; urbanization; coastal zone; fisheries; water quality; water quantity; ecosystem; endangered species; disaster; noise; radioactivity; perception of environmental pollution; water cycle; bio security; resources; commune with nature; (iii) Economic—economic performance; capital and investment; trade; financial status; household financial status; business and industry; eco business; energy use; transportation; material use; waste generation and management; recycling; (iv) Institutional—strategic implementation of SD, environmental management and policy; morality and compliance; international institutions; science and technology; legal administration; SD networks; administration and management. Duck (2000) has proposed certain measures for SD for a country like India, which includes providing school education, sex education and prevention programmes to tackle the problem of population explosion, education provides inspiration for true democratic, pluralistic and secular society, widespread of knowledge by education for conserving natural resources like water, land, air and forest, use of ICT for spreading modern knowledge.

Preethi (1999) is of view that greenhouse gas emissions (CO_2 and CH_4) produced during the bacterial decomposition of flooded peat and forest biomass could be substantial in the case of large reservoirs as has been evident from early data relating to hydro-electric reservoirs in Canada. It is said that the Balbina Dam in Brazil had 26 times more impact on Global warming than emissions from an equivalent coal fired station. The disturbance caused by the construction of a catchment area and the dam and its related components, the tremendous loss of biodiversity, displacement of people, the erasing of their cultural history and in some cases their distinctive identity caused by inundation of fertile cropland and ancient forests have been recorded in the cases of large dams around the world. The Balbina Dam in Brazil inundated an area of 2750 square kms, the Srisailam project flooded 43,300 ha of farmland taking away the livelihood of 100,000 displaced farmers. And this is hardly the only instance where dams have impacted India. Sidhu (2007) opined that the consumption of energy is directly proportional to the progress of the mankind. With ever growing population, improvement in the living standard of the humanity, industrialization of the developing countries, the global demand for energy is expected to increase rather significantly in the near future. The primary source of energy is fossil fuel, however the finiteness of fossil fuel reserves and large-scale environmental degradation caused by their widespread use, particularly global warming, urban air pollution and acid rain strongly suggests that harnessing of non-conventional, renewable and environment friendly energy resources is vital for steering the global energy supplies towards a sustainable path. India must give more thrust to the research and development in the field of non-conventional energy sources not only to mitigate greenhouse effect but also to lessen dependence on oil/gas import.

Archibong (2007) conducted a study on the problems related to the issues of climate extremes, Nigerias experiences in air safety and air accident, contribution of the meteorological agency to extremes in weather and safer air transport. Wazed and Islam (2007) in their study on the design and fabrication of solar air heater, have constructed a solar air heater to make winter sunlight adequate for providing a significant portion of the heat for shelter. It was constructed so as to let sunlight in and prevent as much heat loss as possible. Dimitriou, Christidou and

Hatzinikita (2007) conducted a study on pupils' ideas about reducing air pollution and the results showed that pupils recognize practices and actions at both individual and societal level towards the reduction of air pollution, which also referred the sustainable and technology-based measures involving industrial prevention, land planning, transportation control, protection of forest, sustainable use of energy and waste management. Also public awareness is an important factor for effective participation towards the reduction of air pollution.

Shallcross et al. (2006), in their study on promoting sustainable development through whole school approaches: on International, Intercultural teacher education research and Development Project, focused on a British council funded Higher Education Link project involving three institutions—one in UK and two in South Africa. The link was a research and development project that has three main research strands: contextual profiting that will enable the applicability of a European teacher education project to the South African context, evaluative materials developed and piloting predicated on a respect for indigenous and contextual knowledge, and impact analysis that will examine the role of multidirectional intergenerational mentoring in disseminating messages about sustainable lifestyles.

Sharma (2007) found out that the density of white-backed vulture—Gyps bengalensis around the buffer zones of Corbett Tiger reserve forest was 74 individuals in 2005 as compared to 34 in year 2006, which indicates that some disturbances are responsible for it. Singha (2007) conducted a case study on degrading wetlands—intervention for sustainable development; a case study of Silsako wetlands of Guwahati. Dash, Mishra and Satapathy (2008), conducted a study on the attitude of 450 secondary (243 pre-service and 207 in-service) school teachers from Odisha towards sustainable development through a Likert type five-point attitude scale and was found that both pre- and in-service teachers had a positive attitude for sustainable development. Except low, middle and high socio-economic categories of Arts female in-service teachers, all categories had favourable attitude for sustainable development. Since teachers were more favourable than females and there was increase in attitude score with increase in socio-economic condition. Looking into the dimensions (economic efficiency, environmental harmony, resource conservation, local self-reliance and equity and social justice) of the attitude scale, all pre-service teachers and science in-service teachers were found to have favourable attitude for all the five dimensions of attitude scale. However, in-service arts teachers had positive attitude for economic efficiency and local self-reliance but not for environmental harmony, resource conservation and equity and social justice. Pre-service teachers irrespective of their years of training showed positive attitude. Two years programme teachers were more favourable than one year and four year pre-service teachers. Regarding the relationships between age, teaching experience and socio-economic status and attitude towards sustainable development, it was noted that age and socio-economic status contributed more for the development of attitude towards sustainable development than teaching experience.

Maruyaa (2008) conducted a case study in Turkey on Education to enrich social capital for sustainable development. The study emphasized that through ESD, the fulfillment of the social aspect should also be emphasized. One need to emphasize creating good interpersonal relations as well as networks that connect regions. From educational point of view, ESD brings an opportunity to integrate local indigenous wisdom into modern education. The discussion focuses on the social and traditional factors that support the citizens' activities among Turkish people. Pandey, Tyagi and Goel (2008), are of the opinion that ESD has connections with other programmes and concerns in education. They also opine that sustainable development requires a comprehensive, integrated approach. It is not a new programme but a call for a process to reorient educational policies, programmes and practices so that education plays its part in building the capacities of all members of society to work together to build a sustainable future. Many teaching and learning strategies already used in school geography encourage effective ESD. These includes approaches that are: learner centred, develop autonomous and critical thinking, develop skills of enquiry, creativity, imagination and collective decision-making, use a range of text and media resources. These all contribute to the ability of students to envision the sort of future that they want for themselves and for society.

Mitchell (1994) conducted a study on Sustainable Development at the Village Level in Bali, Indonesia. Using a stress-capability framework, the problems and opportunities for sustainable development at the village level in Bali were examined. Balinese culture incorporates a traditional form of local government which emphasizes cooperation, consensus building, and balance. These aspects provide a strong foundation for sustainable development initiatives. At the same time, many decisions are being taken external to the villages, and even to Bali which may lead to problems for development initiatives. The village study results associated with the Bali Sustainable Development Project indicate both encouraging and disturbing patterns on sustainable development. On the positive side, based on the experiences in Kesiman Kertalangu, Buahan, and Yeh Kuning, as well as in the other five villages, it appears that traditional ways of life based on agriculture are continuing, and that traditional culture and governance systems are flourishing. For many of the villages, especially those at a distance from the south where tourism accommodation is concentrated, the impact of tourism has been relatively minor. Since traditional Balinese culture emphasizes the importance of harmony among people, between people and their environment, and between people and their god, the prospects are good for balancing economic, environmental, and social considerations in development. Furthermore, traditional organization such as gotong royong (voluntary work groups), subaks (irrigation groups), and banjars (neighbourhood organizations) and the desa adat (traditional villages), all based on cooperation and consensus building, provide a strong foundation on which to implement sustainable development ideas. With reduction of agricultural land, village farmers are using Green Revolution technology to increase production. Increasing amounts of waste represent a growing problem in Bali, especially in Denpasar. For these villages, waste disposal particularly metal and plastic containers, are becoming a problem. One outcome of the Bali Sustainable Development Project is anticipated to be some pilot initiatives related to waste management at the village level. A major concern for the villages is that many of the development decisions with the greatest potential impact are beyond their control.

Suda (2002), questions how the current global environmental movement is perceived and portrayed by news media. From a constructionist perspective, the news media have potential to help different groups to create and define issues in the global environmental movements through the process of news making. The study combines the conceptual frameworks of globalization and news construction together. The study examines news coverage of an environmental conflict over the World Bank sponsored hydroelectric dam, the Pak Mun, in a northeastern province of Thailand. The subjects of the study are news stories printed in local news and feature sections in two Thai language newspapers which were aimed at a local level of readership both inside and outside Thailand. The period of study spans 12 years from 1989 to the first three months of 2001, covering the period from the beginning of construction on the Pak Mun Dam to the month in which the Pak Mun Dam gates were ordered opened by the Thai government to allow water to flow back to the Pak Mun river. The study explores four aspects of the Pak Mun news coverage: reporting frequencies, source dependencies, dominant news frames and differences in the construction of news meanings that may create connections between the local Pak Mun conflict and the global anti-large dam movement.

McDonald and Songer (2008) have examined two critical cases of teachers enacting a technology- rich curriculum focused on the development of complex reasoning about biodiversity for fifth graders. Two elements emerged that significantly impact teacher enactment—their conceptions of authenticity and their view of science. Bhattacharya (2007) is of the view that the pressures of the contemporary world to educate its citizens call for capacity building in pre- and in-service teacher training. It may require refocusing on the existing curriculum and training policies to create a vision for society that is not only environmentally sustainable, but also one that is socially, economically and politically sustainable. Skills, knowledge, values and attitudes in teacher education programmes should be oriented towards this goal, eventually leading to capacity building in life skills, managing resources and community development. In order to make the teacher education programme realistic and practical oriented in nature, and to ensure a controlling role for education for sustainable development (ESD), the curriculum may consist of personal development as well as socio-cultural themes. Personal development themes may include self-identity, courage, conscience, competence, fidelity, caring, love, decision-making, self-respect, compassion, sexuality, health and respect for others whereas socio-cultural themes may include parent relationships, citizenships, human values, gender equality, religious beliefs, freedom, environmental conservation, children relationships and civil rights.

York and Frank (2002) are of the view that growing evidence demonstrating clear threats to the sustainability of the human ecosystem has given rise to a variety of sociological theories from human ecology, political economy, neo-classical economics, ecological modernization, reflective modernization, and world systems, addressing man-environment interactions. They assessed the anthropogenic factors driving the environmental impacts of sociology. The overall findings are supportive of the claims of human ecologists, political economists and contradict the claims of modernization theory. Consistent with the claims of human ecologists, climate affects the scale of anthropogenic environmental impacts. Consistent with the claims of political economists' world systems theory, affluence monotonically increases the ecological footprint and urbanization further increases impacts. Contrary to the theory of neo-classical economists and ecological modernization theorists, increase in technological efficiency does not markedly reduce impacts. Overall findings suggest that in order to achieve sustainability, societies will have to curtail both population and economic growth.

The above studies reflect that there has been number of case studies from different parts of the world that were assuring sustainability. These studies revealed that there are initiatives taking place at certain areas like impact of constructing dams, using alternative energy sources, biodiversity conservation, using ICT towards attaining sustainability and human ecosystem or impact of human population on sustainability. These case studies and initiatives should be comprehensive in nature in order bring about sustainability. There is a need to bring such findings into the notice of the present generation. Hence the present study has attempted to incorporate issues related to sustainable development into the school curriculum.

Studies on ESD and Curriculum

In India, since the mid-1980s efforts have been made to bring the perspective of environmental education in formal education at all levels. The NCERT which is the prime organization for improving the country's education in India has been an active body in making Environmental Education as a part of school curriculum. In 2000, the NCERT had recommended EE as a separate discipline to be introduced at elementary level. National Curriculum Framework (NCF 2000 and 2005) has considered Environmental Education to be given priority. The NCF (2005) in its National Focus Group Position Paper on 'Habitat and Learning' stressed the curriculum for Environmental education for schools. Prior to this, in 1998 the National Curriculum Framework for elementary and secondary education had proposed 'the protection of environment' as one of the core components of school curriculum which has to be reflected in the textbooks at all levels. In 2003, the Hon'ble Supreme Court of India directed that EE should be a compulsory subject at all levels of education. It further directed the National Council of Educational Research and Training (NCERT) to prepare a model syllabus for class I to XII, which shall be adopted by every state in their respective schools. Since it was felt to see environment in a holistic manner, it was started as Environmental Studies (EVS) in order to provide a holistic picture of environment to the students. On January 21, 2003, the UNEP launched state of the environment report for South Asia. It identified five key environmental issues—livelihood security, environmental disasters, industrialization, urbanization and diversity loss. The major recommendation of the international conference on eco-restoration (14-21 October, 2003) held at Dehradun was to express great concern at the rapid degradation of both terrestrial and aquatic ecosystems throughout the world that has caused loss of biodiversity and various goods and services of the natural ecosystems and therefore to incorporate tools of environmental evaluation and to ensure community participation. Jackson (2001) pointed out that EE as introduced in school textbooks reveals many contradictions which cannot be removed without questioning the assumptions about current science and technology that school textbooks project. He was of the opinion that environmental education strategy in India to-date has been the infusion of environmental concerns into the existing curriculum. The paper attempted to assess student learning by an analysis of the NCERT model textbooks (NCERT, 1987-89). It is concluded that the infused material is creating incoherence in the curriculum, and the attempts to remove this incoherence are further creating confusion. It is suggested that to overcome this problem, changes may be required in the existing science syllabus. Also, it was stated that environmental problems are inadequately defined, probably with no clear ideas to students about who is responsible for creating them, who will solve them and how. There is thus a need to define the country's environmental problems more realistically and rigorously and to change our approach to introducing these problems to students.

Vedamani and Exemmal (1988) in their study on developing and testing models of EE in Botany relevant for the socially disadvantaged children in the schools of Kerala, found out that from the point of content and approach, the environmental science textbook did not seem to have made a revolutionary break from what existed 50 years earlier or so at the primary level, but content boundaries were clearly maintained.

Howland and Becker (2002) are of the view that Global Learning and Observations to Benefit the Environment (GLOBE) is an international science and environmental education programme that enables school children to learn about the environment by taking scientific measurements of their natural surroundings and sharing their data with scientists via the Internet. By carefully following protocols and using approved measurement devices, students around the world are developing an archive of standardized data that can also be used in professional research. GLOBE is divided into several separate "investigations", each focused on a different aspect of the environment. They include land cover, soil, hydrology, phenology, haze, and the atmosphere. Each investigation has a team of scientists who have worked with students and teachers to develop detailed protocols for the students to collect data. In addition, the scientists are exploring ways of using that data in their own research. Howland's article is about the work of GLOBE scientists—with some students and teachers. It is intended to provide an overview of the scientists' efforts to develop a meaningful learning experience around gathering environmental data for research.

Chung Ko and Lee (2003), conducted a study which was an exploratory study of Hong Kong secondary school integrated Science teachers' perceptions of environmental education. In this study, the teachers were classified according to their scores of attitudes, perceived barriers, and current emphasis on teaching environmental education. It was found that Integrated Science teachers' attitudes toward environmental education, skills of teaching environmental education, beliefs in the relevance of Integrated Science to environmental education, and intentions of teaching environmental education in Integrated Science classes were associated with their actual ways of teaching of environmental education. Teachers tended to teach more environmental education if they held more favourable attitudes toward environmental education, had more skills of teaching environmental education, believed more in the relevance of Integrated Science to environmental education, and would actually want to teach more environmental education in Integrated Science classes if there were fewer constraints. Moreover, variations in the teaching of environmental education were reflected by teachers' emphasis on teaching environmental education, and their use of a variety of teaching methods and their regular practices of extracurricular activities on environmental education.

Pacific Education for sustainable development framework (2006) have identified a priority area in formal education and training which focused on structured learning initiatives for improved knowledge and understanding to support implementation of sustainable practices where the objectives of promoting quality education in all member countries was given focus. It will be through development of education policies and strategies research and development of innovative models and resources that support ESD in pacific contexts, inclusion of learning outcomes that focus on sustainability, development of strategies to assess student understanding of sustainability, development and identification of appropriate ESD resources to support this priority area using appropriate information and communication technology tools.

Kalimuthu (1991) in a study on developing a video programme on environmental pollution in biology for higher secondary students found out that the higher secondary students taught through the video programme learnt more of the concepts on environmental pollution than those who were taught by the lecture method. Annakodi (2008) studied the effectiveness of an instructional package for environmental education on high school students and found that it was equally effective for all the schools irrespective of school types and the awareness on 'environmental actions' and 'environment friendly actions' was significantly higher in experimental group than in the control group and the boys and girls were equally benefited from the study. Exemmal (1980) conducted a study to find out the efficacy of environmental approach, in which it was found that the environmental approach was superior to the formal approach. It was also found that students of rural and low SES group were significantly better in profiting from such instruction than their counterparts in urban areas and coming from high SES. Also the environmental approach stimulated cognitive growth in pupils.

Atkinson (2007) conducted a study in bringing practical environment and development education materials into the schools of transition countries, whereby the project was implemented within a wide group of stakeholders from national government, education institutes, environmental organizations, teachers, NGOs, filmmakers, designers and artists—the study focuses on the importance of partnership of stakeholders involved in adapting and integrating the materials nationally and the development of local ownership of the product to ensure sustainability and upgrading. The lessons used in the classroom from the package are also covered by showing the process of national dissemination and teacher training adopted to enable the use of the different multimedia elements and the new interactive approaches within the kit. Al-bashaireh (2007) investigated the effect of a programme on environmental education based on a systemic approach on the achievement of educational Sciences students at Mu'tah University/Jordan. The study sample comprised of 113 students of first semester of the environmental education course during the scholastic year 2006-07. They were divided into two groups, one group was taught using a systemic approach programme, while the other group was taught by the conventional method. The systemic approach programme and achievement test was validated. The result showed that there was difference on the achievement of the students post-test in favour of those who were taught by the systemic approach programme. No differences were found attributed to students' gender or educational level.

Tapas and Sunanda (2007) suggest that the climate issue dealt with in the textbooks of Bangladesh briefly compare to the present requirements. The Social Development Research Centre (SDRC) and Action Aid Bangladesh have developed a board game as part of a co-curricular activity for the secondary level. The learning kit when utilized by communities can play an effective role as an entry point into the raising of awareness on climate challenges in general, and in demonstrating how risks can be addressed and managed in community specific contexts. Hyogo Framework for Action (HFA) has also suggested the introduction of the issue in the community in a non-formal way. Bishnu (2007) found that institutional support is vital for the continuity of the projects in schools. Even the activities that involved all the students and teachers together with the community were found to ensure continuity of the projects. The involvement of the whole school and community in an environmental fair is a good way to arouse the interest of the people in new interventions. The goal of EE is to direct the change in human behaviour towards natural resource management and consumption patterns. To achieve this goal, the EE intervention should be conducted in such a way that it elicits sustained effect. One single intervention in EE may not be sufficient to achieve the EE goal; thus institutionalization of EE is the most important aspect to be considered for ensuring that the goals of EE are achieved. Baharul (2007) presents an innovative ICT based Environment Education Project (IEEP) being piloted in Assam that is primarily focused on using an institution's surroundings and environment as a framework within which students can construct their own learning, guided by teachers and administrators using proven ICT driven educational practices. IEEP uses environment as the integrating context for learning, designates pedagogy that employs natural and socio-cultural environments as the context for learning, and shares some fundamental educational strategies.

Iyengar (2007) suggested that reorienting the education towards ESD is a proposal that is useful, but require careful consideration in each country and differently. One will have to consider whether ESD should become part of curriculum or it should be taught separately. There is a danger for instance that if it is incorporated in the curriculum then its teaching would be left to the whims and fancies of the teacher. Dharmani (2007) suggested that at the primary level interdisciplinary approaches to be adopted and should be integrated into each subject area. Ahir Kinjal (2007) has conducted a study on the role of higher education in SD which is a case study of Ganghidham taluk. Nakum and Patel (2007) have stressed the importance of structuring and placing ESD in the curriculum.

Ismail, Karpudiwan, and Mohamed (2007) conducted a study on integrated approach in Chemistry in teacher education programme and found out that the integration of active learning and green chemistry experiments into the Chemistry teaching methods course enabled students to be more aware of the environmental issues, which in turn brought about a change in values.

Munjanganja (2010) is of the view that a variety of approaches are employed to impart knowledge about ESD in TVET (Technical and Vocational Education and Training). Common among the approaches are the following: problem-solving, projects, demonstration, role-playing and role-modelling. Other methods are drama, dance, study tours, industrial placements, and ICT tutorials. In addition, there is wide use of conventional methods such as lectures, seminars and workshops.

Bacha (2006) studied the means of contributing to ESD through second language education; the author describes a university-level content-based English language curriculum that incorporates ESD into second language learning. The curriculum aims to build students' language skills as they learn about topics related to sustainable development (SD), including culture, religion, international affairs, globalization, and the environment. Through experiential and interactive learning, curriculum methodology also promotes SD by encouraging respect for personal and cultural values, raising awareness of global perspectives, and developing students' critical and systemic thinking skills, all of which are essential for building and leading a sustainable livelihood. Within the discussion, the author provides suggestions for adapting ESD into second language curricula in primary and secondary education. Specific methodology is also highlighted which transcends subject matter and can be used to promote SD in other academic subjects. In conclusion, the author outlines the challenges and lessons learned in gaining departmental support for an ESD-related curriculum.

An Ecovillage Design Curriculum was developed by Global Ecovillage. Educators for a sustainable earth which provides the basis for a four-week comprehensive course on the fundamentals of ecovillage design. This was a curriculum that has the endorsement of the United Nations Institute of training and research. The characteristics of this curriculum are: to have a thorough and objective assessment of the state of planet by regional, community and place-based solutions; to empower individuals and communities with the knowledge for shaping their worlds to become self-reliant; universal in scope but local in application, preserve precious cultural diversity; investigative theory followed by practical application; imparte life skills; relevant to people in urban and rural regions; promote healthful planetary evolution along with well-being and quality of life; explore and expand the limits of human potential; enable community based visions of a sustainable human civilization as well as the means to turn such vision into reality during the course of the 21st century.

Prahalad (2007) conducted a study using the Ecovillage Design Curriculum developed by Global Ecovillage Educators for a sustainable earth, whereby Auroville which is an international spiritual and ecological community in Tamil Nadu, India by conducting courses in Ecovillage design curriculum. The course shows how to incorporate sustainable values as one try to transit from a post-industrial society to a unsustainable society. It encourages hands-on exercises to promote experiential learning within the local and Indian ecological and cultural context. Visits to various demonstration sites within Auroville in the fields of renewable energy (solar, wind, biogas), reforestation, natural building, organic farming, rainwater harvesting, experiential education, comparative philosophies, deep ecology, healing and yoga are part of the curriculum.

Fadeeva and Mochizuki (2010) quote that as its major contribution to the UNDESD, 2004-2014, the United Nations University (UNU) has promoted the establishment of Regional Centres of Expertise (RCE) on ESD and their networking to build innovative multi-stakeholder platforms for ESD locally and globally. In the first half of the UNDESD, UNU acknowledged 74 RCEs around the world. As an introduction to the special section on RCEs, their article highlights diverse roles that RCEs have taken and presents issues and challenges they have faced. It discusses RCEs as an engine for mobilising diverse stakeholders for ESD, a co-coordinator and an intermediary support structure for local regional ESD activities and related initiatives in the region, and a facilitator of 'social learning'. Glasser (2010) says that Grand Rapid is the first United Nations University (UNU) Regional Centre of Expertise (RCE) on ESD in the United States. It builds on the region's long history and deep foundation in research, planning and problem-solving to build a sustainable future. His article explores the concept of RCEs as social learning for sustainability communities of practice in the context of experiences with creating the first flagship project, the city high/middle centre for economicology. This model is used to broach the question of evaluation, indirectly by suggesting the importance of identifying early indicators of likely success. It closes with 6 'mediations' that were used to guide the flagship project and which may have wider relevance to the global RCE community. These were, responding to SD challenges and enduring ways that can benefit from systems thinking; while the future can neither be foreseen exactly nor controlled perfectly, it can be envisioned and brought into being with love, care and respect; values, good intentions, basic knowledge and sincere commitments in support of SD goals; addressing the prevailing mood of criticism, creating the 'motivation, will and vitality' to effectively target the challenges; knowledge can be used to 'enslave' as well as 'liberate', creating continuous improvements in quality of life for all.

Hartungi (2010) analysed the strengths and constraints of various evaluation methods in SD projects with emphasis on participatory evaluation. An international literature review is used to analyse the application of traditional and participatory approaches. The paper endeavours to be productively proactive as a catalyst for choosing the right evaluation methods. The results also shed light on important impediments to the performance of evaluations and on the role played by various stakeholders in the evaluation process. It was recommended that the participatory evaluation should be used in a complementary way with traditional evaluation. Ding and Shen (2010) are of opinion that existing environmental performance assessment approaches focus on the overall performance to reflect sustainability of built projects. However, the impacts caused by construction activities on the environment occur throughout a project's life cycle which may be different at different stages. Similarly, the economic benefits and social impacts from implementing a construction project may also be different in different project stages. They present a model of the Sustainable Development Value (SDV) which integrates sustainability assessment into the building process. SDV measures the significance of the concerned project to the attainment of SD value at different stages of a building life cycle and the SDV at each stage will be amalgamated into the model of SD ability (SDA). SDA is used as a prototype to demonstrate the extent of sustainable performance to aid decision-making. They present a methodological framework of SDV and SDA and the implementation was demonstrated using a case study.

Shamim (2007) says that AOSED has implemented an awareness programme for secondary school students in the south west coastal region of Bangladesh between March 2003 and March 2005. Under this project, two illustrated easy to read booklets, two flip charts for different levels and teacher guidelines were developed to support the teaching method. Awareness of climate change has been enhanced among 15,000 students of 65 schools and their families and neighbours through this initiative. Kholia et al. (2010) in the article 'International year of Biodiversity—revisiting curricula for conservation', say that every year a large number of students are taken on educational excursions to biodiversity rich areas. These students, who are mostly untrained in proper field and herbarium techniques, tend to collect more and more plants of different species and live materials for practical. They also remove/uproot several rare, endemic and endangered plants of that area which are unknown to them. Similarly in the curriculum of Zoology, Entomology and other related sciences, a large number of animals are dissected throughout the world. Considering the scale of these activities and their educational importance, the following points were suggested in order to achieve the targets of the international year of Biodiversity:

- During herbarium excursions, besides collecting, the practice of digital records (pictures), drawings and painting of live plants and flowers should be encouraged. At the time of practical exams/viva voce these should be assessed.
- Establishment of miniature Botanic gardens should be promoted at college and university levels. It should have representatives of all families, genera and species of the particular area.
- The dissection work at the school or college levels is not useful for many of the students who drop out or change stream at a later stage in pursuit of a suitable job. Therefore, in the wider interest, it is suggested that this type of destructive laboratory work may be reduced in the curriculum.
- If dissection is necessary at the graduate and postgraduate level, only those animals should be kept which are amenable to easy culture.

Bell and Morse (2007) opine that Problem Structuring Methods (PSMs) are widely applied across a range of variable but generally on small scale organizational contexts. However, it has been argued that they are seen and experienced less often in areas of wide ranging and highly complex human activity—specifically those relating to sustainability, environment, democracy and conflict (or SEDC). In an attempt to plan, track and influence human activity in SEDC contexts, the authors make the theoretical case for a PSM, derived from various existing approaches. They show how it could make a contribution in a specific practical context—within sustainable coastal development projects around the Mediterranean which have utilized systemic and prospective sustainability analysis or, as it is now known, Imagine. The latter is itself a PSM but one which is 'bounded' within the limits of the project to help deliver the required 'deliverables' set out in the project blueprint. The authors argue that sustainable development projects would benefit from a deconstruction of process by those engaged in the project and suggest one approach that could be taken—a breakout from a project-bounded PSM to an analysis that embraces the project itself. The paper illustrates the issues by grounding the debate within a set of projects facilitated by Blue plan of Mediterranean coastal zones. It also shows how the analytical framework could be applied and what insights might be generated.

The studies reviewed above focused on various interventions in the form of integrating environmental education in the existing curriculum or studying the effectiveness of an approach to environmental education such as environmental approach, ICT based approach or any other interventions. It also reveals that various approaches were tested to transact EE in schools, colleges and other educational institutions. It is observed that there are few countries that have taken effort either to incorporate EE or ESD into their curriculum. The ecovillage design curriculum developed by Global ecovillage education for a sustainable earth is a notable one. The studies reveal the need for an integrated action at all levels, especially to have ESD embedded in science as a core subject in school and Teacher Education courses. Some countries have made efforts to include climate change, disaster management, biodiversity conservation etc. into their curriculum. Methodologies like Problem Structuring Methods were used for curriculum transaction. But there were no studies where a curriculum was made by integrating the various components of ESD. In India no studies were found where there has been some initiative for integrating ESD into the curriculum.

Studies on the Effect of Pedagogical Approaches over Education for Sustainable Development

Much of today's work in sustainable development can be traced back for several decades. Many milestones have marked the journey towards sustainable development which include the 'United Nations Conference on Human Environment', Stockholm (1972) which led to the establishment of the organization—United Nations Environmental Programme (UNEP). The Brundtland Commission (1987) has first endorsed the concept of Sustainable Development. From then onwards the UN General assembly explored the parallel concept of education to support sustainable development. From 1987-1992, the concept of sustainable development matured as committees discussed, negotiated and wrote the 40 chapters of Agenda 21. Thoughts concerning education and sustainability were initially captured in chapter 36 of Agenda 21 (Rio summit, 1992).

Chapter 36 of Agenda 21 has identified four major thrusts of education to support a sustainable future. They are: improving access to quality basic education, reorienting existing education programmes, developing public understanding and awareness of sustainability and providing training. In order to implement these and to move forward, the United Nations Decade of Education for Sustainable Development has suggested seven strategies which are: Vision building and advocacy, Consultation and ownership, Partnership and networks, Capacity-building and training, Research and innovation, Use of Information and Communication Technologies (ICTs), Monitoring and evaluation.

Pellicer (2007) conducted a study for designing a methodology for developing critical thinking among young children to address air quality issues. He opines that awareness is not the only component of environmental education; there is also the need to develop knowledge, skills and attitudes towards current environmental issues. This can be attained by fostering critical thinking skills to emphasize the complexity of environmental problems, such as urban air quality. The study proposes a methodology based on the main steps of the scientific method and constructionist educational theories. The methodology is called 'Constructing Environmental Understanding' (CEU) and it suggests generating an adequate learning environment in which children are able to observe their local environment, choose a specific problem related to air quality, study that problem through research and interaction with the physical environment, determine its causes and effects, and then construct personal ideas on how to address that problem. The methodology was implemented at a high school with 37 students from the 11th grade. The result shows that most of the children participating in the study have gained a deeper understanding of air quality issues and have been able to address those issues in a local context.

McDonald and Songer (2008) have viewed that translating written curricular materials into rich, complex, learning environment is an under theorized area in science education. The study examines two critical cases of teachers enacting a technology-rich curriculum focused on the development of complex reasoning about biodiversity for fifth graders. Two elements emerged that significantly impact teacher enactment—their conceptions of authenticity (authentic learning/ authentic science) and their view of science (descriptive/inferential). The results suggests that disentangling the common conflation of these two elements supports a broader definition of inquiry science teaching that is more sensitive to context and individual teacher enactment.

Atkinson (2007) conducted a study in bringing practical environment and development education materials into the schools through a multimedia package and interactive approaches on the process of national dissemination; which was adopted by teacher training institutions also. Al-bashaireh (2007) investigated the effect of a programme on environmental education based on a systemic approach on the achievement of educational Sciences students at Mu'tah University/ Jordan. The result showed that there was difference on the achievement of the students post-test in favour of those who were taught by the systemic approach programme.

Behara (2007) in a study on plea for sustainable learning through Vygotsky's approach of constructivism suggested that teaching-learning process should be linked with the development of problem-solving, critical thinking, empathy, inter-personal relationships and communication skills which will help in SD. A sustainable development model was prepared by employing the five E's i.e. Engage, explore, explain, elaborate and evaluate. Pellicer (2007) developed a methodology called 'constructing environmental understanding' and it suggests generating an adequate learning environment in which children are able to observe their local environment; choose a specific problem related to air quality, study that problem through research and interaction with the physical environment, determine its causes and effects and then connect personal ideas on how to address that problem. Result shows that most of the children participating in the study have gained a deeper understanding of air quality issues and have been able to address those issues in local context.

Storhaug (2007) found that the storyline method in education for a sustainable future helps in building attitudes and empowering students for future citizenship. Marie (2002) conducted a study to investigate the relationship of constructivist learning environment and standards-based teaching practices to student achievement and attitudes (self-efficacy, intrinsic value and learning strategies) in Biology. The result provide a strong support for a positive relationship between constructivist learning environment and student attitudes, but little support for a direct relationship to student achievement. Multiple regression findings showed that neither overall constructivist learning environment nor standard-based teaching practices predicted achievement in any of the content areas. Overall constructivist learning environment and standard-based teaching practices were significant positive predictors of student intrinsic value and learning strategies, after controlling for student and classroom demographic variables. Standard-based teaching practices were a significant positive predictor of student self-efficacy in Biology. No specific dimensions of constructivist learning environment were consistently related to student achievement. However several dimensions of constructivist learning environments emerged as significant predictors of student attitudes, including personal relevance, shared control and student negotiation.

Binkley (2003) conducted a study on the frequency of use of constructivist teaching strategies and its effect on academic performance, student social behaviour in relationship to class size. The findings indicated that there was no significant correlation between the use of constructivist teaching strategies and student academic performance as measured by each middle school's grade (A, B, C, D, E and F) on the states mandated grading of schools scale. A small negative correlation between the use of constructivist teaching strategies and the number of student behavioural referrals indicated that higher the teachers use constructivist strategies, the lower the number of referrals per year. It was also determined that as class size decreased, the use of constructivist teaching strategies increased. Munjanganja (2010) is of the view that approaches employed to impart knowledge about ESD in TVET (Technical and Vocational Education and Training) are problem-solving, projects, demonstration, role-playing and role-modelling. Other methods are drama, dance, study tours, industrial placements, and ICT tutorials. In addition, there is wide use of conventional methods such as lectures, seminars and workshops.

Ye Zhao (2003) analyzed the characteristics of environmental science and the teaching methods of Beijing Norman University and discussed how to use constructivist-teaching models in environmental science teaching. It was found that during teaching and learning in environmental science, both the concept map and mind map are useful tools to promote active learning and students' abilities to integrate knowledge; and that problem based learning and the use of case studies can effectively motivate students' learning curiosity and develop certain abilities. It was also found that constructivist teaching, models and perspectives can improve EE reform in Chinese Universities. James (2002) in the study on pursuing sustainable grassroots development in a Thai marginalized periphery looks at the question of sustainability in grassroots development which analyzed that there are many obstacles to grassroots development in rural area.

Petrov and Marina (2007) in their study on vision of a new educational paradigm: meeting the goals of ESD, suggested the vision of new educational paradigm as the mechanism of socio-cultural continuity and development, the basis for reproduction of spiritual potential of the mankind and development of a person, a mechanism of reproduction and development of science and culture, a basis of preservation of historical and national-ethnic self-identification of peoples; the historical-genetic basis on which the future of the mankind grows up. Andrew (2007) outlines the need and nature of education to cultivate 'deep intelligence'. It involves consciously changing and transcending concepts, definitions, beliefs and patterns which limits how we perceive ourselves, others and the world. Such programmes go beyond cognition, into experience.

Samarapungavan, Mantzicopoulôs and Patrick (2008) in their paper examines the nature of kindergarten students' science learning from an inquiry unit. The results indicate that the students developed a functional understanding of scientific inquiry processes and life science concepts during their investigations. Analysis of Science Learning Assessment (SLA) data indicate that the intervention group showed significantly better understanding of scientific inquiry processes than the comparison group. Rogers, Abell (2008), conducted a study to understand one case of undergraduate inquiry-based instruction through the words and actions of students and instructors. The data sources included field notes from 16 of 29 classes, two sets of student and instructor interviews (beginning and end of the semester), and a collection of artifacts, such as the laboratory manual, lecture handouts and the course syllabus. The participants for this study included four faculty instructors and two purposively selected student groups, with a total of eight students. They found the instructors' two course goals, (a) teaching students how scientists do science and (b) using an interdisciplinary approach to develop students' content knowledge of the big ideas in science, were consistent with their observations and the students' descriptions of their experience in the course. However, they observed, and the students also noted, an important feature of the course that the instructors did not describe as a course goal was its reliance on the social nature of learning. This telling case demonstrates that inquiry based instruction is achievable in undergraduate science education.

Apedoe (2008) in his paper reports the synthesis of three case studies of students' engagement in inquiry-based learning activities in an upper level undergraduate geology course. Details of how students engaged in scientific questions, gave priority to evidence, formulated explanations, evaluated explanations and communicated and justified their findings are presented. Data for his study included classroom observations and field notes of classroom practices, questionnaires, archival data (e.g. Student work samples), and audiotapes and transcripts of interviews conducted with the student participants throughout the course. The findings suggest that although these students were able to successfully appropriate inquiry practices (e.g. Giving priority evidence), it was not without its challenges (e.g. perceived lack of guidance). A detailed discussion of the ways in which students were successful, and where they had challenges engaging in inquiry is presented, with the goal of helping direct practitioners and researchers to strategies whereby students' inquiry experiences can be improved.

Hunter, Laursen and Seymour (2007), in an ethnographic study of summer undergraduate research (UR) experience at liberal arts colleges, where faculty and students work collaboratively on a project of mutual interest in an apprenticeship of authentic science research work, analysis of the accounts of faculty and student participants yields comparative insights into the structural elements of this form of UR programme and its benefits for students. Comparison of the perspectives of faculty and their students revealed considerable agreement on the nature, range and extent of students' UR gains. Specific student gains relating to the process of 'becoming a scientist' were described and illustrated by both groups. Faculty framed these gains as part of professional socialization into the sciences. In contrast, students emphasized their personal and intellectual development, with little awareness of their socialization into professional practice. Viewing the findings through the lens of social constructivist learning theories demonstrates that the characteristics of these UR programmes, how faculty practice UR in these colleges, and students' outcome including cognitive and personal growth and the development of a professional identity—strongly exemplify many facets of these theories, particularly, student centred and situated learning as part of cognitive apprenticeship in a community of practice.

Dass and Deal (2007) report that in the USA high school students are interestingly and actively involved in environmental education and conservation efforts in their community, they are engaged in special projects that involve researching a theme/aspect of conservation for which they can take specific action, designing, conducting and reporting an original development and implementing an original action plan within the local community. Student have worked very diligently and found the project very rewarding. The Science Technology Society (STS) instructional approach, which has been characterized by the National Science Teachers Association (NSTA) as the teaching and learning of science and technology in the context of human experience. The NSTA position statement on STS status: The bottom line in STS is the involvement of learners in experiences and issues which are directly related to their lives. STS develops students with skills which allow them to become active, responsible citizens by responding to issues which impact their lives. The experience of science education through STS strategies will create a scientifically literate citizenry for the twenty-first century (NSTA, 1990-91: 48). The STS approach calls for the students to 'feel and act like scientists'.

Santi, Troy and Saysomdeth (2007) conducted a study on community outreach using radio for biodiversity conservation in Lao People's Democratic Republic. To evaluate the programme success, staff members used structured interviewing technique to interview 2380 people in five provinces. Survey groups consisted of government officials, traders, rural villagers and urban dwellers. Qualitative indicators revealed that the listening audience gained new information from the programme. They also found that 67% of the respondents listen to the radio; 18% of respondents listen to the Friends of wildlife programme; and among the various demographic groups interviewed, rural villagers listened to it more than any other.

Murtezan et al. (2007) conducted a study on the analysis of the new curriculum content of Macedonian High schools. The study consists of content analysis to examine the extent to which environment and sustainable development issues are addressed within the curricula. The analysis was fully comprehensive and investigated the entire curricula for all subjects and at all levels in the new secondary schools in the Republic of Macedonia. Results have shown a lot of weakness and gaps in the new curricula. Ecological concepts and principles for sustainability must be included in the curriculum in a thorough and comprehensive manner.

Mohd Nor and Assanarkutty (2007) conducted a study about the moral reasoning on environmental issues with emphasis on the well-being of wildlife in Malaysia. The study focused on

13 and 16 years old school children along the Perak river in the district of Perak Tengah in which the Bota Kanan River Terrapin Wildlife conservation centre run by the Department of Wildlife and National Parks is located. Moral reasoning regarding wildlife provides a relevant locus for exploring pupils' environmental ethic and in formulating environmental education in Malaysia. The results of a structured survey and open-ended questions regarding wildlife dilemmas offered insights into the way the children react toward environmental issues. The study demonstrates that Malaysian children were more likely to choose a teocentric perspective in dealing with environmental issues compared to the anthropocentric or biocentric point of view. However an analysis of the way the environmental issues are presented in the textbook show that it adheres more to an anthropocentric view. The paper also argues to create an effective environmental education, it must be based on the actual way that pupils interpret their experiences, and their feelings towards environmental issues should be its central focus. The study hence concludes that environmental education in the Malaysian context should be presented through a teocentric approach to provide better and more effective results.

From the above studies, it may be concluded that various pedagogical approaches have been used in transacting certain issues related to ESD, out of which interdisciplinary, STS, constructivist approach and inquiry play a predominant role. Though these approaches were found effective in transacting certain contents related to ESD, it has been made use in the present study to transact the integrated ESD contents.

Discussion

The purposive literature review made clear that there are number of gaps existing in the area of Education for sustainable development. Looking back into the studies conducted, one can infer that it was environmental education that was given more priority in the earlier days. Since environmental education was a compulsory subject of study in many educational institutions, there were quite a number of studies pertaining to environmental awareness and environmental attitude. Such studies were conducted at school level, teacher education institutions and other higher educational institutions. Also there were studies on role of gender on environmental awareness and attitude. Even the rural children had better environmental awareness than their urban counterparts. Environmental education is slowly giving way for sustainable development. Educating people about the concept of sustainable development is the scope of education for sustainable development. Since ESD is an emerging area with one of the component as environmental education, it has been reviewed to know the trend.

There were few studies that cater to sustainable development which include the indicators of sustainability. Review of literature revealed that there have been studies undertaken on sustainable development in the areas of Energy (production, demand and supply), poverty alleviation, agriculture, drought, soil erosion, deforestation, desertification, pollution etc. The studies give emphasis to specific areas that hinder sustainability or help in attaining sustainability. Many areas that need sustainability are yet to be explored and researched upon in order to solve issues related to sustainable development. Each country should adopt such sustainability practices that are geographically suitable for the place. Some case studies which are effective in some places may not suit another place. So selecting those case studies that are relevant to their locality should be done while transacting ESD in classroom. UNESCO has listed out all the areas to be addressed under sustainable development. There were no much documents pertaining to the areas to be considered under sustainability, except for the document by UNESCO. Hence, these areas were considered in the present study in order to incorporate the components of ESD into the science and social science curriculum of VII standard.

The studies on sustainable development reflect that there has been number of case studies from different parts of the world that were assuring sustainability. These studies revealed that there are initiatives taking place at certain areas like impact of constructing dams, using alternative energy sources, biodiversity conservation, using ICT towards attaining sustainability and human ecosystem or impact of human population on sustainability. These case studies and initiatives should be comprehensive in nature in order bring about sustainability. There is a need to bring such findings into the notice of the present generation. Hence the present study has attempted to incorporate issues related to sustainable development into the school curriculum. Some of these case studies can be used in classroom interaction to make the students aware of the sustainability practices happening in the world.

The studies reviewed on ESD and curriculum mainly focuses on various curricular reforms in Environmental Education in the form of integrating environmental education in the existing curriculum. Effectiveness of various approaches to environmental education such as environmental approach, ICT based approach on some variables was also reviewed. It also reveals that various approaches were experimented to transact EE in schools, colleges and other educational institutions. It is observed that there are few countries that have taken effort either to incorporate EE or ESD into their curriculum. The ecovillage design curriculum developed by global ecovillage education for a sustainable earth is a notable one. The studies reveal the need for an integrated action at all levels, especially to have ESD embedded in science as a core subject in school and Teacher Education courses. Some countries have made efforts to include climate change, disaster management, biodiversity conservation etc. into their curriculum. Methodologies like Problem Structuring Methods were used for curriculum transaction. But there were no studies where a curriculum was made by integrating the various components of ESD. In India no studies were found where there has been some initiative for integrating ESD into the curriculum.

It was also found from the studies reviewed, that various pedagogical approaches have been used in transacting certain issues related to ESD, out of which interdisciplinary, STS, constructivist approach and inquiry play a predominant role. Though these approaches were found effective in transacting certain contents related to ESD, it has been made use here to transact the integrated ESD contents.

Chapter 3

Identifying Units and Preparing Syllabus

This Section of the book deals with identifying the units and preparing the complete syllabus that is used for transacting in an integrated manner. This is the Developmental Phase I of the study where by the materials are developed. At this phase, the identified ESD components and the appropriate learning experiences were developed and integrated. Hence this phase consist of the following stages:

(a) Identify the components of sustainable development that can be incorporated in the contents of science and social science.

(b) Content analysis to arrive at where ESD can be integrated.

(c) Identifying units in science and social science where there is scope for integrating the concepts of sustainable development.

(d) Identify the plug points to integrate the concepts of sustainable development.

(a) Identify the components of sustainable development that can be incorporated in the contents of science and social science: The components of sustainable development that can be integrated in science and social science were identified based on various reviews and the recommendations of the United Nations Division for Sustainable Development. The areas identified falling within the scope of sustainable development are listed in Table 3.1.

Table 3.1: The Areas Identified Falling within the Scope of Sustainable Development

Themes	Areas
Social & Economic	Industry, Poverty, SCP: Sustainable Consumption and Production Patterns, Sustainable Tourism, Trade, *Demographics*, Health, Human Settlements.
Natural Resources Management	Agriculture, Desertification and Drought, Rural Development, Biodiversity, Forests, Oceans and Seas, Sanitation, Water/ Freshwater, Atmosphere, Climate Change, Energy, Transport, Disaster Reduction and Management, Land, Mountains, Chemicals, Toxic Chemicals, Waste (Hazardous), Waste (Radioactive) and Waste (Solid).
Stakeholders	Major Groups, SIDS (Small Island Development States), Partnerships for Sustainable Development.

Means of Implementation	Capacity-building, Education and Awareness, Finance, Indicators, NSDS (National Sustainable Development Strategies), Information for Decision-making and Participation, Institutional Arrangements, Integrated Decision-making, International Law, International Legal Instruments and Mechanisms, Biotechnology, Science, Technology Consumption and Production Patterns, Demographics, Health Human Settlements, Industry, International Cooperation for Enabling Environment, Land Management, Mountains, Poverty, Sustainable Tourism, Technology, Trade and Environment.
Regional Dimensions	Africa, SIDS: Small Island Developing States.

Source: United Nations Division for Sustainable Development, retrieved from http://www.un.org/esa/dsd susdevtopics/sdt_index.shtml

Among the components listed in Table 3.1, the following were selected for integration into the present study: Agriculture, Atmosphere, Biodiversity, Biotechnology, Climate Change, Demographics, Desertification and Drought, Disaster Reduction and Management, Energy, Finance, Forests, Freshwater, Health, Human Settlements, Indicators, Industry, International Law, Land Management, Oceans and Seas, Poverty, Sanitation, Sustainable Tourism, Technology, Toxic Chemicals, Trade and Environment, Transport, Waste (Hazardous), Waste (Radioactive) and Waste (Solid) and water.

(b) Content analysis to arrive at where ESD can be integrated: Content analysis was done for the units in science and social science textbooks to find out the units and content areas that had the scope for integrating concepts of Sustainable Development.

(c) Identifying units in science and social science where there is scope for integrating the concepts of sustainable development: The contents from science and social sciences were selected after a thorough analysis of the content and identifying the plug points where the concepts of sustainable development can be integrated meaningfully. The topics for the experimental treatment were selected from the science and social science textbooks prescribed for seventh standard students of CBSE schools following the NCERT syllabus for the academic year 2010-11. After integrating the concepts of sustainable development into the existing curriculum of science and social sciences, it was validated by giving to the experts and teachers working in the area. Teachers were consulted to know more about the students' understanding level, suitability of the topics and to ensure that the units taught in the experimental groups would be the same as that are taught in the control group during the experimental period.

Science textbook of VII standard contained eighteen units out of which nine units had more scope of integrating the concepts of sustainable development (Nutrition in plants; Fibre to Fabric; Heat; Weather, climate and adaptations of animals to climate; Wind, storms and cyclones, soil, Water: A precious resource; Forests: our lifeline; Waste water story). This worked out to be about 50% of the entire science syllabus. These nine units were analysed to integrate the concepts of sustainable development meaningfully.

Social Science textbook of class VII is divided into three textbooks, namely: History, Civics and Geography. No units were selected from History as the content become too crowded. Out of the ten units in civics two units had the scope for integrating the concepts of sustainable development (On Equality; Role of the Government in health). Geography had ten units out of which eight units had the scope for integrating concepts of sustainable development (Environment; Inside our earth; Our changing earth; Air; Water; Natural vegetation and wildlife; Human environment—Settlement, transport and communication; Human environment—Interactions; The Tropical and the Subtropical Region). These ten units of social science constitute about 40% of the entire social science syllabus in which the integration of concepts of sustainable development were done meaningfully.

The selected units were classified into eight major units by taking similar units in Science and Social science. The major units are Climate and Climatic changes, Nutrition, Soil, Our earth, Fibre to Fabric, Water management, Air, Human environment—Interaction, settlement, transportation and communication. The selected units are given in Table 3.2.

Table 3.2: Major Units and Selected Topics in each Subject

Sl. No.	Major Units	Science Units	Social Science Units
1.	Climate and Climatic changes	• Heat • Weather, Climate and adaptations of animals to climate • Wind, storms and cyclones	
2.	Nutrition	• Nutrition in plants	• Role of Government in Health
3.	Soil	• Soil	
4.	Our earth	• Forests—Our lifeline	• Environment • Inside our earth • Our changing earth • Natural vegetation and wildlife
5.	Fibre to Fabric	• Fibre to fabric	
6.	Water management	• Water—A precious resource • Waste water story	• Water
7.	Air		• Air
8.	Human environment—Interaction, settlement, transportation and communication		• Human environment-Settlements, Transport and communication • Human environment-Interaction, the tropical and sub-tropical region • On Equality

When analyzed, all the above units were found to have a scope for integrating the concepts of sustainable development.

(d) Identify the plug points to integrate the concepts of sustainable development: In the above selected units, wherever there is a scope of integrating the concepts of sustainable development, it is further analyzed to find out the exact places where the integration can be done meaningfully. The content to be integrated were identified and integrated from the suggestions and committees of UNESCO on ESD, the publications of Centre for Environment Education (CEE) and also from the opinion of experts. It was done keeping in mind the psychological aspects of the population by consulting with the teachers and experts who are working in the area of Education for Sustainable Development.

An example showing the plug points identified for integrating the concepts of sustainable development are given in the syllabus as follows:

Syllabus

Major Area I: Climate and Climatic Changes

Unit 1: Heat

(a) Introduction

(b) Hot and cold

  i. What is temperature and how is it measured
  ii. Heat and climatic change
  iii. Heat and human health

(c) Measuring temperature

  i. What is a clinical thermometer and its importance
  ii. Heat illness
  iii. Heat cramps and heat stroke

(d) Laboratory thermometer

  i. What is laboratory thermometer and its importance

(e) Transfer of heat

  i. What is conduction and conductors
  ii. What are insulators
  iii. What is convection
  iv. What is sea breeze and land breeze
  v. Radiation from the sun
  vi. Use of Cu in wires
  vii. Non-conventional power plants
  viii. Changes in sea breeze and land breeze
  ix. Solar energy for domestic purposes

(f) Kinds of clothes we wear in summer and winter
   i. Global temperature increasing
   ii. Health

Unit 2: Weather, Climate and Adaptations of Animals to Climate

(a) Weather
   i. What is weather
   ii. What are the elements in weather
   iii. Maximum and minimum temperature and how is it recorded
   iv. Length of days in summer and winter
   v. Changing weather patterns
   vi. Adverse weather conditions
   vii. Greenhouse effect and its impact

(b) Climate
   i. What is climate
   ii. What is hot climate
   iii. What is hot and wet climate

(c) Climate and adaptation
   i. What is adaptation
   ii. Polar regions
      - Characteristics of polar region
      - Animals found in polar region and their characteristics
      - Climatic changes and melting of ice caps
      - Impacts of melting of polar ice caps
   iii. Tropical rain forests
      - Characteristics of tropical rain forests
      - Animals found in tropical rain forests and their characteristics
      - Deforestation
      - Endangered species—its causes, effects and preventive measures
      - Climatic change and its influence on life forms

Unit 3: Wind, Storms and Cyclones

(a) Introduction
   i. Meaning of wind
   ii. Movement of air
   iii. Wind currents
   iv. Wind energy as an alternative source of energy
   v. How to harvest wind energy

(b) Air exerts pressure
(c) High speed winds are accompanied by reduced air pressure
(d) Air expands on heating
(e) Wind currents are generated due to uneven heating on the earth
   i. Uneven heating between equator and poles
      - Which region gets the maximum temperature
      - Movement of wind during summer
      - Movement of wind during winter
      - Monsoon winds
      - Heating of earth due to pollutants
      - Greenhouse effect
      - Impact of heat on polar regions
      - Difference in climate due to changes in wind patterns
   ii. Uneven heating of land and water
(f) Thunderstorms and cyclones
   i. What is a thunderstorm
   ii. How a thunderstorm becomes a cyclone
   iii. Hurricanes like typhoon, tornado, flood and drought
   iv. Timely warnings
(g) Destruction caused by cyclones or heavy rainfall
   i. Outbreak of epidemics
   ii. Type of houses to be constructed in cyclone prone areas
(h) Effective safety measures
   i. Cyclone forecast and warning services
   ii. Cyclone shelters in cyclone prone areas
   iii. Importance of technology in forecasting and warning services
   iv. Action on the part of the people
   v. Precautionary measures to be taken
(i) Advance technology has helped
   i. Satellites and radars help in providing cyclone alert
   ii. Science and technology for a sustainable society

Major Area II: Nutrition

Unit 4: Nutrition in Plants

(a) Nutrients
   i. Major nutrients
   ii. Importance of nutrients in maintaining proper health

iii. Percentage of food production versus population
iv. Malnutrition and poverty
v. Use of chemicals in agriculture
vi. Food production, management and food preservation

(b) Plants make their own food but animals cannot
i. Man destroying nature for satisfying his needs
ii. Loss of soil fertility

(c) Mode of nutrition in plants
i. How plants prepare food
ii. What is nutrition
iii. What are autotrophs and heterotrophs
iv. How do plants transport the nutrients
v. Mineral degradation in the soil
vi. Food scarcity
vii. Nutrient deficiency
viii. Hybrid varieties and its impact
ix. Impact of excessive usage of pesticides and weedicides
x. Chemical fertilizers and soil quality

(d) Photosynthesis-food making process in plants
i. Factors needed for photosynthesis
ii. Importance of photosynthesis
iii. Replenishing the soil nutrients
iv. Usable water getting reduced
v. Solar energy as an alternative source of energy
vi. Amount of various gases in the atmosphere and impact
vii. Climatic change
viii. Importance of protecting plants
ix. Reforestation and human settlement
x. Crop rotation
xi. Plant proteins

(e) Other modes of nutrition in plants
i. Heteromorphic mode of nutrition
ii. Insectivorous plants
iii. Biodiversity—importance of preserving it

(f) Saprotrophs
i. What is saprotrophs

ii. Lichens
iii. Its use in various industries

(g) How nutrients are replenished in the soil
i. Farmers using manures and fertilizers
ii. Nutrients get replenished
iii. Importance of rhizobium
iv. Use of natural manures
v. Crop rotation
vi. Environmentally friendly activities
vii. Nitrogen fixing symbiotic and free living micro-organisms
viii. Amount of food produced for the population
ix. Agricultural land converting into buildings and industries
x. Conversion of agrarian culture into consumerism
xi. Rural habitation shifting to urban
xii. Self-employment of farmers are disturbed

Major Area III: Soil

Unit 5: Soil

(a) Introduction
i. Important natural resource
ii. Supports growth of plants and many organisms
iii. Soil depletion
iv. Soil erosion—causes, effects and preventive measures

(b) Soil treming with life
i. Treasure of living organisms

(c) Soil profile
i. Layers of soil
ii. What is humus
iii. Weathering of soil
iv. What is soil profile
v. Characteristics of A – horizon, B – horizon and C – horizon
vi. Bedrock
vii. How loss of humus soil occurs
viii. Mining and its effect on soil profile

(d) Soil types
i. Products of weathering
ii. Parent rock

iii. What is soil
iv. Sandy soil, clayey soil, loamy soil—characteristics
v. Water and weathering
vi. Soil erosion and transport
vii. Lichens and weathering
viii. Chemical weathering and mechanical weathering
ix. Need to preserve soil

(e) Properties of soil
   i. Percolation rate of water
   ii. Percolation of water versus various chemicals in the soil
   iii. Soil water content and infiltration rates

(f) Moisture in soil
   i. Nature of water vapour above the soil in summer
   ii. Drainage on run off and flood
   iii. Soil moisture and agriculture

(g) Absorption of water by soil
   i. What is soil moisture?

(h) Soil and crops
   i. Types of soil in different parts of India
   ii. Factors affecting soil
   iii. Climatic factors and vegetation
   iv. Types of soil for various crops like, wheat, gram, paddy, lentils, pulses, cotton etc.
   v. Weather and climate
   vi. Run off potential
   vii. Soil erosion and slope failure
   viii. Reservoir management
   ix. Geotechnical engineering
   x. Water quality
   xi. Soil management and crop management
   xii. Soil fertility and crop nutrition
   xiii. Soil-borne diseases
   xiv. Soil salinity, pH, and Nutrient requirement
   xv. Organic fertilizers and soil fertility

Major Area IV: Our Earth

Unit 6: Inside our Earth

(a) Introduction
   i. Earth—a dynamic planet
(b) Interior of the earth
   i. Nature of crust, core and mantle
   ii. Impact of mining on different layers of earth
(c) Rocks and minerals
   i. Types of rocks
   ii. What is rock
   iii. Types of rocks—igneous rocks (intrusive and extrusive rocks), sedimentary rocks and metamorphic rocks
   iv. Rocks and groundwater conservation
   v. Phosphate rocks for sustainable agriculture
   vi. Quarrying and environmental impact
   vii. Depleting of igneous, sedimentary and metamorphic rocks due to over usage by human beings.
   viii. Sustainable development of mineral resources
   ix. Rock cycle
   x. Over exploitation of minerals—how it influences the nature and life forms on earth.

Unit 7: Our Changing Earth

(a) Introduction
   i. Lithospheric plates
   ii. Movement of lithospheric plates
   iii. Endogenic forces
   iv. Exogenic forces
   v. What is volcano and earthquake
   vi. What is focus and epicentre
   vii. Man's activity affecting the earth
   viii. Tsunami—a natural calamity
   ix. Emission of gases in a volcanic eruption and how it harms our environment
   x. Improved technology as a helping agent in predicting natural calamities
(b) Major land forms
   i. Weathering and erosion
   ii. Soil erosion—its causes and effects

(c) Work of a river
  i. What is waterfall
  ii. What are Meanders, ox bow lake, delta, levees, flood plain and distributaries
  iii. Human activities and water pollution
  iv. Flood: its importance and its impact on life forms

(d) Work of sea waves
  i. What are sea waves, arches, stacks and sea cliff
  ii. Tsunami waves: Its causes, effects and how to prevent such natural calamities

(e) Work of ice
  i. Glaciers and glacial moraines
  ii. Greenhouse effect and its effect on glaciers and coastal areas

(f) Work of wind
  i. Wind as an active agent for erosion
  ii. What are mushroom rocks, sand dunes and loess

Unit 8: Forests—Our Lifeline

(a) Introduction
  i. Forests as green lungs
  ii. Forests as an important renewable natural resource

(b) Visit to a forest
  i. Top canopy
  ii. Shrubs and herbs
  iii. Various food chains
  iv. Creepers and climbers
  v. Various animals, insects, spiders, squirrels found
  vi. Decomposers
  vii. Transpiration
  viii. Green lungs
  ix. Tribes and forest
  x. Seed dispersal by animals
  xi. Forest as a natural absorber of rainwater
  xii. Role of forests in controlling floods
  xiii. Role of forests in controlling soil erosion
  xiv. Role of forests in bringing rainfall
  xv. Role of forests in reducing noise pollution
  xvi. Forests and wildlife for maintaining ecological balance
  xvii. Chief forest products

xviii. Tropical and sub-tropical forests getting disturbed
xix. Reasons for destruction of forests
xx. Forests and ecological balance
xxi. Desertification
xxii. Deforestation
xxiii. Afforestation
xxiv. Plants and soil fertility
xxv. Impact of increase in CO_2 in the atmosphere
xxvi. Forest and economy
xxvii. Aesthetic value of forest
xxviii. Eco-tourism

Unit 9: Natural Vegetation and Wildlife

(a) Introduction
   i. Classification of natural vegetation into forests, grasslands and shrubs
   ii. What is biodiversity
   iii. Rio Declaration (1992)
   iv. Richer biodiversity in the tropics
   v. Distribution of species in the polar regions

(b) Forests: Tropical evergreen forests
   i. Also called as tropical rainforests
   ii. Place is hot and receive heavy rainfall
   iii. Hardwood trees are found here
   iv. Flora and fauna vary depending on climate, altitude, soil
   v. Hotspots of biodiversity
   vi. Changing biological diversity
   vii. Climate and trees found

(c) Tropical Deciduous forest
   i. Monsoon forests
   ii. Trees shed their leaves in the dry season
   iii. Climate and trees found
   iv. The hardwood trees found
   v. Biology of rare and declining species
   vi. Restoration of ecology through *ex-situ* conservation
   vii. Determining patterns and indicators of ecological response to stress

(d) Temperate evergreen forests
   i. Located in the mid-latitudinal coastal region
   ii. Climate and trees found

(e) Temperate deciduous forests

i. Found towards higher latitudes
ii. The common trees found
iii. Ecosystems that are heavily affected by human beings
iv. Restoration of the degraded ecosystem in an environmentally friendly manner
v. Climate and trees found

(f) Mediterranean vegetation

i. Found in the west and southwest margins of the continents
ii. Climate and trees found here
iii. United nations conservation of biological diversity
iv. Monitoring the impact of deforestation and various forms of pollution

(g) Coniferous forests

i. Found in the higher latitudes (50°–70°) of Northern hemisphere
ii. Climate and trees found
iii. Conservation and wise use of world's biodiversity for sustainable development
iv. Endemic species and its conservation

(h) Grasslands: Tropical grasslands

i. These grow on either side of the equator and extend till the tropics
ii. Climate and trees found
iii. Animals found
iv. Conserving species which are vulnerable, endangered, rare, threatened and lower risk
v. Various causes of loss of biological diversity
vi. Environmental pollution disturbs the food chain and food web, which lead to destruction of flora and fauna

(i) Temperate grasslands

i. These are found in the mid-latitudinal zones and in the interior part of the continents
ii. Plants and animals found
iii. Reasons for loss of biodiversity

(j) Thorny bushes

i. These are found in the dry desert like regions
ii. Climate found
iii. Plants and animals found
iv. Measures taken in India for conservation of biodiversity including the legal framework
v. Promoting *ex-situ* conservation and *in-situ* conservation
vi. Human activities responsible for loss of plant diversity
vii. Policy measures for conservation and suitable utilization of forest biodiversity

Unit 10: Environment

(a) What is environment?

i. What is environment?
ii. What is natural environment?
iii. What is man-made environment?
iv. Human environment
v. Human influence on natural environment
vi. Influence of human activities on land, climate, vegetation and wildlife

(b) Natural environment

i. Components of natural environment
ii. Nature of lithosphere, hydrosphere, atmosphere and biosphere
iii. Depletion of the natural environment by various natural and human influences
iv. How the topsoil of the lithosphere get washed away
v. Major landforms of earth
vi. Inter-relationship of the realms (Lithosphere, Hydrosphere, Atmosphere and Biosphere) of the earth
vii. How climate changes influences the earth's atmosphere and its life forms
viii. Need for conserving natural vegetation and wildlife

(c) What is Ecosystem?

i. Meaning of ecosystem
ii. Develop sensitivity towards environment
iii. How an ecosystem gets vanished, polluted and destroyed

(d) Human environment

i. Transition of man from ancient to modern
ii. Human settlement, transport and communication—how it causes hindrance to natural environment
iii. Changes in the environment; like global warming, greenhouse effect, ozone depletion etc.
iv. Changing world due to globalization, commercialization, urbanization etc. and how it can influence the life forms
v. Measures to control industrialization, urbanization etc.
vi. Need to sustain the natural environment for the well-being of all life forms on earth

Major Area V: Fibre to Fabric

Unit 11: Fibre to Fabric

(a) Introduction

i. Animals that produce wool and silk
ii. Importance of wool

(b) Animal fibres—wool and silk
   i. The wool yielding animals
   ii. Two types of fibres: 1. the coarse beard hair, 2. the fine soft under hair
   iii. Selective breeding is done for producing offspring of special characteristics
   iv. Growth of farm animals—its importance in eradicating poverty and attaining growth of economy
   v. Selective breeding for producing disease resistant varieties, high yielding varieties

(c) Animals that yield wool

(d) From fibre to wool
   i. Rearing and breeding of sheep
   ii. Some of the breeds of sheep reared

(e) Processing fibre into wool
   i. Steps in wool processing
   ii. Satisfy the needs (of fibre) of human beings without destroying or harming the population of sheep

(f) Silk
   i. What is sericulture
   ii. Sericulture industry and its potential in India

(g) Life history of silk moth
   i. Life cycle
   ii. Silkworm rearing and its importance in economy
   iii. Silk industry
   iv. Silk export
   v. New technology in sericulture

(h) From cocoon to silk

(i) Rearing silkworms
   1. Process of silkworm rearing
   2. Rearing of silkworm resulting in killing of pupa
   3. Conservation of silkworm genetic resources
   4. Development of appropriate technology for silkworm rearing
   5. For sustainable development of sericulture and progressive increase in productivity
   6. Processing silk

Major Area VI: Water Management

Unit 12: Water

(a) Introduction
   i. Water cycle
   ii. One of the five elements—earth, fire, air, space and water

iii. Modern development and mismanagement of water

iv. Shortage of water leads to epidemics, hunger, despair and death

(b) Distribution of water bodies

i. Watershed projects

ii. Rainwater harvesting

iii. Activities to prevent runoff water

iv. Avoiding concretizing the land

(c) Ocean circulation

i. Waves, tides and currents

(d) Waves

i. What are waves?

ii. What is Tsunami?

iii. Construction of dams, buildings, destruction of forests and natural land etc. as the cause of earthquake and volcanic eruptions

iv. Reasons for occurrence of Tsunami

(e) Tides

i. What is tide?

ii. High tide and low tide

iii. Spring tide and neap tide

(f) Ocean currents

i. What are ocean currents?

Unit 13: Water—A Precious Resource

(a) Introduction

i. World water day

ii. Amount of water recommended per person per day

iii. Water scarcity—its causes, effects and preventive measures

iv. Need for a more oriented and integrated approach to water management and development

v. Different ways of managing water

vi. Managing water at individual level, within cities and between states and countries

(b) How much water is available

i. 71% of earth's surface is covered with water

ii. Most of this water is not fit for human consumption

iii. Freshwater

iv. Decreasing the amount of usable water on earth

v. Impact of water depletion

vi. How water gets polluted?
vii. Eutrophication
viii. No. of rivers in the state
ix. Nationalizing rivers
x. Water becoming a political issue
xi. Bloodshed occurred on water issues
xii. Greed for water and equal distribution of water

(c) Forms of water
i. Water cycle
ii. Solid, liquid and gaseous forms of water on earth
iii. Various projects to protect water
iv. How human settlements pollute water
v. Industrialisation and water pollution
vi. Water quality management issues
vii. Reutilisation and recycling of waste water
viii. Water pollution control through law
ix. Assessment of water quality
x. Use of solar power for cleaning polluted water

(d) Groundwater as an important source of water
i. Water table
ii. Infiltration
iii. Aquifer
iv. Future of groundwater resources at risk
v. Acid rain
vi. Rainwater harvesting
vii. Constructing pits for conserving and percolation of water
viii. Water management in kitchen
ix. Water management in garden
x. Active participation at individual level

(e) Depletion of water table
i. Depletion of water table
ii. Increasing population and groundwater
iii. Population pressure on agriculture forces increasing use of groundwater
iv. Changing climatic patterns
v. Concrete buildings, mining and flooring reduce the percolation of water into the soil
vi. A sustainable agriculture is needed to sustain the needs of the increasing population

(f) Distribution of water
   i. Excessive rainfall causes floods, whereas the absence of rain results in drought
   ii. The water available for use varies widely

(g) Water management
   i. How wastage of water occurs
   ii. Use water economically
   iii. Ways of water harvesting or rainwater harvesting
   iv. What is Bawri and drip irrigation
   v. Sustainable water use
   vi. Sustainable criteria for water

(h) What role can you play? Effect of water scarcity on plants
   i. Plants wilt and ultimately dry up if they are not watered
   ii. Create awareness among the community
   iii. Ones role at home and school

Unit 14: Waste Water Story

(a) Introduction
   i. What is waste water
   ii. Stagnant waste water causes different contagious diseases
   iii. Replication of mosquitoes in stagnant water

(b) Water, Our lifeline
   i. Accessibility to safe drinking water
   ii. Increasing scarcity of freshwater is due to population growth, pollution, industrial development, mismanagement and other factors
   iii. The period 2005-15 as the International Decade for Action on 'Water for life'
   iv. Sewage treatment
   v. Chemical and microbial contamination of water
   vi. Awareness among public about the steps to be taken for maintaining safe drinking water
   vii. Over exploitation and pollution of water

(c) What is sewage?
   i. Meaning of sewage
   ii. Organic and inorganic impurities in the sewage
   iii. Proper disposal of wastes
   iv. Improper disposal of wastes from hospitals, industries etc. into water bodies and its impact on environment
   v. Mixing of degradable and non-degradable wastes

vi. Proper recycling of wastes
vii. Sewage disposal in highly polluted places
viii. Avoiding sewage disposal in areas of human settlements

(d) Water freshens up—an eventful journey
i. Treatment plant
ii. Regular checking of sewage pits to prevent the outbreak of contagious diseases

(e) Waste water treatment plant (WWTP)
i. Treatment of waste water involving physical, chemical and biological processes
ii. Role of technology in waste water treatment
iii. Convert sewage into usable forms like Biogas
iv. Avoid direct discharge of wastes into water bodies

(f) Become an active citizen
i. Participatory behaviour of public

(g) Better housekeeping practices

(h) Sanitation and disease
i. Poor sanitation and contaminated drinking water is the cause of a large number of diseases
ii. Untreated human excreta are a health hazard, cause water pollution and soil pollution
iii. Diseases like cholera, typhoid, Polio, Meningitis, Hepatitis and Dysentery
iv. Outbreak of various diseases like Malaria, Chikunguniya, etc. due to unhygienic waste disposal and due to stagnant water

(i) Alternative arrangements for sewage disposal
i. Low cost onsite sewage disposal systems

(j) Sanitation at public places
i. Railway stations, bus depots, airports, hospitals are places where large amount of waste is generated
ii. The government has laid down certain standards of sanitation

(k) Conclusion
i. Adopting good sanitation practices
ii. Individual initiative
iii. Collective action

Major Area VII: Air

Unit 15: Air

(a) Introduction
i. What is atmosphere?
ii. Importance of atmosphere
iii. One of the important element in the five elements—earth, fire, air, space and water

(b) Composition of the atmosphere

i. The composition of gases in the atmosphere needs to be maintained in a balance

ii. Atmosphere gets polluted due to different poisonous gases

iii. Need to plant more trees which is suitable for each place

iv. Planting of more suitable trees to prevent the excessive accumulation of carbon dioxide in the atmosphere

v. Increase in carbon dioxide level leading to greenhouse effect and global warming and its impact on the environment.

(c) Structure of the atmosphere

i. Troposphere, Stratosphere, Mesosphere, Thermosphere and Exosphere

ii. How troposphere, stratosphere, mesosphere, thermosphere and exosphere get affected by human activities

(d) Weather and climate

i. What is climate

ii. Monitor the impact of climate change, deforestation and various forms of pollution

(e) Temperature

i. What is temperature?

ii. What is insolation?

iii. Changes in climatic patterns

iv. Trapping of solar energy for domestic purposes

v. Temperature fluctuations causing global warming and its impact

vi. Industrialization, modernization, globalization and its relation to increase in temperature

(f) Air pressure

i. What is air pressure?

ii. Cyclones and its impact

(g) Wind

i. What is wind?

ii. Permanent wind, seasonal wind and local wind

iii. What is loo?

iv. Changes occurring in various seasons like heavy rains during monsoon, rains during summer, lack of rain, rain in desert etc.

(h) Moisture

i. Water vapour

ii. How is rain formed

iii. Rains that are not seasonal and its impact on environment

Major Area VIII: Human Environment—Interaction, Settlements, Transportation and Communication

Unit 16: Human Environment—Settlements, Transport and Communication

(a) Introduction
   i. What are settlements?
   ii. Early life
   iii. Permanent and temporary settlements
   iv. Rural settlements, compact settlements and scattered settlements
   v. The early man and how they lived a life in accordance with nature
   vi. How exploiting of nature by man started
   vii. Need for a sustainable development to satisfy the needs of man and without exploiting other organisms
   viii. Compact settlements in big cities—how it creates pollution of various types
   ix. Rural life—need of developments in these areas
   x. Urban life—has many differences—culturally, environmentally, morally

(b) Transport
   i. What is transportation?
   ii. Early transportation
   iii. Modern transportation
   iv. Modern transport causing various types of pollution
   v. Exploiting natural resources

(c) Roadways
   i. What are roadways?
   ii. Metalled and unmetalled roads
   iii. Subways or under paths

(d) Railways
   i. The invention of the steam engine and the Industrial Revolution
   ii. Diesel and electric engines have largely replaced the steam engines
   iii. Superfast trains
   iv. Advanced technological skills
   v. It is the largest in Asia

(e) Waterways
   i. Inland waterways and sea routes
   ii. Important ports of the world
   iii. Oil leakage into water bodies from vessels moving in the sea
   iv. Big ships causes harm to water-living organisms

(f) Airways
   i. Importance of airways
   ii. Air traffic is adversely affected by bad weather
   iii. Important airports

(g) Communication
   i. Information revolution in the world
   ii. Newspapers, radio and television—Mass communication
   iii. Importance of satellites
   iv. Electronic mails or e-mails

Unit 17: Human Environment—Interaction, the Tropical and Sub-tropical Region

(a) Life in the Amazon
   i. Climate
      1. Hot and wet climate
   ii. Rainforests
      1. Thick forests grow that create dense roof and does not allow the sunlight to reach the ground
      2. Plants and animals found
      3. Deforestation of these rainforests
      4. Conversion of these forests to agricultural lands
      5. Remote sensing technology helping in conservation of Amazon
   iii. People of the rainforest
      1. Crops that are cultivated
      2. The indigenous population
      3. Large area of the rainforest has been disappearing annually in the Amazon basin due to developmental activities
      4. Culture and lifestyles of the people are well adapted to the environment
      5. Threat to the Amazon basin is deforestation and cattle ranching

(b) Life in the Ganga-Brahmaputra basin
   i. Monsoon climate
   ii. Crops that are cultivated
   iii. Vegetation varies according to the landforms
   iv. Mangrove forests
   v. Variety of wildlife
   vi. Animals found
   vii. Tourism
   viii. Water resource management approach

ix. Surplus water and flooding
x. International conflicts and co-operation
xi. Environmental factors affecting quality and quantity of water
xii. Flood control programmes in India
xiii. The environmental value and the geomorphic importance of floods

Chapter 4

How to Integrate ESD

This Unit includes the following stages of the content development. This is the Developmental Phase II which includes the following stages:

(a) Integrating the concepts of sustainable development meaningfully
(b) Preparation of concept maps for the selected units
(c) Planning the pedagogical approaches and the learning activities for the selected units
(d) Unit planning
(e) Preparation of lesson plans
(f) Planning for assessment

After analysing the plug points in the selected units, the concepts of sustainable development were integrated meaningfully in the desired places. Example of the integration carried out for one unit each in Science and Social Science is summarised in the Tables 4.1 and 4.2 to show how ESD was integrated.

Table 4.1: Integration of the Concepts of Sustainable Development in Science

UNIT–NUTRITION IN PLANTS

Concepts in the Textbook	Sub-Concepts in the Textbook	ESD Integrated
Nutrients	Proteins. Fats. Vitamins. Minerals.	What is the importance of nutrients in maintaining proper health. Malnutrition and poverty. Percentage of food production versus population. Today no fruits and vegetables are there without chemicals. Causes bio-magnification. Food production, Food management and Food preservation.
Plants make their own food but animals cannot		How man destroys nature for satisfying his needs. Loss of soil fertility.

Contd....

Mode of nutrition in plants	Plants prepare food by themselves using water. Carbon dioxide and minerals. Nutrients help in building their bodies, to grow, repair damaged parts and providing energy. Nutrition is the mode of taking food by an organism and its utilization by body. The mode of nutrition in which organisms make food themselves is called Autotropic organisms. Eg. Plants. Heterotrophs are organisms that depend on others for food. Where are food factories of plants located? How plants obtain raw materials? How do they transport them?	Importance of water not only to plants, but also for other organisms. Degradation of minerals in soil. Food prepared by plants are being used by human and food scarcity. Nutrient deficiency leading to various diseases. The plants upon which we depend on the food we eat, for the oxygen we breathe depends in turn upon the soil (which supplies with the mineral elements they use). Proper nutrients to be needed in appropriate quantity. Introducing of hybrid varieties and its impact. Excessive use of pesticides and weedicides and its impact like causing of more diseases. Continuous use of fertilizers and pesticides reduces the quality of soil.
Photosynthesis—food making process in plants	Leaves are food factories Water and mineral in soil are absorbed by roots. Carbon dioxide is taken from air through stomata. Chlorophyll helps leaves to capture energy of sunlight. Sun is the ultimate source of energy for all living organisms. Photosynthesis (photo = light and synthesis = to combine) is a process in which the chlorophyll containing leaves in the presence of sunlight use carbon dioxide and water to synthesize carbohydrates (food-starch).	Replenishing the soil nutrients by various ways. Usable water getting reduced. Amount of various gases in atmosphere and its impact on earth. Use of solar energy as a major source of energy (solar cooker, solar heater etc.). Amount of oxygen reducing and how it influences life. Climatic change. Importance of protecting plants and trees.

Contd....

	$CO_2 + H_2O \xrightarrow[\text{chlorophyll}]{\text{Sunlight}}$ Carbohydrates + O_2 Oxygen, which is essential for survival of all living organisms, is produced during photosynthesis. Leaves other than green also perform photosynthesis. Synthesis of plant food other than carbohydrates (proteins and fats) is by using nitrogen from the soil.	Reforestation and human settlements. Agriculture—Crop rotation. Plant protein as a source of food for animals including humans.
Other modes of nutrition in plants	Some plants have heterotrophic mode of nutrition. Plants like Cuscuta are parasitic over other plants (host). Insect eating plants are called Insectivorous plants.	Biodiversity—Importance of preserving it.
Saprotrophs	The mode of nutrition in which organisms take in nutrients in solution form from dead and decaying matter is called saprotrophic nutrition and such plants are called saprotrophs, e.g. Fungi. Some organisms live together and share shelter and nutrients, which is called symbiotic relationship. In Lichens, a chlorophyll containing partner, which is an algae, and a fungus live together.	In industries like paper industry, beverages etc...its uses and harm to nature.
How nutrients are replenished in the soil	Farmers spread manure or fertilizers in the field. Since plants absorb mineral nutrients from soil, it gets replenished. Fertilizers contain Nitrogen, potassium, phosphorus etc. A bacterium called Rhizhobium can convert atmospheric nitrogen to its soluble form, which can be used by plants.	How can Rhizobium improve the yield of agricultural crops? Use of Natural manures in agriculture. Crop rotation as a means of improving soil fertility. Environment friendly. Avoiding soil depletion in a natural way.

Contd....

	Rhizobium lives in the roots of leguminous plants in the form of symbiotic association with plants. This is helpful for farmers since they need not add nitrogen fertilizers in the soil.	Microorganisms that can fix atmospheric nitrogen can be classified into two main groups as symbiotic microorganisms and free-living microorganisms (e.g. Cyanobacteria). How much agricultural land is available. Amount of food produced per population. Agricultural land getting converted into buildings and industries. Conversion of agrarian culture into consumerism. Who should take care of agriculture. Selling of agricultural land and migrating to towns. Wasting agricultural land causes taking away of self-employment of farmers and converting it into IT companies and industries.

UNIT–FIBRE TO FABRIC

Introduction	Wool is obtained from the fleece (hair) of sheep or Yak. Silk fibres come from cocoons of the silk moth.	Use of wool in colder parts of the world.
Animal fibres—wool and silk	Wool: It comes from sheep, goat, yak and some other animals. The wool yielding animals bear hair on their body, which trap a lot of air. Air is a poor conductor of heat. So hair keeps these animals warm. The hairy skin of the sheep has two types of fibres: (1) the coarse beard hair (2) the fine soft under hair. Selective breeding is done for producing offspring of special characteristics.	Growth of farm animals—its importance in eradicating poverty and attaining growth of economy. Livestock production. Selective breeding for producing disease resistant varieties, high yielding varieties, etc.

Contd....

Animals that yield wool	Angora wool is obtained from angora goats found in hilly regions as Jammu and Kashmir. Wool is obtained from goat hair. Fur (hair) on the body of camels is also used as wool. Llama and Alpaca found in South America also yield wool.	
From fibre to wool	Rearing and breeding of sheep. Sheep are herbivores and prefer grass and leaves. Some of the breeds of sheep reared in our country are Lohi, Rampur bushair Nali, Bakharawal, Marwari, and Patanwadi.	
Processing fibre into wool	Step 1: The fleece of the sheep along with a thin layer of skin is removed from its body (shearing). Step 2: The sheared skin with hair is thoroughly washed in tanks to remove grease, dust and dirt (scouring). Step 3: The hairy skin is sent to a factory where hair of different textures are separated or sorted (sorting). Step 4: Small fluffy fibres called burrs are picked out from the hair. The fibres are scoured again and dried. Step 5: The fibres can be dyed in various colour, as the natural fleece of sheep and goat is black, brown or white. Step 6: The fibre are straightened, combed and rolled into yarn.	Satisfy the needs (of fibre) of human beings without destroying or harming the population of sheep.
Silk	Silkworms spin the silk fibres. The rearing of silkworms for obtaining silk is called 'Sericulture'.	Sericulture industry and its potential in India.

Contd....

Life history of silk moth	The female silk moth lays eggs, from which hatch larva which are called caterpillar or silkworms. Caterpillar moves to the next pupa stage where it first weaves a net to hold itself. It swings its head from side to side in the form of a figure '8'. During the movements of the head the caterpillar secretes fibres made of a protein, which hardens on exposure to air and becomes silk fibre. The caterpillar completely covers itself by silk fibres called cocoon. Silk fibres are used for weaving silk cloth, which is obtained from the cocoon of silk moth. Tassar silk, Mooga silk, Kosa silk etc. are obtained from cocoons spun by different types of moths. The most common silk moth is the Mulberry silk moth. India produces plenty of silk on a commercial scale.	Silkworm rearing and its importance in economy of a country. Silk industry. Providing employment. Silk export. New technology in sericulture.
From cocoon to silk	For obtaining silk, moths are reared and their cocoons are collected to get silk threads.	
Rearing silkworms	A female silkworm lays hundreds of eggs at a time. Eggs are stored carefully on strips of cloth or paper and sold to farmers. Keep eggs under hygienic conditions and suitable conditions of temperature and humidity. Eggs are warmed to suitable temperature for the larvae to hatch from eggs. The worms are kept in clean bamboo trays along with fleshy chopped mulberry leaves.	Rearing of silkworm resulting in killing of pupa inside the cocoon. Conservation of silkworm genetic resources. Development of appropriate technology for silkworm rearing and egg production. For sustainable development of sericulture and progressive increase in productivity.

Contd....

	After 25-30 days caterpillar stop eating and move to tiny chambers of bamboo in the tray to spin cocoon. Small racks or twigs may be provided on which cocoon get attached. Caterpillar or silk moth spins the cocoon inside which develops silk moth.	
Processing silk	A pile of cocoon is used for obtaining silk fibres. Cocoons are kept under sun or boiled or exposed to steam. The silk fibres separate out. The process of taking out threads from the cocoon for use as silk is called reeling the silk (done by special machines). Silk fibres are then spun into silk threads, which are woven into silk cloth by weavers.	

UNIT–HEAT

Introduction	Woolen clothes keep us warm and we wear light coloured clothes when it is hot.	
Hot and cold	How do we decide which object is hotter than the other? A reliable measure of the hotness of an object is its temperature. Temperature is measured by a device called Thermometer.	Climate change turning up the heat. Heat beyond a limit can kill human beings. In extreme heat and humidity evaporation is slowed down and the body must work extra hard to maintain normal temperature.
Measuring temperature	The thermometer that measures our body temperature is called Clinical thermometer. A clinical thermometer consists of a long, narrow, uniform glass tube with a bulb at one end having mercury.	Older adults, young children and those who are sick or overweight are more likely to succumb to extreme heat. Fever and rise in body temperature of human body.

Contd....

	Outside the bulb, a small shining thread of mercury can be seen. The scale use is the Celsius scale (°C) which reads temperature from 35°C to 42°C. The normal temperature of human body is 37°C. This could be slightly higher or slightly lower. Normal temperature is the average body temperature of a large number of healthy persons. The clinical thermometer is designed to measure the temperature of human body only. The temperature of human body does not go below 35°C or above 42°C.	Importance of thermometer in maintaining health consciousness. People living in urban areas may be at greater risk from the effect of prolonged heat waves than those living in rural areas. Asphalt and concrete store heat longer and gradually release heat at night which can produce higher night time temperature known as 'urban heat island effect'. Heat stroke or sun stroke and its impact. How to prepare oneself from extreme heat. Usually in high temperature, high humidity or rigorous exercise in hot weather, the natural cooling system (sweating) begin to fall which may result in heat illness, which can come in the form of heat cramps, heat exhaustion or heat stroke.
Laboratory Thermometer	The range of a laboratory thermometer is generally from –10°C to 110°C. The temperature must be read while the thermometer is in water in a laboratory. In clinical thermometer there is a kink that prevents mercury level from falling on its own.	
Transfer of heat	Heat flows from a hotter object to a colder object. The process by which heat is transferred from the hotter end to the colder end of an object is known as conduction. The materials that allow heat to pass through them easily are conductors of heat, e.g. Al, Fe, Cu.	Use of copper in wires and the various insulators being used. Non-conventional power plants. Development of environmentally friendly cables. How geothermal heat pumps could power the future.

Contd....

	The materials that do not allow heat to pass through them easily are poor conductors of heat, which are called as insulators, e.g. Plastic, wood, water, air. When water is heated the water near the flame gets hot. Hot water rises up, cold water from the sides moves towards the source of heat. This water also gets hot and rises and water from the sides moves down. This mode of heat transfer is called convection. In coastal areas during day, the land gets heated faster than water. The air over the land becomes hotter and rises up, cooler air from sea rushes towards the land. Warm air from land move towards sea. The air from the sea is called sea breeze. At night it is reverse. The water cools down more slowly than land. So the cool air from the land moves towards the sea. This is called land breeze. From the sun the heat comes to us by a process called radiation. The transfer of heat by radiation does not require any medium. When heat falls on some object, a part of it is reflected, a part is absorbed and a part may be transmitted.	Seasonal land—sea temperature, in conjunction with certain weather patterns, can significantly affect wind speed. Often such changes causes changes in air mass stability or sea or land breeze development. Trapping of solar energy for domestic purposes like in solar heater, solar cooker etc.
Kinds of clothes we wear in summer and winter	Dark surfaces more heat and hence one feel comfortable with dark coloured clothes in winter. Light coloured clothes reflect most of the heat that falls on them and hence feel more comfortable wearing them in summer.	Global temperature increase due to increase in carbon dioxide. Importance of maintaining proper health.

Contd....

	Wool is a poor conductor of heat. There is air trapped in between the wool fibres, which prevents the flow of heat forms our body to the cold surrounding. Hence we feel warm in winter.	

UNIT–WEATHER, CLIMATE AND ADAPTATIONS OF ANIMALS TO CLIMATE

Weather	The day-to-day condition of the atmosphere at a place with respect to the temperature, humidity, rainfall, wind speed etc. is called the weather at that place. The temperature, humidity and other factors are called the elements of the weather. Weather is a complex phenomenon that it can vary over very short periods of time. The maximum and minimum temperature can be recorded everyday using a maximum and minimum thermometer. The maximum temperature of the day occurs in afternoon while the minimum temperature occurs in early morning. Days are shorter in winter than summer.	Changing weather patterns in different parts of the world. Adverse weather conditions like drought, flood etc. in some places. Greenhouse effect and its impact.
Climate	The average weather pattern taken over a long time, say 25 years is called the climate of the place. If temperature at a place is high most of the time, then we say that the climate of that place is hot. If there is rainfall on most of the days in the same place, then we can say that the climate is hot and wet, e.g. In India, Kerala—very hot and wet. J&K—moderately hot and wet.	

Contd....

	Rajasthan (typical desert)—Hot and dry. NE India—Wet.	
Climate and adaptation	Animals are adapted to survive in the conditions in which they live. Animals living in very hot and cold climate must possess special features to protect themselves against extreme cold or heat. Features and habits that help animals to adapt to their surroundings are a result of the process of evolution, e.g. Animals of polar regions and tropical rainforests.	
Polar regions	e.g. Canada, Greenland, Iceland, Norway, Sweden, Finland, Alaska in USA and Siberian region of Russia. Polar regions present an extreme climate, which is covered with snow. For 6 months the sun does not rise and for 6 months does not set. In winter the temperature can be low as –37°C. Polar bear found here have white fur which protects them from predators. To protect from extreme cold, they have thick layers of fur. They also have a layer of fat under their skin, which insulates the body from cold and keeps it warm. It has long curved and sharp claws, which help to walk in ice. It has a strong sense of smell, which helps to locate and catch its prey. Penguin is also white which has thick skin and lot of fat to protect from cold.	Climate change and the melting of polar ice caps, its impacts. If polar ice caps melts how it affects the life in polar regions.

Contd....

	Penguins are also good swimmers. Other animals living in the polar regions are many types of fishes, foxes, oxen, reindeers etc. They migrate to warmer regions when winter sets in, e.g. Siberian Crane comes to India.	
Tropical rainforest	e.g. Malaysia, Indonesia, Brazil, Republic of Congo, Kenya, Uganda and Nigeria. Tropical region has a hot climate because of its location around equator. The coldest month has temperature less than 15°C and in summer it may cross 40°C. Days and nights are almost equal in length. They receive plenty of rainfall and has tropical rainforests. It is found in Western ghats and Assam in India, Southeast Asia, central America and central Africa. Major type of animals living here are monkeys, apes, gorillas, lions, tigers, elephants, leopards, lizard, snakes, birds and insects. The climatic conditions are highly suitable for supporting an enormous number and variety of animals. e.g. Touchan (bird) and its characteristics. Many tropical animals have sensitive hearing, sharp eyesight, thick skin and a skin colour, which helps them to camouflage by blending with the surroundings. e.g. Big cats, Lion, tigers, etc. Lion tailed macaque and its characteristics. Elephant and its characteristics.	Deforestation. Destruction of species leading to endangered species. How these species can be affected as a result of deforestation. How change in climatic conditions influence the life forms in tropical rainforest. What are endangered species and its causes, effects and preventive measures.

Contd....

UNIT–WIND, STORMS AND CYCLONES

Introduction, Air exerts pressure, High-speed winds are accompanied by reduced air pressure, Air expands on heating	The moving air is called wind. Air exerts pressure. High-speed winds are accompanied by reduced air pressure. Air moves from the region where the air pressure is high to the region where pressure is low. Air expands on heating. Warm air is lighter than the cold air. Wind currents are generated due to uneven heating on the earth.	Use of wind energy as an alternative source of energy. Wind turbines for harvesting wind energy.
Wind currents are generated due to uneven heating on the earth Uneven heating between equator and poles	Regions near the equator get maximum heat from the sun. Air in these regions gets warm which rises up and the cooler air from the regions in the 0-30 degrees latitude belt on either side of the equator moves in. These winds blow from the north and south towards the equator. At the poles the air is colder than that at latitudes about 60 degrees. The warm air at these latitudes rises up and the cold wind from the polar regions rushes in, to take its place.	Heating of earth, due to the pollutants. Greenhouse effect and global warming. Impact of heat on the polar regions, which ultimately affect the low-lying areas and coastal areas. Changes in wind patterns causing difference in climate.
Uneven heating of land and water	In summer, near the equator the land warms up faster and most of the time the temperature of the land is higher than that of water in the oceans. The air over the land gets heated and rises. This causes the winds to flow from the oceans towards the land. In winter, the direction of the wind gets reversed. The monsoon wind carries water and it rains.	

Contd....

Thunderstorms and cyclones	Thunderstorm develops in hot, humid tropical areas like India. The rising temperature produce strong upward rising winds, which carry water droplets, upwards, when they freeze and fall down again. The swift movement of the falling water droplets along with the rising air creates lightening and sound. This is called Thunderstorm.	Hurricanes like Typhoon, Tornado, flood and drought leading to human sufferings, loss of lives, economic damage. Timely warnings are essential for mitigating the disastrous impact on population and economy. Information provided by National Meteorological and hydrological services is crucial for sustainable development in all countries.
How a thunderstorm becomes a cyclone	Before cloud formation, water takes up heat from atmosphere to change into vapour. When water vapour changes back to liquid (raindrops) heat is released to the atmosphere, which warms the air around. The air tends to rise and cause a drop in pressure. More air rushes to the centre of the storm. This chain of events ends with the formation of a very low-pressure system with very high speed winds revolving around it. It is called a cyclone. Wind speed, wind direction, temperature and humidity contribute to the development of cyclones.	
Destruction caused by cyclones	Strong winds push water towards the shore even if the storm is hundreds of kilometers away. Low pressure in the eye lifts water surface in the centre where water may rise as high as 3-12 meters, which appear like a water wall moving towards the shore. As a result seawater enters the low-lying coastal areas causing severe loss of life and property, which can also reduce fertility of soil.	Weather, climate and water resources have a drastic impact on socio-economic development and well-being of human kind. Cause drowning of human beings and livestock, erode beaches and embankments, destroy vegetation and reduce soil fertility. Floods and coastal inundation pollute drinking water and cause outbreak of epidemics.

Contd....

	Continuous heavy rainfall may worsen the situation. It can damage houses, telephones, other communication systems, trees etc. Tornadoes: Tornadoes is a dark funnel shaped cloud that reaches from the sky to the ground. A violent tornado can travel at a speed of about 300 km/hour. It may form within cyclones. The whole coastline of India is vulnerable to cyclones, particularly the east coast.	Measures to be taken during a cyclone hit. The type of houses to be constructed in places which are prone to cyclones.
Effective safety measures	Cyclone forecast and warning service. Rapid communication of warnings to the government agencies, port, fisherman, ships and public. Construction of cyclone shelters in cyclone prone areas.	Importance of technology in forecast and warning services.
Action on the part of the people	Should not ignore the warnings issued by meteorological department. Make necessary arrangements to shift essential goods. Avoid driving vehicles through standing water. Keep ready phone number for emergency services. Precautions to be taken if one is staying in a cyclone hit area.	
Advance technology has helped	Due to satellites and radars, a cyclone alert or cyclone watch is issued 48 hours in advance of any expected storm and a cyclone warning is issued 24 hours in advance.	Science and technology for a sustainable society.

Contd....

UNIT–SOIL

Introduction	Soil is one of the most important natural resources. It supports growth of plants. It is home for many organisms. It is essential for agriculture, which provides food, clothing and shelter for all.	Depleting of soil, which is rich in nutrients. Soil erosion: its causes, effects and preventive measures.
Soil treming with life	Soil is a treasure of living organisms like microbes, plants, animals etc.	
Soil profile	Soil is composed of distinct layers. The rotting dead matter in the soil is called humus. Soil is formed by the breaking down of rocks by the action of wind, water and by a process called weathering. A vertical section through different layers of the soil is called soil profile. Each layer (horizon) differs in texture, colour, depth and chemical composition. The uppermost horizon is dark in colour and rich in humus and minerals, which makes the soil fertile and provides nutrients to growing plants. This layer is soft, porous and retains more water which is called topsoil or A-horizon, which provides shelter for many living organisms such as worms, rodents, moles, beetles. The next layer has a lesser amount of humus, but more of minerals. This layer is harder and more compact and is called B-Horizon or middle layer.	Loss of humus soil due to various natural disasters like flood. Soil erosion etc. How mining affects the soil profile?

Contd....

	The third layer is the C-horizon, which is made up of small lumps of rocks with cracks and crevices. Below this layer is the bedrock, which is hard and difficult to dig.	
Soil types	Weathering of rocks produces small particles of various materials like sand and clay. The relative amount of sand and clay depends upon the rock from which the particles were formed i.e. the parent rock. The mixture of rock particles and humus is called the soil. If soil contains greater proportion of big particles it is called sandy soil. If the proportion of fine particles is relatively higher, then it is called clayey soil. If the amount of large and fine particles is about the same, then the soil is called loamy. Sandy soil tends to be light, well aerated and dry. Clay particles are much smaller, can pack tightly leaving little space for air. Water can be held in tiny gaps. The best topsoil for growing plants is loam. Loamy soil is a mixture of sand, clay and silt. It has humus in it, which has the right water holding capacity for growth of plants.	Importance of water in weathering. Soil erosion and transport (Sediments on move). Importance of lichens in weathering of rocks. –Chemical weathering –Mechanical weathering Aggregate water stability of sandy and clayey loam soils. Plants growing in loamy and clayey soils. Need to preserve the soil.
Properties of soil	Percolation rate of water in soil. Glucose $\xrightarrow{\text{without the use of oxygen}}$ Alcohol+ CO_2 ı Energy	Water percolation being affected by various chemicals in the soil. The soil water content influences infiltration and percolation rates.

Contd....

Moisture in soil	On a hot summer day, the vapour coming out of the soil reflects the sunlight and the air above the soil seems to shimmer.	Influence of drainage on run off and flooding. Soil moisture and its impact on agriculture.
Absorption of water by soil	Soil holds water in it, which is called soil moisture.	
Soil and crops	Different types of soil are found in different parts of India. Soil is affected by wind, rainfall, temperature, light and humidity. The climatic factors and components of soil determine the various types of vegetation and crops grown. Clayey and loamy soils are both suitable for growing cereals like Wheat and Gram. For paddy, soils rich in clay and organic matter and having good capacity to retain water are ideal. For lentils and other pulses, loamy soils, which drain water easily, are required. For cotton, sandy loam or loam which drain water easily and can hold plenty of air are more suitable. Crops such as wheat are grown in the fine clayey soils because they are rich in humus and are very feeble.	Weather and climate. Run off potential and flood control. Soil erosion and slope failure. Reservoir management. Geotechnical engineering. Water quality. Soil management and crop management. Soil fertility and crop nutrition. Soil-borne diseases. Soil salinity, pH, and Nutrient requirement. Organic fertilizers and soil fertility.

UNIT–RESPIRATION IN ORGANISMS

Why do we respire	Each cell of an organism performs certain functions such as nutrition, transport, excretion and reproduction for which they need energy. The food has stored energy, which is released during respiration. All living organisms respire to get energy from food.	Carbohydrates (glucose), proteins (amino acids) and fats (fatty acids) are broken down during respiration. Fat need more oxygen for its complete breakdown. High deposit of fats in human body increases ones weight and is difficult to oxidize.

Contd....

	The air we breathe in contain oxygen and that we breathe out is rich in carbon dioxide. The air we breathe in is transported to all parts of the body and ultimately to each cell. In the cells, oxygen in the air helps in the breakdown of food with the release of energy by a process called cellular respiration. Cellular respiration takes place in the cells of all organisms. In the cell, the food (glucose) is broken down into carbon dioxide and water using oxygen. When breakdown of glucose occurs with the help of oxygen, it is called aerobic respiration. Food can also be broken down, without using oxygen, which is known as anaerobic respiration. Breakdown of food releases energy. $\text{Glucose} \xrightarrow{\text{without the use of oxygen}} CO_2 + H_2O + \text{Energy}$ Organisms like yeast survive in the absence of air, which are called as anaerobes. Here in the absence of O_2, glucose breaks down into alcohol and carbon dioxide. $\text{Glucose} \xrightarrow{\text{without the use of oxygen}} CO_2 + H_2O + \text{Energy}$ Anaerobic respiration takes place in muscle cells. $\underset{\text{(In muscle)}}{\text{Glucose}} \xrightarrow{\text{in the absence of oxygen}}$ Lactic acid + Energy The accumulation of lactic acid causes muscle cramps.	Need of proper exercise to maintain a proper amount of carbohydrates, protein and fats in the body. Industrial metabolism—recycling of materials. Use of anaerobes in fermentation in various industries like paper industry, textile industry etc. Active exercise to reduce muscle fatigue.

Contd....

	Hot water bathos massage improves circulation of blood, which results in increase in the supply of oxygen to the muscle cells. The increase in the supply of oxygen results in the complete breakdown of lactic acid into carbon dioxide and water.	
Breathing	Breathing means taking in air rich in oxygen and giving out air rich in carbon dioxide with the help of respiratory organs. The taxing in of air rich in oxygen into the body is called inhalation. Giving out of air rich in carbon dioxide is known as exhalation. The number of times a person breathes in a minute is termed as the breathing rate. A breath means one inhalation plus one exhalation. Whenever a person needs extra energy, he or she breathes faster, so that more oxygen is supplied to our cells.	Increase in CO_2 content in the atmosphere. Resulting in building oxygen parlours in big cities and towns. Breathing problems due to changing lifestyles.
How do we breathe	We take in air through our nostrils. When we inhale air, it passes through our nostrils into the nasal cavity. From the nasal cavity, the air reaches our lungs through the windpipe. Lungs are present in the chest cavity, which is surrounded by ribs on the sides. A large muscular sheet called diaphragm forms the floor of the chest cavity. Breathing involves the movement of the diaphragm and the rib cage.	Various diseases of respiratory system due to changes in environment.

Contd....

	During inhalation, ribs move up and outwards and diaphragm moves down, which increases space in the chest cavity and air rushes into the lungs. During exhalation, ribs move down and inwards, while diaphragm moves upto its former position, which reduces the size of chest cavity and air is pushed out of the lungs.	
Breathing in other animals	Animals such as elephant, lions, cows, goats, frogs, lizards, snakes, birds have lungs in their chest cavities like the human beings. Cockroach: A cockroach has small openings on the sides of its body, which are called spiracles. Insects have a network of air tubes called tracheae for gas exchange. Oxygen rich air rushes through spiracles into the tracheal tube diffuses into the body tissue and reaches every cell of the body. Similarly carbon dioxide from the cells goes into the tracheal tubes and moves out through spiracles. Earthworm: Skin of an earthworm feels moist and slimy on touching. Gases can pass through them. Frogs have pairs of lungs, they can also breathe through their skin which is moist and slippery.	
Breathing under water	Gills in fish help them to use oxygen dissolved in water. Gills are projections of the skin. Gills are well supplied with blood vessels for exchange of gases.	

Contd....

Do plants also respire	Plants take in oxygen from the air and give out carbon dioxide. In the cells, oxygen is used to breakdown glucose into carbon dioxide and water as in other organisms. The leaves of the plants have tiny pores called stomata for exchange of oxygen and carbon dioxide. Roots take up air (oxygen) from air spaces present between the soil particles.	Global climate change and its effect on coastal areas, changes in current vegetation.

UNIT–WATER—A PRECIOUS RESOURCE

Introduction	March 22 is celebrated as the world water day. The amount of water recommended by the United Nations for drinking, washing, cooking and maintaining proper hygiene is a minimum of 50 litres per person per day. In some places there is an acute shortage of water especially during summer. It is estimated that in a few years from now more than one-third of the people in the world could face water scarcity.	Water supports ecosystems, economic development, community well-being and cultural values. Water scarcity: its causes, effects and preventive measures. Need for a more oriented and integrated approach to water management and development. Different ways of managing water. Managing water at individual level, within cities and between states and countries.
How much water is available	71% of earth's surface is covered with water. Almost all the water on the earth is contained in the seas and oceans, rivers, lakes, ice caps, as ground water and in the atmosphere. Most of this water is not fit for human consumption. The water that is fit for use is freshwater.	Decreasing the amount of usable water on earth. Protect freshwater sources. What would be the impact of water depletion? How water gets polluted? Eutrophication: its causes and effects. Number of rivers in the state. Nationalizing rivers. Water becoming a political issue.

Contd....

		Bloodshed occurred on water issues (Kaveri issue). Scarcity of water and it is not any ones property. No greed for water and equal distribution of water.
Forms of water	Water on the earth has been maintained for millions of years by various processes, which make the water cycle. When water circulates through the water cycle, it can be found in all the three forms—solid, liquid and gas at any given time somewhere on the earth. Solid form, snow and ice is present as icecaps at the poles of the earth, snow covered mountains and glaciers. Liquid water is present in oceans, lakes, rivers and underground. Gaseous form is the water vapour present in the air around us. The continuous cycling of water among its three forms keeps the total amount of water on the earth constant.	Various projects to protect water sources like Ganga action plan, Yamuna action plan etc. How human settlements pollute water. Industrialisation and water pollution. Water quality management issues. Reutilisation and recycling of wastewater. Water pollution control through law. Assessment of water quality including coastal water quality. Use of solar power for cleaning polluted water.
Groundwater as an important source of water	Water table is the upper limit of the soil where all the space between particles of soil and gaps between rocks are filled with water. The rainwater and water from other sources such as rivers and ponds seeps through the soil and fills the empty spaces and cracks deep below the ground by a process of infiltration. At places the groundwater is stored between layers of hard rock below the water table, which is known as aquifer.	Future of groundwater resources at risk. Acid rain as a phenomenon of pollution. Rainwater harvesting for conserving water. Constructing pits for conserving and percolation of water. Water management in kitchen. Water management in garden and other domestic purposes. Need of active participation at individual level.

Contd....

Depletion of water table	The water table does not get affected as long as we draw as much water as is replenished by natural processes. Depletion of water table occurs due to many reasons like, increase in population, industrial and agricultural activities, deforestation, decrease in the effective area for seepage of water, scanty rainfall. Increasing population has resulted in consuming more groundwater and allowing lesser water to seep into the ground. The number of industries is increasing continuously where water is drawn from the ground. Population pressure on agriculture forces increasing use of groundwater day-by-day resulting in depletion of water table.	Changing climatic patterns. Concrete buildings, mining and flooring reduce the percolation of water into the soil. A sustainable agriculture is needed to sustain the needs of the increasing population.
Distribution of water	Some regions have excessive rains while others have very little rainfall. Excessive rainfall causes floods, whereas the absence of rain results in drought.	The water available for use varies widely overtime due to both natural fluctuations in the global hydrological cycle and the non-natural fluctuations caused by human interventions.
Water management	Wastage of water occurs during the supply of water through pipes, leaking taps and other places. Unnecessary use of water and overdrawing from groundwater should be avoided. Individuals should use water economically. Rainwater can be used to recharge the groundwater, which is known as water harvesting or rainwater harvesting.	A sustainable water use: which means the use of water that supports the ability of human society to endure and flourish into the indefinite future without undermining the integrity of the hydrological cycle or the ecological systems that depend on it. (Gleick et al. 1995). Sustainable criteria for water can be • A minimum water requirement will be guaranteed to all humans to maintain human health.

Contd....

	Some ways of rainwater harvesting are through bawris and drip irrigation. Bawri is a traditional way of collecting water. Drip irrigation is a technique of watering plants by making use of narrow tubings, which deliver water directly at the base of the plant.	• Sufficient water will be guaranteed to restore and maintain the health of ecosystem. • Water quality will be maintained to meet certain minimum standards. • Human actions will not impair the long term renewability of fresh water stocks and flows. • Data on water resources availability, use and quality will be collected and made accessible to all parties. • Institutional mechanisms will be set up to prevent and resolve conflicts over water. • Water planning and decision making will be democratic, ensuring representation of all affected parties and fostering direct participation of affected interests.
What role can you play? Effect of water scarcity on plants	Plants wilt and ultimately dry up if they are not watered for a few days.	How to create awareness among the community. Ones role at home and school.

UNIT–FORESTS—OUR LIFELINE

Introduction	Forests serve as green lungs and water purifying systems in nature.	Forests are important renewable natural resource.
Visit to a forest	Forest is a system comprising various plants, animals and microorganisms. The different treetops forms green covers over the land, which is not uniformly green. In forest, the trees form the uppermost layer, followed by shrubs. Herbs form the lowest layer of vegetation. The trees are covered with different types of creepers and climbers.	Forests and wildlife are essential for ecological balance of an area. The chief products that forests supply are wood, minor forest products etc. The major reduction in the forest is in tropical and sub-tropical regions (40.2%).

Contd....

	The branchy part of a tree above the stem is known as the crown of the tree (canopy). Trees have crowns of different types and sizes. These have created understoreys in the forest. Giant trees constituted the top layer, followed by shrubs and tall grasses and herbs formed the lowest layer. Various animals, insects, spiders, squirrels, various other small animals are found in the forest. All animals whether herbivores or carnivores depend on plants for food. Organisms which feed on plants often get eaten by other organisms. Many food chains can be found in a forest. All food chains are linked. If any one food chain is disturbed, it affects other food chains. Mushrooms, tiny insects, millipedes, ants, beetles and microorganisms in the soil feed upon the dead plant and animal tissues and convert them into dark coloured substances called humus. The microorganisms, which convert the dead plants and animals to humus, are known as Decomposers. The presence of humus ensures that the nutrients of the dead plants and animals are released into the soil. From these the nutrients are again absorbed by roots of the living plants. Plants release oxygen through the process of photosynthesis, which are used by animals for respiration.	Problems such as overgrazing, indiscriminate felling of trees, overexploitation of land resources leads to destruction of forest which ultimately lead to desertification. When forests die, the ecological balance maintained by nature breaks away; and flood or drought are the terrible consequences. Plants reduce evaporation; thus allowing water to remain in soil for a long time. India is losing about 1.5 million hectares of forest cover each year. Forests are destroyed for agriculture, river valley projects, industrial uses, road construction and miscellaneous uses. Desertification causes a steady rise in the atmospheric temperature. Afforestation—a strategy to restore the forests. Role of plants in maintaining soil fertility. Impact of increasing carbon dioxide in the atmosphere—green-house effect and global warming—its causes and effects on the environment. How the seedlings grow in a forest in natural way. Destruction of any one species in the ecosystem disturbs the total balance of ecosystem. Forest is an important component of our environment and economy, it checks air pollution and soil erosion, save hill slopes from land slides and in deserts trees reduce soil erosion by checking wind

Contd....

	Plants maintain the balance of oxygen and carbon dioxide in the atmosphere. Hence forests are called "Green lungs". Trees take in water through their roots and release water vapour into the air through evaporation. The people living in the forest (tribes) depend on forests for their food, shelter, water and medicines. The animals disperse the seeds of certain plants and help the forest to grow and regenerate. The decaying animal dung also provides nutrients to the seedlings to grow. With greater variety of plants, the forest provides greater opportunities for food and habitat for herbivores. Larger number of herbivores means increased availability of food for carnivores. Wide variety of animals helps the forest to regenerate and grow. Decomposers help in maintaining the supply of nutrients, to the growing plants. Hence forest is a living entity. Forest acts as a natural absorber of rainwater and allows it to seep and helps to maintain water table throughout the year. Forests help in controlling floods and maintain the flow of water in the streams so that we get a steady supply of water. Roots of trees bind the soil together, which prevent soil erosion. Forests help in bringing good rainfall in neighbouring areas. Noise pollution can be less due to forests.	velocity, water holding capacity of soil, maintain soil fertility, regulate earth's temperature regimes and water cycle, shifting of sand and silting and reduce flood havoc. It also has aesthetic and tourist values and serve as gene reserve of important species—Eco tourism.

Contd....

	If we do things wisely, we can preserve forests and environment as well as have development.	

UNIT–WASTE WATER STORY

Introduction	Water which is rich in lather, mixed with oil, black brown water that goes down the drains from sinks, showers, toilets, laundries which are dirty is called wastewater.	Stagnant waste water causes different contagious diseases. Cause the replication of mosquitoes in stagnant water.
Water, Our lifeline	Clean water is not available to all. It has been reported that one billion of our fellow human beings have no access to safe drinking water, which cause water related diseases and deaths. The increasing scarcity of freshwater is due to population growth, pollution, industrial development, mismanagement and other factors. On March 22, 2005, the General Assembly of the UN proclaimed the period 2005-2015 as the International Decade for Action on 'Water for life'. The decade aims to reduce by half the number of people who do not have access to safe drinking water. Cleaning of water is a process of removing pollutants before it enters a water body or is reused. This process of waste water treatment is known as 'sewage treatment'.	Chemical and microbial contamination of water. Create awareness among public about the steps to be taken for maintaining safe drinking water. Over exploitation and pollution of water should be controlled.
What is sewage	Sewage is waste water released by homes, industries, hospitals, offices and other users. It also includes rainwater that has run down the street during a storm or heavy rain. Sewage is a liquid waste, which has majority of water with dissolved, and suspended impurities called contaminants.	Proper disposal of wastes for maintaining proper hygiene. Improper disposal of wastes from hospitals, industries etc. into water bodies and its impact on environment. Sewages also mix with rainwater and is carried to other water bodies like river and oceans.

Contd....

	Sewage is a complex mixture containing suspended solids, organic and inorganic impurities, nutrients, saprotropic and disease causing bacteria and other microbes. Organic impurities are human faeces, animal waste, oil, urea (urine), pesticides, herbicides, fruit and vegetable waste etc. Inorganic impurities are nitrates, phosphates, and metals. Nutrients are Phosphorus and Nitrogen. Bacteria are such as which causes Cholera and Typhoid. Other microbes are such as which cause dysentery.	Avoid mixing of degradable and non-degradable wastes. Maintain separate bins for degradable and non-degradable wastes. Separate each impurities based on their degrading ability and its proper recycling should be recommended. Protect ones locality from stagnant water. Sewage disposal in highly polluted places. Avoid sewage disposal in areas of human settlements.
Water freshens up—an eventful journey	In home or a public building generally one set of pipes brings clean water and another set of pipes takes away waste water. A network of big and small pipes called sewers, forming the sewerage is present. It carries sewage from the point of being produced to the point of disposal i.e. Treatment plant. Manholes are located at every 50m to 60m in the sewage, at the junction of two or more sewers and at points where there is a change in direction.	Regular checking of sewage pits to prevent the outbreak of contagious diseases.
Waste Water Treatment Plant (WWTP)	Treatment of waste water involves physical, chemical and biological processes, which remove physical, chemical and biological matter that contaminates the waste water. 1. Waste water is passed through bar screens. Large objects like rags, sticks, cans, plastic packets, napkins are removed.	Role of technology in waste water treatment. Convert sewage into usable forms like Biogas. Avoid direct discharge of wastes into water bodies.

Contd....

	2. Water then goes to a grit and sand removal tank. The speed of the incoming waste water is decreased to allow sand, grit and pebbles to settle down. 3. Water is then allowed to settle in a large tank which is sloped towards the middle. • Solids like faeces settle at the bottom and are removed with a scraper which is called sludge. • A skimmer removes the floatable solids like oil and grease. • Water so cleared is called clarified water. • The sludge is transferred to a separate tank where it is decomposed by anaerobic bacteria, which produce biogas. 4. Air is pumped into the clarified water to help aerobic bacteria to grow and it can consume human waste, food waste, soaps and other unwanted matter remaining in clarified water. Dried sludge is used as manure, returning organic matter and nutrients to the soil. The treated water has a very low level of organic material and suspended matter. • It is discharged into a sea, a river or into the ground. • Nature cleans it up. • It may be necessary to disinfect water with chemicals like chlorine and ozone before releasing it into the distribution system.	

Contd....

Become an active citizen	To be an enlightened citizen, one can approach the municipality or the gram panchayat and insist them to cover the open drains etc.	Participatory behaviour of public to be promoted for cleaning drains, proper plastic disposal etc.
Better housekeeping practices	One of the ways to minimize or eliminate waste is to see what one is releasing down the drain. Cooking oil and fats should not be thrown down the drain as it can harden and block the pipes. Chemicals like paints, solvents, insecticides, motor oils, medicines should not be thrown down the drain as it may kill microbes that help purify water. Used tealeaves, solid food remains, soft toys, cotton, sanitary towels etc. should be thrown in the dustbin.	Avoid or minimize using plastics. Substitute polythene bags with paper bags, which are eco-friendly. Oils and grease if thrown directly in water bodies can affect the organisms living in water, which will not get enough oxygen.
Sanitation and disease	Poor sanitation and contaminated drinking water is the cause of a large number of diseases. A very large fraction of our people defecates in the open, on dry riverbeds, on railway tracks, near fields or directly in water. Untreated human excreta are a health hazard, cause water pollution and soil pollution. It becomes the most common route for water-borne diseases like cholera, typhoid, Polio, Meningitis, Hepatitis and Dysentery.	Outbreak of various diseases like Malaria, Chikunguniya etc. due to unhygienic waste disposal and due to stagnant water.
Alternative arrangements for sewage disposal	To improve sanitation, low cost onsite sewage disposal systems are encouraged, e.g. Septic tanks, chemical toilets, composting pits. Some organizations offer hygienic onsite human waste disposal technology, which do not require scavenging.	Some technology have developed an alternative to dispose human wastes on railway tracks like: • The latrine automatically closes ones the train comes to a halt. • Avoiding using toilets in the railway stations when train is halted.

Contd....

	• Excreta from the toilet seats flow through covered drains into a biogas plant.	
Sanitation at public places	Railway stations, bus depots, airports, hospitals are places where large amount of waste is generated. It must be disposed properly otherwise epidemics may break out. The government has laid down certain standards of sanitation, but unfortunately, they are not strictly enforced. We should not scatter litter anywhere. If there is no dustbin in sight, we should carry the litter home and throw it in the dustbin.	
Conclusion	We all have role in keeping our environment clean and healthy. One must realize ones responsibility in maintaining water sources in a healthy state. Adopting good sanitation practices should be our way of life. As an agent of change, ones individual initiative will make a great difference. A lot can be done if people work together which has a great power in collective action.	

Note: Use Reflective journals on everyday effort shown by students, which can foster Education for Sustainable Development.

Table 4.2: Integration of the Concepts of Sustainable Development in Social Science

UNIT–SOCIAL SCIENCE—OUR ENVIRONMENT AND NATURAL ENVIRONMENT

Concepts	Sub-Concepts	ESD to be Integrated
What is environment	The place, people, things and nature that surround any living organism is called Environment. Environment is a combination of natural and man-made phenomena. The natural environment refers to both biotic and abiotic conditions existing on the earth. Human environment reveals the activities, creations and interactions among human beings.	Environment as the totality of surrounding conditions. It is the surrounding conditions, influences or forces, by which living forms are influenced and modified in their growth and development. How human influences cause danger to natural environment. Influence of land, climate, vegetation and wildlife on human life.
Natural environment	Land, water, air, plants and animals comprise the natural environment. Lithosphere is the solid crust or the hard top layer of the earth, which is made up of rocks and minerals and covered by a thin layer of soil. It is the domain that provides us forests, grasslands for grazing, land for agriculture and human settlements. The domain of water is referred to as hydrosphere, which comprises of different types of water bodies like rivers, lakes, seas, oceans etc. The atmosphere is the thin layer of air that surrounds the earth, which is held due to gravitational force. It protects from the harmful rays and scorching heat of the sun, which consists of a number of gases, dust and water vapour. The changes in the atmosphere produce changes in the weather and climate. Biosphere is a narrow zone of the earth where land, water and air interact with each other to support life and consists of plants and animal kingdom.	Depletion of the natural environment by various natural and human influences. Sustainable development for future prosperity. How the topsoil of the lithosphere get washed away. Major landforms of earth. Interrelationship of the realms (Lithosphere, Hydrosphere, Atmosphere and Biosphere) of the earth. How climate changes influences the earth's atmosphere and its life forms. Need for conserving natural vegetation and wildlife.

Contd....

What is Ecosystem?	All plants, animals and human beings depend on their immediate surroundings. The relation between the living organism, as well as the relation between the organisms and their surroundings form an ecosystem, e.g. Rainforest, grassland, desert, mountains, lake, river, ocean, small ponds, etc.	Develop sensitivity towards environment. How an ecosystem gets vanished, polluted and destroyed.
Human environment	Human beings interact with the environment and modify it according to their need. Early humans adapted themselves to the natural surroundings by leading a simple life and fulfilling their requirements from the nature. When time and need grew, humans learn new ways to use and change environment. They learn to grow crops, domesticate animals and lead a settled life, wheel was invented, surplus food was produced, barter system emerged, trade and commerce developed. Industrial revolution enabled large-scale production; transportation became faster, information revolution made communication easier and speedy. A perfect balance is necessary between the natural and human environment. Humans must learn to live and use their environment in a harmonious way.	Human settlement, transport and communication—how it causes hindrance to natural environment. Changes in the environment; like global warming, greenhouse effect, ozone depletion etc. Changing world due to globalization, commercialization, urbanization etc. and how it can influence the life forms. Measures to control industrialization, urbanization etc. Need to sustain the natural environment for the well-being of all life forms on earth.

UNIT–INSIDE OUR EARTH

Introduction	The earth, our homeland is a dynamic planet. It is constantly undergoing changes inside and outside.	
Interior of the earth	Earth is made up of several concentric layers with one inside another. The uppermost layer over the earth's surface is called the crust.	Mining of silica and alumina—how it influences the lithosphere. Mining can cause severe damage to the earth's crust.

Contd....

	It is the thinnest of all the layers. It is about 35 km. on the continental masses and only 5 km. on the ocean floors. The main mineral constituents of the continental mass are silica and alumina. It is thus called sial. The oceanic crust mainly consists of silica and magnesium; it is therefore called sima. Just beneath the crust is the mantle, which extends up to a depth of 2900 km. below the crust. The innermost layer is the core with a radius of about 3500 km. It is mainly made up of nickel and iron and is called nife which has very high temperature and pressure.	Mining damages the land and pollute the topsoil and contaminate the area with toxic metals and chemicals.
Rocks and minerals	The earth's crust is made up of various types of rocks. Any natural mass of mineral matter that makes up the earth's crust is called a rock, which can be of different colour, size and texture. There are three major types of rocks: igneous rocks, sedimentary rocks and metamorphic rocks. When the molten magma cools, it becomes solid, which are called as igneous rocks (primary rocks); they are of two types—intrusive rocks and extrusive rocks. When the molten lava comes on the earth's surface, it rapidly cools down and becomes solid on the crust, which are known as extrusive igneous rocks, which have a very fine-grained structure. For example, basalt. The molten magma cools down deep inside the earth's crust. Solid rocks so formed are called intrusive igneous rocks. Since they cool down slowly they form large grains. **Granite:** Rocks roll down, crack, and hit each other and are broken down into small fragments called sediments which are transported and deposited by wind, water, etc.	Role of rocks in conserving groundwater. Sustainable groundwater development. Use of phosphate rocks for a sustainable agriculture. Phosphate rocks used in industries. Quarrying and its environmental impacts. Depleting of igneous, sedimentary and metamorphic rocks due to over usage by human beings for building purposes. Steps to be taken for a sustainable development of mineral resources. Igneous and sedimentary rocks being exploited by human beings for constructing buildings. Need for sustainable development of these resources. Rock cycle, which helps in maintaining an ecological balance. Over exploitation of minerals—how it influences the nature and life forms on earth.

Contd....

	These loose sediments are compressed and hardened to form layers of rocks, which are known as sedimentary rocks. For example, sandstone is made from grains of sand. Igneous and sedimentary rocks can change into metamorphic rocks under great heat and pressure. For example, clay changes into slate and limestone into marble. Rocks are useful to us for making roads, houses and buildings. The process of transformation of the rock from one type to another under certain conditions in a cyclic manner is known as the rock cycle. The igneous rocks are broken down into small particles that are transported and deposited to form sedimentary rocks. When the igneous and sedimentary rocks are subjected to heat and pressure they change into metamorphic rocks which are still under great heat and pressure melt down to form molten magma, which can again cool down and solidify into igneous rocks. Minerals are important to mankind. Some are used as fuels (coal, natural gas and petroleum), in industries (iron, aluminium, gold, uranium, etc.), in medicine, in fertilizers etc.	

UNIT–OUR CHANGING EARTH

Introduction	The lithosphere is broken into a number of plates known as the lithospheric plates. Due to the movement of the molten magma inside the earth, the lithospheric plates move around very slowly. The movement of these plates causes changes on the surface of the earth. The earth movements are divided on the basis of the forces, which cause them. The forces that act in the interior of the earth are called as endogenic forces and	Other than natural forces, man also exhibits forces that harm the earth. Human interference on the nature as causation for natural calamities like earthquake. Tsunami—a natural calamity due to the movement of lithospheric plates in the oceans. Emission of gases in a volcanic eruption and how it harms our environment.

Contd....

	that work on the surface of the earth are called as exogenic forces. Endogenic forces sometimes produce sudden movements (Earthquakes and volcanoes) and at the other times produce slow movements (building mountains). A volcano is a vent (opening) in the earth's crust through which molten materials erupts suddenly. When the lithospheric plates move, the surface of the earth vibrates. The vibrations can travel all round the earth, which are called earthquakes. The place in the crust where the movement starts is called the focus. The place on the surface above the focus is called the epicenter. Vibrations travel outwards from the epicenter as waves, where greatest damage is usually closest to the epicenter and the strength of earthquake decreases away from the center. Although earthquakes cannot be predicted, the impact can be minimized if one is prepared beforehand. Some common earthquake prediction methods adopted locally by people include studying animal behaviour; fish in the ponds get agitated, snakes come to the surface.	Human activities like constructing dams, industries, huge buildings, deforestation etc. as a major cause for earthquakes, which cause imbalance to the nature. Improved technology as a helping agent in predicting natural calamities and ways to escape these calamities.
Major landforms	The landscape is being continuously worn away by two processes—weathering and erosion. Weathering is the breaking up of the rocks on the earth's surface. Erosion is the wearing away of the landscape by different agents like water, wind and ice. The process of erosion and deposition create different landforms on the surface of the earth.	Soil erosion—its causes and effects. Apart from Natural erosion, soil erosion occurs due to human activities.

Contd....

Work of a river	The running water in the river erodes the landscape. When the river tumbles at steep angle over very hard rocks or down a steep valley side it forms a waterfall. As the river enters the plain it twists and turns forming large bends known as meanders. Due to continuous erosion and deposition along the sides of the meander, the ends of the meander loop come closer and closer. In due course of time the meander loop cuts off from the river and forms a cut-off lake, also called an ox-bow lake. As the river overflows its banks, it leads to the flooding of the neighbouring areas, which deposits layers of fine soil and other material called sediments along its banks. This leads to the formation of a flat fertile floodplain. The raised banks are called levees. As the river approaches the sea, the speed of the flowing water decreases and the river begins to break up into a number of streams called distributaries. Each distributary forms its own mouth. The collection of sediments from all the mouths forms a delta.	How river gets polluted due to various human activities. River getting polluted as it enters places where human beings are inhabited. Flood: Its importance and its impact on life forms.
Work of sea waves	The erosion and deposition of the sea waves gives rise to coastal landforms. Sea waves continuously strike at the rocks, which develop cracks, which become larger and wider to form hollow like caves called sea caves. As these cavities become bigger and bigger only the roof of the caves remain, thus forming sea arches. Further, erosion breaks the roof and only walls are left which are called stacks. The steep rocky coast rising almost vertically above seawater is called sea cliff.	Tsunami waves: Its causes, effects and how to prevent such natural calamities.

Contd....

Work of ice	Glaciers are "rivers" of ice which too erode the landscape by bulldozing soil and stones to expose the solid rock below. As the ice melts they get filled up with water and become beautiful lakes in the mountains. The material carried by the glacier such as rocks big and small, sand and silt gets deposited which are called glacial moraines.	How Carbon dioxide increase causes Greenhouse effect and its impact on melting of Glaciers and sinking of coastal land.
Work of wind	An active agent of erosion and deposition in the deserts is wind. In deserts you can see rocks in the shape of a mushroom, commonly called mushroom rocks. Winds erode the lower section of the rock more than the upper part, hence such rocks have narrower base and wider top. When the wind blows, it lifts and transports sand from one place to another and when it stops blowing the sand falls and gets deposited in low hill-like structures called sand dunes. When the grains of sand are very fine and light, the wind can carry it over very long distances. When such sand is deposited in large areas, it is called loess.	

UNIT–AIR

Introduction	Our earth is surrounded by a huge blanket of air called atmosphere on which all living beings on the earth depends. It provides us the air we breathe and protects us from the harmful effects of the sun's rays.	Considered as one of the important element in the five elements—earth, fire, air, space and water—it was revered and worshipped and treated by all with respect.
Composition of the atmosphere	Nitrogen and oxygen are two gases, which make up the bulk of the atmosphere. Carbon dioxide, helium, ozone, argon and hydrogen are found in lesser quantities.	The composition of gases in the atmosphere needs to be maintained in a balance for supporting various life forms and ecosystem. Atmosphere gets polluted due to different poisonous gases.

Contd....

	Gases, tiny dust particles are also present in the air. When we inhale, we take some amount of nitrogen into our lungs and exhale it. Plants need nitrogen for their survival, which cannot be taken directly from the air. Bacteria that live in the soil and roots of some plants take nitrogen from the air and change its form so that plants can use it. Humans and animals take in oxygen during breathing and green plants produce oxygen during photosynthesis. Oxygen content in the air remains constant. If we cut trees then this balance gets disturbed. Green plants use carbon dioxide to make their food and release oxygen. Humans or animals release carbon dioxide. The amount of carbon dioxide released by humans or animals seems to be equal to the amount used by the plants, which make a perfect balance. The balance is upset by burning of fuels, such as coal and oil which add billions of tons of carbon dioxide into the atmosphere each year resulting in the increased volume of carbon dioxide which affects the earth's weather and climate.	Oxygen amount in the atmosphere decreases due to human activities. Need to plant more trees which is suitable for each place. Planting of more suitable trees to prevent the excessive accumulation of carbon dioxide in the atmosphere. Increase in carbon dioxide level leading to greenhouse effect and global warming and its impact on the environment.
Structure of the atmosphere	Our atmosphere is divided into five layers starting from the earth's surface, which are Troposphere, Stratosphere, Mesosphere, Thermosphere and Exosphere. Troposphere is the most important layer of the atmosphere. Its average height is 13 km. Almost all the weather phenomena like rainfall, fog and hailstorm occur in this layer. Stratosphere lies above the troposphere, which extends up to a height of 50 km, which is almost free from clouds and	How troposphere, stratosphere, mesosphere, thermosphere and exosphere get affected by human activities.

Contd....

	associated weather phenomenon. It contains a layer of ozone gas. Mesosphere is the third layer above the stratosphere, which extends upto the height of 80 km. Meteorites burn up in this layer on entering from the space. In Thermosphere, temperature rises very rapidly with increasing height. Ionosphere is a part of this layer. It extends between 80-400 km. This layer helps in radio transmission. Exosphere is the uppermost layer of the atmosphere, which has very thin air, light gases like helium and hydrogen.	
Weather and climate	Weather can change dramatically from day to day. The average weather condition of a place for a longer period of time represents the climate of a place.	Monitor the impact of climate change, deforestation and various forms of pollution and explore means of mitigating damages.
Temperature	The degree of hotness and coldness of the air is known as temperature. The temperature of the atmosphere changes not only between day and night but also from season to season. Insolation is the incoming solar energy intercepted by the earth. The amount of insolation decreases from the equator towards the poles. If the earth's temperature rises too high, it would become too warm for some crops to grow. Temperature in cities is much higher than that of villages. The concrete and metals in buildings and the asphalt of roads get heated up during the day.	Change in the climatic patterns in the earth. Trapping of solar energy and using it as an alternative source of energy for domestic purposes. Temperature fluctuations causing global warming and its impact. Industrialization, modernization, globalization and its relation to increase in temperature.
Air pressure	Air pressure is defined as the pressure exerted by the weight of air on the earth's surface.	Cyclones and its impact.

Contd....

	As we go up the layers of atmosphere, the pressure falls rapidly. The air pressure is highest at sea level and decreases with height. In areas where temperature is high, the air gets heated and rises which creates a low-pressure area, which is associated with cloudy skies and wet weather. In areas having lower temperature, the air is cold. It is therefore heavy. Heavy air sinks and creates a high-pressure area. High pressure is associated with clear and sunny skies. The air always moves from high-pressure areas to low-pressure areas.	
Wind	The movement of air from high-pressure area to low-pressure areas is called wind. Winds can be broadly divided into three types. **Permanent winds** are those, which blow constantly throughout the year in a particular direction. For example, Trade winds, Westerlies and Easterlies. **Seasonal winds** are those, which change their direction in different seasons. For example monsoons in India. **Local winds** are those, which blow only during a particular period of the day or year in a small area. For example, land and sea breeze. The hot and dry local wind of northern planes of India is called loo.	Changes occurring in various seasons like heavy rains during monsoon, rains during summer, lack of rain, rain in desert etc.
Moisture	When water evaporates from land and different water bodies, it becomes water vapour. Moisture in the air at any time is known as humidity. When the water vapour rises, it starts cooling. The water vapour condenses causing formation of droplets of water. Clouds are just masses of such water droplets.	Rains that are not seasonal and its impact on environment.

Contd....

	When these droplets of water become too heavy to float in air, then they come down as precipitation. Precipitation that comes down to the earth in liquid form is called rain. Most of the groundwater comes from rainwater. When trees on hillsides are cut, rainwater flows down the bare mountains and can cause flooding of lowlying areas. On the basis of mechanism, there are three types of rainfall: the convectional rainfall, the orographic rainfall and the cyclonic rainfall.	

UNIT–WATER

Introduction	The process by which water continually changes its form and circulates between oceans, atmosphere and land is known as the water cycle. Earth is like a Terrarium, where the same water that existed centuries ago still exists today. The major sources of freshwater are the rivers, ponds, springs and glaciers. The ocean and the seas contain salty water which contains large amounts of dissolved salts, mostly salts of is sodium chloride or the common table salt.	One of the five elements—earth, fire, air, space and water. Modern development and mis-management of water resulted in huge shortage of water. Shortage of water leads to epidemics, hunger, despair and death.
Distribution of water bodies	Three-fourth of the earth surface is covered by water. Distribution of water is Oceans (97.3%) (Saline), Ice-caps (02.0%), Groundwater (0.68%), Freshwater lakes and Inland seas (0.009%), Salt lakes (0.009%), Atmosphere (0.0019%), Rivers (0.0001%) (Freshwater).	Watershed projects for conserving groundwater. Rainwater harvesting and its importance. Activities to prevent run off water. Avoiding concretizing the land to help in easy penetration of water.
Ocean circulation	Ocean water keeps moving continuously and is never still. The movements that occur in oceans can be broadly categorized as: waves, tides and currents.	

Contd....

Waves	When the water on the surface of the ocean rises and falls alternately, they are called waves. During a storm, the winds blowing at very high speed form huge waves, which cause tremendous destruction. An earthquake, a volcanic eruption or underwater landslides can shift large amounts of ocean water, which result in huge tidal wave called tsunami that may be as high as 15m. The largest tsunami ever measured was 150m high. These waves travel at a speed of more than 700 km. per hour. The tsunami of 2004 caused widespread damage in the coastal areas of India. The Indira point in the Andaman and Nicobar islands got submerged after the tsunami.	Construction of dams, buildings, destruction of forests and natural land etc. as the cause of earthquake and volcanic eruptions. Reasons for occurrence of Tsunami. Mans influence on environment and the natural response to these.
Tides	The rhythmic rise and fall of ocean water twice in a day is called a tide. It is high tide when water covers much of the shore by rising to its highest level. It is low tide when water falls to its lowest level and recedes from the shore. The strong gravitational pull exerted by the sun and the moon on the earth's surface causes the tides. The water of the earth closer to the moon gets pulled under the influence of the moon's gravitational force and causes high tide. During the fullmoon and new moon days, the sun, the moon and the earth are in the same line and the tides are highest. These tides are called spring tides. When the moon is in its first and last quarter, the ocean waters get drawn in diagonally opposite directions by the gravitational pull of sun and earth resulting in low tides. These tides are called **neap tides.** The rise and fall of water due to tides is being used to generate electricity in some places.	

Contd....

Ocean currents	Ocean currents are streams of water flowing constantly on the ocean surface in definite directions, which may be warm or cold. The warm ocean currents originate near the equator and move towards the poles. The cold currents carry water from polar or higher latitudes to tropical or lower latitudes. The Labrador Ocean current is cold current while the Gulf Stream is a warm current. The ocean current influences the temperature conditions of the area. Warm currents bring about warm temperature over land surface. The areas where the warm and cold currents meet provide the best fishing grounds.	

UNIT–NATURAL VEGETATION AND WILDLIFE

Introduction	With the change in height, the climate changes and that changes natural vegetation. The growth of vegetation depends on temperature and moisture. It also depends on factors like slope and thickness of soil. Natural vegetation is generally classified into three. Forests are those, which grow where temperature and rainfall are plentiful to support a tree cover. Grasslands are which grow in the region of moderate rain. *Shrubs*: Thorny shrubs and scrubs grow in the dry region.	Biodiversity is 'the variability among living organisms from all sources, including, *inter alia*, terrestrial, marine and other ecosystems and the ecological complexes of which they are part; this includes diversity within species, between species and of ecosystem'—Rio Declaration (1992). Biodiversity is not distributed evenly on earth. It is richer in the tropics. As one approaches the polar regions one finds larger and larger populations of fewer and fewer species.
Forests: Tropical Evergreen forests	These forests are also called tropical rainforests. These forests occur in the regions near the equator and close to the tropics, which are hot and receive heavy rainfall throughout the year. The trees do not shed their leaves altogether.	Flora and fauna vary depending on climate, altitude, soil and the presence of other species. Hotspots of biodiversity. Most hotspots are located in the tropics and most of them are forests.

Contd....

	The thick canopies of the closely spaced trees do not allow the sunlight to penetrate inside the forest even in the daytime, e.g. hardwood trees like rosewood, ebony, mahogany.	Changing biological diversity and how the change will affect community structure and ecosystem processes.
Tropical Deciduous forest	Tropical deciduous are the monsoon forests found in the large part of India, northern Australia and in central America. These regions experience seasonal changes. Trees shed their leaves in the dry season to conserve water. The hardwood trees found in these forests are sal, teak, neem and shisham. Tigers, lions, elephants, langoors and monkeys are the common animals.	Biology of rare and declining species and develop scientific information needed to sustain populations and determine value and viabilities of these species. Restoration of ecology through *ex-situ* conservation. Determining patterns and indicators of ecological response to stress so that technologies needed to assess the status of ecological system, to forecast and assess stress and to monitor the recovery of damaged ecological system.
Temperate Evergreen forests	The temperate evergreen forests are located in the mid-latitudinal coastal region. They are commonly found along the eastern margin of the continents, e.g., In southeast USA, South China and in South East Brazil. They comprise both hard and soft wood trees like oak, pine, eucalyptus, etc.	
Temperate Deciduous forests	These are found towards higher latitudes whereby they shed their leaves in the dry season. These are found in the northeastern part of USA, China, New Zealand, Chile and coastal regions of Western Europe. The common trees are oak, ash, beech, etc. Deer, foxes, wolves are the animals commonly found. Birds like pheasants, monals are also found here.	Ecosystems that are heavily affected by human beings. Restoration of the degraded ecosystem in an environmentally friendly manner.
Mediterranean vegetation	The west and southwest margins of the continents have Mediterranean vegetation, which are found in the areas around the Mediterranean sea in Europe, Africa and	Monitoring the impact of deforestation, various forms of pollution and explore means of mitigating damages.

Contd....

	Asia, and also in California in the USA, southwest Africa, southwestern South America and southwest Australia. These regions are marked for hot dry summers and mild rainy winters. Citrus fruits such as oranges, figs, olives and grapes are commonly cultivated here because people have removed the natural vegetation in order to cultivate what they want to.	United Nations conservation of biological diversity.
Coniferous forests	In the higher latitudes (50°–70°) of Northern hemisphere the spectacular Coniferous forests are found. They have tall, softwood evergreen trees like Chir, pine, cedar. Silver fox, mink, polar bear are the common animals found here.	Conservation and wise use of world's biodiversity for sustainable development. Endemic species and its conservation.
Grasslands Tropical grasslands	These grow on either side of the equator and extend till the tropics. This vegetation grows in the areas of moderate to low amount of rainfall. They can grow very tall, about 3 to 4 meters in height, e.g. savannah grasslands of Africa. Elephants, zebras, giraffes, deer, leopards are the common animals.	Conserving species which are vulnerable, endangered, rare, threatened and lower risk in order to prevent it from becoming extinct. Various causes of loss of biological diversity. Environmental pollution disturbs the food chain and food web, which lead to destruction of flora, due to changed climatic conditions.
Temperate grasslands	These are found in the mid-latitudinal zones and in the interior part of the continents. Usually, grass here is short and nutritious. Wild buffaloes, bison, antelopes are common animals.	Other causes of loss of biodiversity are due to human need, increasing human population, faulty government policies, selfish attitudes of social control authorities, inadequate distribution of lands, lack of public awareness and nature education.
Thorny bushes	These are found in the dry desert-like regions. Tropical deserts are located in the western margins of the continents. The vegetation cover is scarce, because of scanty rain and scorching heat. Polar region is extremely cold. Growth of natural vegetation is very limited here.	Measures taken in India for conservation of biodiversity including the legal framework. Promoting *ex-situ* conservation and *in-situ* conservation whenever needed.

Contd....

	Only mosses, lichens and very small shrubs are found here. It grows during the very short summer, which is called as Tundra type of vegetation. This vegetation is found in the polar areas of Europe, Asia and North America. The animals have thick fur and thick skin to protect from the cold climatic conditions. Seal, walruses, musk-oxen, Arctic owl, Polar bear and snow foxes are some of the animals found here.	Human activities responsible for loss of plant diversity are dam construction and reservoir formation, extension of towns, construction of roads, clearance of vegetation, logging and exploitation of forests, grassland reclamation programmes, overgrazing, over-exploitation of plant species, forest fire, landslides etc. Policy measures for conservation and suitable utilization of forest biodiversity.

UNIT–HUMAN ENVIRONMENT-SETTLEMENTS, TRANSPORT AND COMMUNICATION

Introduction	Early human beings depended entirely on nature for food, clothing and shelter; but with time they learnt new skills to grow food, build homes and develop better means of transport and communication. Settlements are places where people build their homes. Early human beings lived on trees and in caves. When they started to grow crops it became necessary to have a permanent home. The settlements grew near the river valleys as water was available and land was fertile. With the development of trade, commerce and manufacturing, human settlements became larger. Settlement flourished and civilizations developed near river valleys. Settlements can be permanent or temporary. Settlements, which are occupied for a short time, are called temporary settlements, e.g. people living in deep forests, hot and cold deserts, mountains etc. who practice hunting, gathering, shifting cultivation and transhumance. Settlements, where people build homes to live-in are called permanent settlements.	The early man and how they lived a life in accordance with nature. Less resource exploitation was seen in earlier days. How exploiting of nature by man started. Developments creating burden to the nature. Need for a sustainable development to satisfy the needs of man and without exploiting other organisms. Compact settlements in big cities—how it creates pollution of various types and the increased use of natural resources in these areas. Rural life—need of developments in these areas which need to have sustainability. Urban life—has many differences: culturally, environmentally, morally etc.

Contd....

	The villages are rural settlement where people are engaged in activities like agriculture, fishing, forestry, crafts work and trading etc. Rural settlements can be compact or scattered. A compact settlement is a closely built area of dwellings, wherever flat land is available. In a scattered settlement dwellings are spaced over an extensive area, e.g. in hilly tracts, thick forests, and regions of extreme climate. In rural areas, people build houses to suit their environment. In regions of heavy rainfall, they have slanting roofs. Places where water accumulates in the rainy season the houses are constructed on a raised platform or stilts. Thick mud walled houses with thatched roofs are very common in areas of hot climate. The towns are small and the cities are larger urban settlements. In urban areas the people are engaged in manufacturing, trading, and services.	
Transport	Transport is the means by which people and goods move. In the early days, people had to walk long distances and used animals to carry their goods. Invention of the wheel made transport easier. Early traders used either the sea route or the land route, which takes long time. Airplanes have made travel faster. Modern means of transport thus saves time and energy. The four major means of transport are roadways, railways, waterways and airways.	Modern transport causing various types of pollution. Exploiting natural resources and construction of roads, destroying the natural vegetation; but need to have roads only when necessary.
Roadways	This is the means of transport especially for short distances.	

Contd....

	Roads can be metalled (pucca) or unmetalled (kutcha), which are build in terrains like deserts, forests, high mountains etc. Manali-Leh highway in the Himlayan Mountains is one of the highest roadways in the world. Roads built underground are called subways/under paths. Flyovers are built over raised structures.	
Railways	The railways carry heavy goods and people over long distances quickly and cheaply. The invention of the steam engine and the Industrial Revolution helped in speedy development of rail transport. Diesel and electric engines have largely replaced the steam engines. In places superfast trains have been introduced to make the journey faster. Advanced technological skills have enabled laying of railway lines in difficult mountain terrains. Indian railway network is well developed. It is the largest in Asia.	
Waterways	Waterways are the cheapest for carrying heavy and bulky goods over long distances. There are mainly of two types of waterways—*inland waterways* and *sea routes*. Navigable rivers and lakes are used as inland waterways, e.g. the Ganga-Brahmaputra river system, the Great lakes in North America and the river Nile in Africa. Sea routes and oceanic routes are mostly used for transporting merchandise and goods from one country to another. These routes are connected with the ports. Some of the important ports of the world are Singapore and Mumbai in Asia,	Oil leakage into water bodies from vessels moving in the sea or water bodies. Big ships causes harm to water-living organisms.

Contd....

	New York, Los Angeles in North America, Rio de Janerio in South America, Durban and Cape Town in Africa, Sydney in Australia, London and Rotterdam in Europe.	
Airways	It is the fastest way of transport developed in the early twentieth century, which is the most expensive one due to high cost of fuels. Air traffic is adversely affected by bad weather like fog and storms. It is the only mode of transport to reach the most remote and distant areas especially where there are no roads and railways. Helicopters are extremely useful in most inaccessible areas and in time of calamities for rescuing people and distributing food, water, clothes and medicines. Some of the important airports are Delhi, Mumbai, New York, London, Paris, Frankfurt and Cairo.	Too much resource is wasted by various airways.
Communication	It is the process of conveying messages to others. With the development of technology humans have devised new and fast modes of communication. The advancement in the field of communication has brought about an information revolution in the world. Through newspapers, radio and television we can communicate with a large number of people hence called as mass media. Satellites have helped in oil exploration, survey of forest, underground water, mineral wealth, weather forecast and disaster warning. Now one can send electronic mails or e-mails through Internet. Wireless telephonic communications through cellular phones have become very popular today.	

Contd....

	Internet not only provides us with worldwide information and interaction but has also made our lives more comfortable.	

UNIT–HUMAN ENVIRONMENT INTERACTION, THE TROPICAL AND THE SUB-TROPICAL REGION

Life in the Amazon	Tropical region lies very close to the equator; between 10°N and 10°S is referred to as the equatorial region. The river Amazon flows through this region. The place where a river flows into another body of water is called the river's mouth. Numerous tributaries join the Amazon river to form the Amazon basin. The river basin drains portions of Brazil, parts of Peru, Bolivia, Ecuador, Columbia and a small part of Venezuela.	Amazon basin has many unexplored areas with many species of fishes not yet explored.
Climate	Amazon Basin is characterized by hot and wet climate throughout the year. Both day and nights are equally hot and humid. It rains almost everyday, that too without much warning. The day temperatures are high with very high humidity. At night the temperature goes down but the humidity remains high.	
Rainforests	As it rains heavily in this region, thick forests grow that create dense roof and does not allow the sunlight to reach the ground. Only shade tolerant vegetation may grow here. Orchids, bromeliads grow as plant parasites. It is rich in fauna. Birds such as toucans are found here. Animals like monkeys, sloth and ant-eating tapirs are found here. Various species of reptiles and snakes also thrive in these jungles. Several species of fishes including the flesh eating Piranha fish is also found in the river.	Deforestation of these rainforests. Conversion of these forests to agricultural lands. Remote sensing technology helping in conservation of Amazon.

Contd....

People of the rain-forest	People grow most of their food in small areas after clearing some trees in the forest. While men hunt and fish along the rivers, women take care of the crops. They mainly grow tapioca, pineapple and sweet potato. They practice "slash and burn agriculture". The staple food is manioc, also known as cassava that grows under the ground like the potato. They also eat queen ants and egg sacs. Cash crops like coffee, maize and cocoa are also grown. The rainforests provide a lot of wood for the houses. Some families live in thatched houses shaped like beehives. There are other large apartment-like houses called "Maloca" with a steeply slanting roof. In the older days the heart of the forest, could be reached only by navigating the river. In 1970 the Trans Amazon highway made all parts of the rainforest accessible. Aircrafts and helicopters are also used for reaching various places. The indigenous population was pushed out from the area and forced to settle in new areas. It is estimated that a large area of the rainforest has been disappearing annually in the Amazon basin due to developmental activities. The topsoil is washed away as the rains fall and the lush forest turns into a barren landscape.	Culture and lifestyles of the people are well adapted to the environment. Threat to the Amazon basin is deforestation and cattle ranching by larger multinational and corporations. Amazon deforestation jumps to 69% in 2008. Forest cover in Southern Amazon may fall to 20% by 2016. 20% of Brazilian Amazon tree species is going to be extinct (Proceedings of the National Academy of Sciences).
Life in the Ganga-Brahmaputra basin	The tributaries of rivers Ganga and Brahmaputra together form the Ganga-Brahmaputra basin in the Indian subcontinent, which lies in the sub-tropical region, situated between 10°N to 30°N latitudes.	Water resource management approach is required to balance environmental, social and economic considerations. Surplus water and flooding are the perennial problem in this region.

Contd....

	The tributaries of the River Ganga like the Ghaghra, the Sone, the Chambal, the Gandak, the Kosi and the tributaries of Brahmaputra drain it. The plains of the Ganga and the Brahmaputra, the mountains and the foothills of the Himalayas and the Sundarbans delta are the main features of this basin. The area is dominated by monsoon climate. The monsoon brings rains from mid-June to mid-September. The basin area has varied topography. Wherever there are mountain areas with steep slopes, less number of people lives. The plain area provides the most suitable land for human habitation, where soil is fertile, population is high and Paddy is the main crop. Wheat, maize, sorghum, gram, millets, sugarcane, banana are the other crops that are grown. In West Bengal and Assam tea is grown. Silk is produced in Bihar and Assam. The vegetation varies according to the landforms. Tropical deciduous trees grow here along with teak, sal and peepal. The delta area is covered with Mangrove forests. In parts of Uttarakhand, Sikkim and Arunachal Pradesh, coniferous trees like pine, deodar and fir can be seen. There is a variety of wildlife. Elephants, tigers, deer and monkeys, one-horned rhinoceros, Bengal tiger, crocodiles and alligator are found here. It has several big towns and cities. The cities of Allahabad, Kanpur, Varanasi, Lucknow, Patna and Kolkata all with the population of more than ten lakhs are located along the River Ganga.	Eroded materials from uplifted areas are deposited in the down faulted depressions leading to aggradations and shifting of rivers. Increasing demands for water from various sectors and decreasing water availability due to overuse, pollution and inefficient water management leads to conflicts worldwide (over allocation or over environmental issues). International conflicts and co-operation. Environmental factors affecting quality and quantity of water. National water policy and interstate issues. Flood control programmes in India and need to have a river-friendly flood control measures that recognize the environmental value and the geomorphic importance of floods.

Contd....

	The waste water from these towns and industries is discharged into the rivers, which leads to the pollution of the rivers. All the four ways of transport are well developed in this area. Tourism is another important activity of the basin.	

UNIT–LIFE IN THE TEMPERATE GRASSLANDS

Introduction	Grasslands can be defined as a region where grasses form the dominant type of plant life, which make up almost a quarter of the total land surface. As climate plays an important role in the formation of grasslands, it is generally used as a basis to divide the world's grasslands into two broad categories: those that occur in the temperate region and those that occur in the tropical regions.	Overgrazing causes the depletion of grasslands. How fire can destroy the grasslands and how it influences the growth of different flora and fauna.
The Prairies	The temperate grasslands of North America are known as the Prairies. It is a region of flat, gently sloping or hilly land. For the most part, prairies are treeless but, near the lowlying plains, flanking river valleys, woodlands can be found. Tall grass, upto two metres high, dominates the landscape. The prairies are bound by the Rocky Mountains in the west and the Great Lakes in the east. Prairies cover parts of USA (the area is drained by the tributaries of Mississippi) and parts of Canada (drained by the tributaries of Saskatchewan Rivers).	Fire caused by periodic burning cause loss of biodiversity. The North American prairie is one of the most endangered ecosystems on earth. In some areas upto 99 per cent of the prairie has been destroyed in just the last 125-150 years.
Climate	The climate is of continental type with extreme temperature. The summers are warm with temperature around 20°C, while in winter may be –20°C. Annual rainfall is moderate and ideal for growth of grass. Due to the absence of north-south barrier, a local wind 'chinook' blows here.	

Contd....

Flora and fauna	Prairies are practically treeless. Places that receive rainfall of over 50 cm. are suitable for farming as soil is fertile and the major crops are maize, potatoes, soyabean, cotton and alfa alfa. Areas where rainfall is very little or unreliable, grasses are short and sparce which are suitable for cattle rearing. Large cattle farms called ranches are looked after by cowboys. Bison/American buffalo is the important animal which is nearly extinct due to indiscriminate hunting. Other animals are rabbits, coyotes, gophers and prairie dog.	Changes in climatic patterns causing the changes in the vegetation. Reasons for the extinction of these species and to protect them. Mexican prairie dog (an endangered species) was poisoned because they were believed to compete with grazing cattle. Eskimo curlew were also hunted to extinction.
People	The people of this region are hard-working and have harnessed technology to utilize their rich natural resources. Two of the most developed countries in the world—the USA and Canada are located in this region. The prairies are also known as 'Granaries of the world' due to the huge surplus of wheat production. Dairy farming is another major industry. Dairy farming and extensive agriculture promote setting up of food processing industries. Large mineral deposits especially coal and iron and a good network of roads, railways and canals in this region have made it most industrialized region in the world.	Mining of resources like coal and iron should not exceed the limit which will hinder the future to meet their needs.
The Velds	The temperate grasslands of South Africa are called the velds. Velds are rolling plateaus with varying heights ranging from 600m to 1100m, which is found by the Drakensburg mountains on the east and Kalahari desert in the west. On the North east part, 'high velds' are located that attain a height of more than 1600m in some places.	

Contd....

	The velds receive rainfall mainly in the summer months from November to February.	
Flora and fauna	The vegetation cover is sparse. Grasses dominates the landscape. Plants like red grass, acacia and Maroola and animals like lions, leopards, cheetah and kudu are seen here.	
People	Velds are known for cattle rearing and mining. The main crops are maize, wheat, barley, oats and potato. Cash crops like Tobacco, sugarcane and cotton are also grown. Sheep rearing is the important occupation of the people. Sheep is bred mainly for wool and has given rise to wool industry. Merino sheep is a popular species and their wool is very warm. Dairy farming is the next important occupation where dairy products like butter, cheese are produced for both domestic supply and also for export. Velds have rich reserve of minerals. Iron and steel industry has developed where coal and iron are present. Gold and diamond mining are major occupations. Johannesburg is known for being the gold capital of the world and Kimberley is famous for diamond mines.	Mining—should be controlled so that it does not hinder the needs of the future.

UNIT–LIFE IN THE DESERT

Introduction	It is difficult for anyone to live in places where there is no water to drink, where there is no grass for their cattle to feed on and where there is no water to help the crops to grow. Desert areas are characterized by low rainfall, scanty vegetation and extreme temperatures. Depending on the temperatures, there can be hot deserts or cold deserts.	Atleast three common issues are faced by deserts i.e. Maintenance of biodiversity, recycling of waste minimizing the physical deterioration of the environment and the use of water and other resources.

Contd....

	The people inhabit these lands wherever little water is available to practice agriculture.	Three areas to be given focus are: • Sustainability: Developing processes that enable the enjoyment of a quality of life that is in balance with the maintenance and enhancement of local and global life. • Harmony: Developing processes for the effective engagement of western style and indigenous communities that leads to harmonious and successful economic and social advance for all groups. • Wealth creation: Developing viable businesses and employment opportunities capable of supporting an internationally competitive lifestyle for the people of the desert.
The Hot desert-Sahara	Sahara is the world's largest desert which has an area around 8.54 million sq. km. It touches eleven countries like Algeria, Chad, Egypt, Libya, Mali, Mauritania, Morocco, Niger, Sudan, Tunisia and Western Sahara. Sahara desert is covered with gravel plains and elevated plateaus with bare rocky surface.	Oil is extracted from here which is of great importance to economy of the entire country. This mineral exploitation has led to economic growth in Sahara but has lost the indigenous people to lose work.
Climate	The climate is scorching hot and parch dry which has a short rainy season. The sky is cloudless and clear. Moisture evaporates faster than it accumulates. Days are hot and the temperatures during the day may soar as high as 50°C. The nights may be freezing cold with temperatures nearing zero degrees.	
Flora and fauna	Vegetation in the Sahara desert includes cactus, date palms and acacia. In some places there are oasis—green islands with date palms surrounding them. Camels, hyenas, jackals, foxes, scorpions, many varieties of snakes and lizards are the prominent animal species.	Various environment processes and environmental changes that occurred in Sahara. Plant and animal population is sparse.

Contd....

People	Despite of harsh climate, Sahara has been inhabited by various groups of people, e.g. Bedouins and Tuaregs are nomadic tribes rearing livestock such as goats, sheep, camels and horses. They wear heavy robes as protection against dust storms and hot winds. The oasis in the Sahara and the Nile Valley in Egypt supports settled population. Since water is available, the people grow date palms. Crops such as rice, wheat, barley and beans are also grown. Egyptian cotton, famous worldwide is grown in Egypt. The discovery of oil—a product in great demand throughout the world, in Algeria, Libya and Egypt is constantly transforming the Sahara desert. Other minerals of importance that are found in the area include iron, phosphorus, manganese and uranium. The cultural landscape of the Sahara is undergoing change.	According to Archeologists, the Sahara was much more densely populated thousands of years ago when the desert's climate was not as harsh as it is today. The extreme temperature causes difficulty in sustaining life in Sahara. Drip irrigation is a clear and ecologically sustainable way to manage groundwater resources. Carefully using water to irrigate desert species can give the suitable added value to families' economy, needed to develop new profitable use of local resources. Land degeneration caused by salinization has been the main problem constraining the development of oasis. Some of the social problems found here are difference in age classes, low education level and poor livelihood. Desert development leads to gradual decease of basic resources especially water, change in social relations and economical foundation and ultimately to abandoned villages because of out-migration.
The cold desert-Ladakh	Ladakh is a cold desert lying in the Great Himalayas, on the eastern side of Jammu and Kashmir. The Karakoram Range in the north and the Zanskar mountains in the south enclose it. Several rivers flow through Ladakh, Indus being the most important among them. Several glaciers are found in Ladakh, for example the Gangri glacier. The altitude in Ladakh varies from about 3000m in Kargil to more than 8000m in the Karakoram. Due to high altitude, the climate is extremely cold and dry.	Ladakh witnesses the little change in technological level. Agriculture is confined to river valley basins where irrigation is available. Animal husbandry is main occupation. Ladakh possess virtually no normal forests, though along river banks and valleys some greenery does exist. Melting of the glaciers in Ladakh due to Greenhouse effect and global warming and its impact on the globe.

Contd....

	The day temperatures in summer are just above zero degree and the night temperatures well below 30°C. It is freezing cold in the winters when the temperatures may remain below 40°C for most of the time. As it lies in the rain shadow of the Himalayas, there is little rainfall, as low as 10cm every year.	
Flora and fauna	Due to high aridity, the vegetation is sparse. There are scanty patches of grasses and shrubs for animals to graze. Groves of willows and poplars are seen in the valleys. During the summers, fruit trees such as apples, apricots and walnuts bloom. Several species of birds are sighted in Ladakh. Robins, redstarts, Tibetan snowcock, raven and hoopoe are common. Some of these are migratory birds. The animals of Ladakh are wild goats, wild sheep, yak and special kinds of dogs.	Different plant species which are traditional medicinal plants are used against various ailments. The flora and fauna of Ladakh are threatened and protection is vital if ancient ecosystems should survive.
People	The people here are either Muslims or Buddhists. Several Buddhists monasteries dot the Ladakhi landscape with their traditional 'gompas', e.g. Hemis, Thiksey, Shey and Lamayuru. In the summer season the people are busy cultivating barley, potatoes, peas, beans and turnip. The climate in winter months is so harsh that people keep themselves engaged in festivities and ceremonies. The women are very hard-working. Leh, the capital of Ladakh is well connected both by road and air. The National Highway 1A connects Leh to Kashmir Valley through the Zojila Pass. Tourism is a major activity with several tourists streaming in from within India and abroad. Life of people is undergoing change due to modernization.	Tribal groups of Ladakh. Ethno botanical aspects of Ladakh. Medicines that are being used by various tribal groups for curing different ailments. Traditional medicines of cold desert-Ladakh. Remedies for conservation and development of traditional system of medicines. The valley sustain an agrarian population along the course of the drainage system wherever sources of artificial is available.

Contd....

	But the people of Ladakh have over the centuries learned to live in balance and harmony with nature. Due to scarcity of resources like water and fuel, they are used with reverence and care. Nothing is discarded or wasted.	

CIVICS UNIT–ON EQUALITY

Equality and inequality	Equality is a key feature of democracy. What is Universal adult franchise. Casteism. Students being treated unequally based on caste. Inequality based on religion. Indian constitution recognizes every person as equal. According to Indian constitution, every individual in the country including male and female persons from all castes, religions, tribes, educational and economic backgrounds are recognized as equal. Every person is equal before the law. No person can be discriminated against on the basis of their religion, race, caste, place of birth or whether they are male or female. Every person has access to all public places. Untouchability has been abolished.	How inequality hinders the progress of a nation. What if the citizens do not vote. Casteism and development in India. Caste-discrimination that they observe in their locality and its impact. Religious disparity as a hindrance in development. Gender disparity, educational disparity, economic disparity as hindrance in development of a nation.
How the government has tried to implement equality	Through laws and government programmes or schemes. Mid-day meal scheme. Article 15 of Indian Constitution.	
Issues of equality in other democracies	In many democratic countries around the world, the issue of equality continues to be the key issue around which communities struggle. African Americans treated unequally in USA. Civil rights movement.	

Contd....

UNIT–ROLE OF THE GOVERNMENT IN HEALTH

What is health	Health is the ability to remain free of illness and injuries. Clean water and a pollution free environment is essential for being healthy. Without any mental strain.	How food was considered in olden days and also among tribal community. Reasons for the improper health in the modern world. Water logging and its impact on human health. Precautions to be taken during monsoon season to prevent one-self from getting diseases. Community programmes for maintaining a healthy environment.
Health care in India	India has the largest number of doctors in the world. Most doctors settle in rural areas. Health facilities have grown substantially over the years. India has a large number of medical tourists from many countries. India is the fourth largest producer of medicines and the large exporter. We are not able to provide clean drinking water to all. Half of all children in India do not get adequate food to eat and are under-nourished. In order to prevent and treat illness we need appropriate healthcare facilities such as health centres, hospitals, laboratories etc.	How to make doctors equally available in the rural areas too. Healthy being and development of a country. Medical tourists as a source of economic development. Reducing the use of allopathic medicines and using a natural way of treatment. Ways of water conservation to provide clean and safe water. Avoid wastage of food.
Public health services	Public health service is a chain of health centres and hospitals run by the government. At the village level there are health centres where there is usually a nurse and a village health worker. At the district level, there is District hospital that supervises all the health centres. The resources needed to run a public health service centre is from the money that the public pay to the government as taxes. It provides health care services either free or at a low cost.	How public health services help in attaining sustainability in a country. How to improve the conditions of public health centres.

Contd....

	It take action to prevent the spread of diseases such as TB, Malaria, jaundice, cholera, diarrhea, chikungunya etc. It take action to prevent the spread of diseases such as TB, Malaria, jaundice, cholera, diarrhea, chikungunya etc.	
Private health services	It is run by doctors who run them on their own. There are hospitals and nursing homes that are privately owned. There are many laboratories and medical shops that are run privately. Private health facilities are not owned or controlled by the government. In private facilities, patients have to pay a lot of money for every service that they use.	Private facilities to be made use by all classes of people through some concession basis, which leads to progress of a country.
Health care and equality	In India we can find that the private services are increasing, but public services are not. Private services are mostly concentrated in urban areas. At times, cheaper methods, though available are not used. Only 20% of the population can afford all the medicines that they require during an illness. 40% of people who are admitted to a hospital for some illness or injury have to borrow money or sell some of their possessions to pay for the expenses. Poor people are not provided basic necessities like drinking water, adequate housing, clean surroundings etc. that make them likely to fall ill. Women's health concerns are considered to be less important than the health of men in the family.	Impact of discrimination on health care leading to hindrance to sustainable development.
What can be done	It is the responsibility of the government to provide quality health care services to all its citizens, especially the poor and the disadvantaged.	Few examples of some case studies is taken as example where it is exposed to better health facilities.

Contd....

	The Kerala experience where 40% of the entire state budget was given to panchayats which made possible for the village to make sure that proper planning was done for water, food, women's development and education. Anganwadis, heath centres were all improved. The Costa Rican approach is where the Costa Rican Government (in S. Africa) took a decision and decided to spend the money that the army would have used, on health, education and other basic needs of the people.	

Chapter 5

ESD Themes Addressed

The themes that are addressed in the modules are as follows. Each theme focus on the different Questions to be addressed pertaining to sustainability, followed by the content outline.

THEME 1: POPULATION AND SUSTAINABILITY

Questions to be addressed

- How is the population growth related to poverty? List out the strategies for eliminating poverty in India.
- How is population growth related to the global community? How does the growth in population affect the global community?
- What is the status of population growth in developing, developed and under-developed countries of the world? How does it influence the earth?
- How is population growth related to the quality of life? How can you ensure a sustainable population growth along with a better quality of life?
- Does population education help in attaining sustainability? If yes, how?
- Why is it important to control the population growth? What are the consequences that one will face if the population growth continues at a faster rate?
- How are population, environment, resources and development related? What are the ways by which we can have a sustainable development?
- What are the roles of women in a society for attaining a sustainable society?
- What are the different strategies that one can adopt to alleviate poverty and how far each individual have attempted to eradicate poverty?
- Find out the different policies in India that are related to population. What could be the reason for giving importance on policies related to population?
- What are the reasons for imbalanced distribution of population and what are the main reasons for international migrations. How can you make use of the native people in bringing about development in their country in a sustainable manner?
- What are the different ways by which we can balance the population dynamics, socio-economic development, natural resources and environmental quality?
- What are the different environmental problems that are faced by the world due to the rapid population growth?

- What are the consequences that people has to face living in marginal and vulnerable areas? How can you provide rehabilitation for such people?
- What are the main reasons for people moving towards metropolitan cities? How can you assure developments in rural areas also so that the metropolitan crowd can be reduced?
- How is population and food production related? What are the measures that one can take to have a balance between food production and population growth.
- How is population and family planning related? Should family planning be considered in bringing out a sustainable society?
- What are the main reasons for the raise in mortality rates in the modern world?
- How are population and HIV/AIDS related? What are the steps that one has to follow for leading a healthy life and why is it important?
- Which are the ecosystems that are highly affected by human activities and what are the main causes for such destruction?

Content outline

- Relationship between population growth and poverty
- Population and global community
- Population in developing, developed and under-developed countries
- Relationship between population growth and environment
- Population growth and quality of life
- Importance of population education
- Controlling the population growth
- Relationship between population, resources, environment and development
- Role of women and gender equality
- Alleviation of poverty
- Policies on population
- Imbalanced population distribution and international migration as the major problems
- Balancing population dynamics, socio-economic development, the use of natural resources and environmental quality
- Environmental problems due to population growth
  - Land degradation
  - Deforestation
  - Air and water pollution
  - Threats to bio-diversity
  - Habitat destruction
  - Rising sea level due to greenhouse effect
- Human settlements in marginal and vulnerable areas
- People concentrating on large metropolitan cities

- ➢ Population versus food production
- ➢ Importance of education, health and human resource development for quality life
- ➢ Women empowerment
- ➢ Family planning and population
- ➢ Population and mortality rates
- ➢ Population and HIV/AIDS
- ➢ Eco-systems that are heavily affected by human beings.

THEME 2: AGRICULTURE, NUTRITION AND SUSTAINABILITY

Questions to be addressed

- How is population and food production related? What are the measures that one can take to have a balance between food production and population growth.
- How is malnutrition and poverty related? What are the strategies that can be adopted for providing proper nutrition for all the people?
- What are the impacts of using chemical fertilizers in the agricultural field? How can we reduce the impact of chemical fertilizers?

Content outline

- ➢ Percentage of food production versus population
- ➢ Malnutrition and poverty
- ➢ Use of chemicals in agriculture
- ➢ Food production, management and food preservation
- ➢ Loss of soil fertility
- ➢ Mineral degradation in the soil
- ➢ Food scarcity
- ➢ Nutrient deficiency
- ➢ Use of hybrid varieties in agriculture and its impact
- ➢ Impact of excessive usage of pesticides and weedicides
- ➢ Chemical fertilizers and soil quality
- ➢ Replenishing the soil nutrients
- ➢ Crop rotation
- ➢ Plant proteins
- ➢ Rhizobium as a natural fertilizer
- ➢ Use of natural manures
- ➢ Nitrogen fixing symbiotic and free living microorganisms
- ➢ Amount of food produced for the population
- ➢ Agricultural land getting converted into buildings and industries
- ➢ Conversion of agrarian culture into consumerism

- Self-employment of farmers are being disturbed
- Soil depletion
- Soil erosion
- How loss of humus soil occurs
- Soil management and crop management
- Soil fertility, crop rotation and crop production
- Soil borne diseases
- Soil salinity, pH and nutrient requirements
- Organic fertilizers and soil fertility
- Sericulture industry and its potential
- Sustainable agriculture
- Agrarian population
- Prospects for food security
- Soil moisture and agriculture
- Phosphate rocks for sustainable agriculture
- Conversion of forests to agricultural lands
- Animal husbandry.

THEME 3: SUSTAINABILITY AND URBANISATION

Questions to be addressed

- What are the social changes that are anticipated in movement of people from rural to urban?
- How do globalisation, commercialisation, urbanisation etc. influence the life forms
- Sericulture helps in improving a country's economy—Explain?
- How can we reduce the water pollution caused by industrial wastes?

Content outline

- Reservoir management
- Movement of people from rural to urban areas
- Importance on anaerobes in various industries like paper, textiles etc.
- Changing world due to globalisation, commercialisation, urbanisation etc. and how it can influence the life forms
- Measures to control industrialisation, urbanisation etc.
- Sericulture industry and its potential in India
- Silk industry, silk export and new technologies in sericulture
- Silkworm rearing and its importance to economy
- Industrialisation and water pollution

- Industrialisation, modernisation, globalisation and its relation to increase in temperature
- Urban life having difference in culture, environmentally and morally.

THEME 4: RURAL DEVELOPMENT

Questions to be addressed

- Why are developments occurring very rarely in rural areas? What solutions can you suggest for bringing about developments in rural areas?
- What are the reasons for the rural people shifting to urban areas? How can we bring about development both to urban and rural areas in a sustainable manner?

Content outline

- Causes for lack of development in rural areas
- Rural habitation shifting to urban
- Self-employment of farmers being disturbed
- Growth of farm animals and its importance in eradicating poverty and attaining growth of economy
- Selective breeding for producing disease resistant varieties and high yielding varieties in agriculture
- Rural life—Need for developments in these areas
- Culture and lifestyles of the people are well adapted to the environment
- Life of tribes getting modernised.

THEME 5: INTERNATIONAL UNDERSTANDING AND PEACE

Questions to be addressed

- How can we resolve conflicts in the name of water? How can we assure good drinking water to all the living beings?
- How do constitutional provisions help in conserving biodiversity?

Content outline

- Rio declaration
- Measures taken in India for conservation of biodiversity including the legal framework
- International conflicts in the name of water and need for co-operation.

THEME 6: GENDER EQUALITY AND HUMAN RIGHTS

Questions to be addressed

- What are the various issues pertaining to human rights in India?
- What are the different ways to stop the Human Rights Violations of Marginalized/ Disadvantaged Groups?
- What are the reasons for giving more focus on Human rights education?
- What are the various means and ways to protect human rights?

Content outline

- ➢ Human Rights education
- ➢ Human Rights in the Indian Constitution
- ➢ Human Rights Violations of Marginalized/Disadvantaged Groups
- ➢ Globalisation: Impact on Human Rights
- ➢ Emerging Issues in Human Rights
- ➢ Human Rights Protection Mechanism in India
- ➢ Promotion of Human Rights Education.

THEME 7: HEALTH PROMOTION

Questions to be addressed

- How do increase in temperature has an impact on human health?
- What are the importance of nutrients in maintaining proper health? How can we assure food security to all?
- How is malnutrition linked with poverty? How can we overcome poverty?
- Obesity is a common disease in the modern world. What are its causes and explain the ways to overcome it?
- What are the importance of exercise in the daily life?
- How are respiratory diseases linked with industrialisation?

Content outline

- ➢ Heat and human health
- ➢ Heat illness
- ➢ Heat cramps and heat stroke
- ➢ Increase in global temperature and health problems
- ➢ Importance of nutrients in maintaining proper health
- ➢ Malnutrition and poverty
- ➢ Food production, management and food preservation
- ➢ Why fats require more oxygen for its breakdown
- ➢ Fat deposition and body weight
- ➢ Obesity
- ➢ Need for proper exercise
- ➢ Active exercise to reduce muscle fatigue
- ➢ Breathing problems and changing lifestyles
- ➢ Diseases of respiratory system.

THEME 8: ENVIRONMENTAL CONSERVATION AND PROTECTION

Sub-theme 1: Water Management

Questions to be addressed

- What are the different sources of water and what is its present condition? What is the main cause for the depletion of water bodies and how can you conserve the water sources?
- Why is it necessary to maintain a balance between oceans and lands? What are the impacts if such balance is disturbed?
- What is the importance of hydrological cycle and how is it helpful in maintaining a balance on the earth?
- What are the different water resources in India? How much of groundwater and surface water is used per person and why is it important to conserve them?
- Why is it necessary to maintain a proper management of water resources? What would happen if it is not taken seriously?
- List out some of the places which experienced conflicts in the name of water. Why are such conflicts occurring and how can we solve such crisis in the future?
- Is nationalising rivers a boon or a curse? Why?
- What are the physical and chemical parameters of water and how is it getting disturbed due to modern developments?
- How do the radiations affect water resources? What are its harmful effects and how can it be reduced?
- How are the water distributed in the world and why is it been disturbed? What are the causes for such changes?
- What are the different ways to attain a sustainable development of water resources?
- How does increase in population affects the water resources? What are the steps to be taken to reduce water depletion?
- What are the reasons for water scarcity in different parts of the world? What is the condition of water scarcity in India?
- What are the different ways to provide access to safe drinking water and better sanitation for the population? Why is it essential?
- Why the national policy on water has been introduced? What are the reasons for giving such priority for water?
- What is the main purpose for construction of dams? What are the criteria that one should keep in mind while planning to construct dams?
- How do modern developments cause hindrance to the proper water management? How can one assure a better water management in an area?
- What is the status that has been given to water in the ancient Indian literatures? How much changes have occurred in the modern world?

- What are the various impacts on human beings due to scarcity of water? How can you prevent such disasters in the future?
- Why are various watershed projects being introduced in India? Why are they gaining priority in the modern world?
- Why rainwater harvesting is gaining priority and how can you practice rainwater harvesting at home?
- What are the different activities that you can undertake to prevent runoff water?
- What are the implications on land by concretizing the land? How can you bring awareness in your community regarding its ill effects?
- What are the impacts on the environment due to construction of dams? How can you assure development by protecting the environment?
- What are the reasons for water scarcity in various parts of the world? What are the strategies that you can adopt for preventing water scarcity in the future?
- What are the different ways of water management and why is it important?
- What are the different strategies that you can adopt for managing water at the individual level, within cities, between states and countries? Why should you look into these impacts globally?
- How does the amount of usable water on the earth get decreased? What can you do to prevent the groundwater depletion?
- What are the different ways of water being polluted? What are the steps that one can take to prevent water pollution?
- Why water has become a political issue in many places and why bloodshed had occurred in many parts of the world. How can we reduce the pressure on water resources?
- How can you prevent water pollution in areas of human settlements? Find out few strategies to prevent water pollution in such areas?
- How can you maintain water quality in areas of human settlements and how can you assess the quality of water?
- What are the ways for converting wastewater into usable forms? How has technology helped in recycling of wastewater?
- What are the different laws pertaining to prevention of water pollution? Why the Governments are giving more priority for protecting water?
- How can you have a better wastewater management in kitchens and gardens? List out few methods for it?
- What are the causes for acid rains in certain areas? What are its causes and effects? How can you prevent acid rains in the future?
- What roles can one play at home and school for conserving water? List out few ways that you can adopt at school and homes for water conservation.
- How can you undertake few activities in order to bring awareness in the community regarding water conservation?

- What are the ill effects of stagnant water in some places? Why is it very essential to keep your surroundings clean?
- How does the water get polluted from different sources? What are the different agents of pollution? How can you prevent such pollutions and why is it essential?
- List out few activities that can be undertaken by the community for safeguarding freshwater, groundwater etc.
- How do water help in weathering of rocks? How does water act as a main agent that need to be protected for the formation of soil?
- What will happen during heavy rains in places having no proper drainage system? How can it affect the life in those areas?
- How do floods affect the life in an area? What are the precautionary measures that one can take in flood hit areas?
- What is the different flood control programmes undertaken in India? Why is it been given more importance?
- How can drip irrigation help in conserving groundwater? How can you adopt them in your locality to conserve groundwater?

Content outline

- Different sources of water
- Water balance of oceans and lands
- Hydrological cycle and water balance on earth
- Water resources of India (how much groundwater and surface water is used per person)
- Utilisation of water
- Water crisis leading to conflicts
- Nationalisation of rivers
- Water quality (both physical and chemical parameters)
- Radiological effects of water
- The world water distribution
- Water and sustainable development
- Population and water stress
- Water scarcity in different countries and specific to India
- Access to safe drinking water and sanitation in developing countries
- National water policy
- Construction of dams
- Impact of modern development on water management system
- Water as one of the five elements in ancient India—Earth, Fire, Air, Space and Water
- Shortage of water leading to epidemics, hunger, despair and death
- Watershed projects

- Rainwater harvesting
- Activities to prevent run of water
- Avoiding concretizing the land
- Construction of dams, destruction of nature as the cause of earthquake and volcanic eruptions
- Water scarcity—its causes, effects and preventive measures
- Need for a more oriented and integrated approach to water management and development
- Different ways of managing water
- Managing water at individual level
- Water management within cities, between states and countries
- Decreasing the amount of usable water on earth
- Impact of water depletion
- How water gets polluted
- Eutrophication
- Water as a political issue
- Bloodshed occurred on water issues
- How human settlements pollute water
- Water quality management issues
- Re-utilization and recycling of water
- Water pollution control through law
- Assessment of water quality
- Use of solar energy for cleaning polluted water
- Acid rain
- Constructing pits for conserving and percolation of water
- Water management in kitchen and garden
- Sustainable water use
- Ones role at home and school for conserving water
- Creating awareness among the community on water conservation
- Stagnant water and its impact on human health
- Chemical and microbial contamination of water
- Role of technology in wastewater treatment
- Participatory behaviour of public
- Diseases that are spread due to stagnant water
- Usable water getting reduced
- Water and weathering of rocks
- Percolation of water versus various chemicals in the soil

- ➢ Drainage on run of and flood
- ➢ Surplus water and flooding
- ➢ Environmental factors affecting quality and quantity of water
- ➢ Flood control programmes in India
- ➢ Environmental value and geomorphic importance of floods
- ➢ Drip irrigation to manage groundwater.

Sub-theme 2: Biodiversity/Forest

Questions to be addressed

- What is the present condition of forest cover in India? What are the different ways to conserve them and increase the forest cover?
- How does wildlife get affected due to forest destruction? Enumerate some measures to overcome it?
- How do climatic changes affect the plant and animal species of the Polar Regions?
- What are the reasons for species becoming endangered? How can we restore them?
- What are the ways to control deforestation?
- What is the importance of growing endemic plant species other than imported plant varieties?
- What are the reasons for conserving of hot spot areas?

Content outline

- ➢ Importance of protecting and preserving biodiversity
- ➢ Forests as an important renewable resource
- ➢ Forests and wildlife for maintaining ecological balance
- ➢ Tropical and sub-tropical forests getting disturbed
- ➢ Reasons for destruction of forests
- ➢ Desertification, Deforestation and Afforestation
- ➢ Forest and economy
- ➢ Aesthetic value of forests
- ➢ Eco-tourism
- ➢ Richer biodiversity in the tropics
- ➢ Distribution of plant and animal species in the polar regions
- ➢ Flora and fauna vary according to climate, altitude and soil
- ➢ Hot spots of biodiversity
- ➢ Changing biological diversity
- ➢ Biology of rare and declining species
- ➢ Restoration of ecology through ex-situ conservation

- ➢ Restoration of the degraded ecosystem in an environmentally friendly manner
- ➢ Importance of conserving trees
- ➢ Endangered species—its causes, effects and preventive measures
- ➢ Man destroying nature for satisfying his needs
- ➢ Importance of reforestation
- ➢ Some of the environmentally friendly activities
- ➢ Determining patterns and indicators of ecological response to stress
- ➢ Conservation and wise-use of world's biodiversity for sustainable development
- ➢ Endemic species and its conservation
- ➢ Conserving species which are vulnerable, endangered, rare, threatened and lower risk
- ➢ Various causes of loss of biological diversity
- ➢ Promoting ex-situ conservation and in-situ conservation
- ➢ Policy measures for conservation and suitable utilization of forest biodiversity
- ➢ Influence of human activities on land, climate, vegetation and wildlife
- ➢ Need to plant more trees which is suitable for each place
- ➢ Remote sensing technology helping in conservation of forests like Amazon
- ➢ Threats to Amazon, temperate grasslands, deserts etc.
- ➢ Overgrazing causes the depletion of grasslands
- ➢ How fire can destroy the grasslands
- ➢ Changing climatic patterns leading to changes in the vegetation
- ➢ Endangered species—Reasons for extinction
- ➢ Maintenance of biodiversity
- ➢ Areas that need to give focus for its conservation and protection
- ➢ Various environment processes and environmental changes that occurred in Sahara
- ➢ Traditional medicines—Ethnobotany
- ➢ Remedies for conservation and development of traditional system of medicines.

Sub-theme 3: Renewable Energy

Questions to be addressed

- What are the alternative sources of energy? How can it help in satisfying our energy needs?
- Harvesting of wind energy and tidal energy are some ways to conserve energy—Discuss.
- Nuclear energy plants help in satisfying our energy needs—But what are the challenges behind nuclear plants?
- Do Water and Forest belong to Non-renewable sources of energy—Justify?

Content outline

- Importance of non-conventional power plants
- Solar energy for domestic purposes
- Harvesting of wind energy and tidal energy
- How to harvest wind energy and tidal energy
- How to harvest solar energy for domestic purposes
- Nuclear energy and its consequences
- Hydro energy and its impact.

Sub-theme 4: Land Management

Questions to be addressed

- What are the impacts of Mining on soil profile, water and living beings?
- What are the causes and impacts of Soil erosion?
- What are the environmental impact of Quarrying?
- What are the causes and effects of soil depletion?

Content outline

- Mineral degradation in the soil
- Soil depletion; soil erosion
- Mining and its effect on soil profile
- Soil water content and infiltration rates
- Soil erosion and slope failure
- Impact of mining on different layers of earth
- Quarrying and environmental impact
- Causes for soil erosion and soil depletion
- Soil erosion and transporting to water bodies
- Lichens and weathering of rocks
- Impact of mining on different layers of earth
- Quarrying and its impact on environment
- Causes for soil depletion and soil erosion
- Soil erosion and transporting to water bodies
- Lichens and weathering of rocks
- Impact of mining on different layers of earth
- Quarrying and environmental impact
- Major landforms of earth
- How the topsoil of the lithosphere get washed away

- Compact settlements in big cities—how it creates pollution of various types
- Land degeneration caused by salinization.

Sub-theme 5: Climatic Change

Questions to be addressed

- What are the causes for Global temperature increasing or Global warming?
- What are the Changing weather patterns in the present world? What are its main causes?
- Climatic changes and main cause for melting of ice caps—Justify.
- Why are different species getting endangered? What are its causes, effects and preventive measures?
- Industrialisation and climatic change are interlinked—Discuss.
- How are the amount of various gases in the atmosphere changing and what are its impact?
- How do improved technology a helping agent in predicting natural calamities?

Content outline

- Heat and climatic change
- Global temperature increasing
- Changing weather patterns
- Adverse weather conditions
- Greenhouse effect and its impact
- Climatic changes and melting of ice caps
- Impacts of melting of polar ice caps
- Deforestation
- Endangered species—its causes, effects and preventive measures
- Climatic change and its influence on life forms
- Heating of earth due to pollutants
- Difference in climate due to changes in wind patterns
- Hurricanes like typhoon, tornado, flood and drought
- Importance of technology in forecasting and warning services
- Deforestation and climatic change
- Industrialisation and climatic change
- Tsunami—a natural calamity
- Impact of increase in CO_2 in the atmosphere
- Greenhouse effect and its impact
- Causes for global warming
- Why global warming is given more priority now-a-days

- ➢ Impact of global warming on life, polar regions and coastal areas
- ➢ Amount of various gases in the atmosphere and its impact
- ➢ Improved technology as a helping agent in predicting natural calamities
- ➢ Impact of increase in CO_2 in the atmosphere
- ➢ Cyclones and its impact
- ➢ Changes occurring in various seasons like heavy rains during monsoon, rains during summers, lack of rain, rain in deserts etc.
- ➢ Rains that are seasonal and its impact on the environment.

Sub-theme 6: Waste Management, Toxic Chemicals

Questions to be addressed

- How do science and technology help in waste disposal?
- What are the ways for proper disposal and recycling of wastes?
- What are the different ways of sewage disposal in highly polluted places?
- What is the role of technology in wastewater treatment?
- What are the diseases spread through unhygienic waste disposal?
- What are the ways for participatory behaviour of public in waste management?

Content outline

- ➢ Importance of science and technology in proper waste disposal
- ➢ Recycling of wastes for minimizing the physical deterioration of the environment
- ➢ Industrial metabolism
- ➢ Proper disposal and recycling of wastes
- ➢ Impact of mixing degradable and non-degradable wastes
- ➢ Sewage disposal in highly polluted places
- ➢ Avoiding sewage disposal in areas of human settlements
- ➢ Regular checking of sewage pits to prevent the outbreak of contagious diseases
- ➢ Role of technology in wastewater treatment
- ➢ Convert sewage into usable forms like biogas
- ➢ Avoiding direct discharge of wastes to water bodies
- ➢ Participatory behaviour of public in waste management
- ➢ Conversion of sewage to useful forms
- ➢ Diseases spread through unhygienic waste disposal.

Sub-theme 7: Sustainable Use of Natural Resources

Questions to be addressed

- What are the ways for restoration of the degraded ecosystem in an environmentally friendly manner

- How do Human influence natural environment
- Why are Forests considered as an important renewable natural resource
- How does depletion of natural environment happen by various natural and human influence
- What are the techniques to develop sensitivity towards environment.

Content outline

- ➢ Natural resources are limited
- ➢ Oxygen parlours as a result of lesser no. of trees
- ➢ Sustainable development of mineral resources
- ➢ Depleting of igneous, sedimentary and metamorphic rocks due to over usage by human beings
- ➢ Overexploitation of minerals—how it influences the nature and life forms on earth
- ➢ Forests as an important renewable natural resource
- ➢ Restoration of the degraded ecosystem in an environmentally friendly manner
- ➢ Human influence on natural environment
- ➢ Depletion of natural environment by various natural and human influence
- ➢ Develop sensitivity towards environment
- ➢ How an ecosystem gets vanished, polluted and destroyed
- ➢ The early man and how they lived a life in accordance with nature
- ➢ How exploiting of nature by man started
- ➢ Extraction of oil from different deserts
- ➢ Mineral exploitation though lead to economic growth, it can lose the work of indigenous people.

Sub-theme 8: Air Pollution

Questions to be addressed

- How does emission of gases in a volcanic eruption harm our environment
- How can we monitoring the impact of deforestation and various forms of pollution on life forms and how can we overcome the same?
- Critically analyse Greenhouse effect, ozone depletion, acid rain in the present context
- How do troposphere, stratosphere, mesosphere, thermosphere and exosphere get affected by human activities?
- Does Planting of more suitable trees helps to prevent the excessive accumulation of CO_2 in the atmosphere—Justify.

Content outline

- ➢ Emission of gases in a volcanic eruption and how it harms our environment
- ➢ Monitoring the impact of deforestation and various forms of pollution

- Greenhouse effect, ozone depletion, acid rain—its causes and effects
- Air as one of the main elements among the five elements in the ancient time—earth, fire, air, space and water
- Need for maintaining a balance in composition of gases in the atmosphere
- Different gases that pollutes the environment
- Planting of more suitable trees to prevent the excessive accumulation of CO_2 in the atmosphere
- Increase in CO_2 leading to Greenhouse effect and global warming
- How the troposphere, stratosphere, mesosphere, thermosphere and exosphere get affected by human activities
- Monitor the impact of various forms of pollution.

Sub-theme 9: Transport

Questions to be addressed

- How do Modern transportation facilities deteriorate our environment and resources?
- How modern transportation causes various types of pollution?
- How natural resources get exploited due to transportation and what are its consequences?
- How are Oil leakage from different vessels in the water bodies harmful for marine and land organisms?

Content outline

- Modern transportation
- How modern transportation causes various types of pollution
- How natural resources are exploited due to transportation
- Oil leakage from different vessels in the water bodies
- Big ships causing harm to organisms living in the water.

Chapter 6

How to Transact ESD

This section of the book deals with the planning of each chapter which has the integrated ESD content. Each unit consist of scope of the unit, focus points, issues to be raised, learning objectives, Resources and Activities. Some of the activities from the Science and Social Science Textbook of VII standard of NCERT syllabus is also included in order to maintain a proper continuity in the lessons.

UNIT 1: NUTRITION IN PLANTS

Scope

The unit deals with the various modes of nutrition in plants like, autotrophs, heterotrophs, saprotrophs and symbiotic relationships. It also describes about the food making process in autotrophic plants i.e., Photosynthesis that helps in the synthesis of carbohydrates. They also synthesize other components of food such as proteins and fats.

Focus points

1. Malnutrition and health
2. Organic nutrients in the soil getting depleted
3. Reasons for the soil nutrient depletion
4. Concentration of CO_2 in the atmosphere and how it gets disturbed
5. Reasons for usable water getting reduced
6. What is crop rotation? What is the role of farmers in food production?
7. Ways of utilising solar energy for domestic work
8. Need for protecting plants and trees
9. What happens if chemical fertilizers are used in excess in the soil
10. Food production versus Population. How food distribution is managed in India?
11. How can we improve the fertility of soil eco-friendly

Issues to be raised

1. What are the causes of malnutrition?
2. What is the importance of nutrients in maintaining proper health?

3. What will happen to plants if nutrients are less in the soil?
4. How do soil nutrients deplete?
5. What are the various gases in the atmosphere and how it influences the environment?
6. How do usable water in the soil get reduced?
7. How can you use solar energy in our domestic work?
8. What are the importance of protecting plants and trees?
9. Why is it important to preserve biodiversity?
10. What are the disadvantages of using fertilizers in the soil?
11. What is Rhizobium and what is its importance?
12. How can you reduce the use of chemical fertilizers?
13. What are the ways of improving the fertility of soil?
14. What are the advantages of using organic manure?

Learning objectives

The pupil

- Infer the causes of malnutrition.
- Identifies the reasons for degradation of minerals in the soil.
- List out the various reasons for depletion of usable water in the soil.
- Analyse the uses of solar energy in various domestic purposes.
- Discuss the importance of protecting plants and biodiversity.
- Analyse the importance of saprotrophs in different industries.
- Interpret the disadvantages of using fertilizers in the soil to increase fertility.
- Mention ways to reduce the use of chemical fertilizers.
- List out ways of improving soil fertility in an eco-friendly manner.

Resources

Pictures of various deficiency diseases (both plants and animals), potted plants, iodine solution, newspaper cuttings on water conservation, fungus, root nodules of leguminous plants, visit to a paddy field, bread slice, microscope, magnifying glass.

Activities

Activity 1: Pupil will be asked to list out the various nutrients needed by organisms for living. They are asked to collect about the different functions of these nutrients. They are also asked to collect pictures of diseases caused due to the deficiency of these nutrients (both in plants and animals). Pupils are asked to explore into the causes for malnutrition in the country and to come out with solutions to tackle the problem. Pupil will be asked to get recent news from newspaper regarding the food shortage and malnutrition in different places of the country and present in the classroom and maintain a record of the collected material.

Activity 2: Pupil will be asked to compare the nutritional behaviour in animals and plants. They are asked to observe the plants and find out how they prepare food. They will be asked to discuss on the following questions:

- Where do plants get the various nutrients?
- How do plants transport the raw materials?
- How is water important for plants?
- Where are food factories of plants located?
- How does the mineral in the soil degrade?

They are asked to reflect upon why plants are called as Autotrophs? They will be asked to observe the surroundings and find out the varied colour plants and are asked to find out how they too prepare food?

Activity 3: Pupil is asked to collect information about plants that are used as medicines for common diseases (grandma's medicine) from earlier days onwards. They are asked to collect few plants which are to be pasted in the science diary. It can be followed by maintaining an herbal garden in the school.

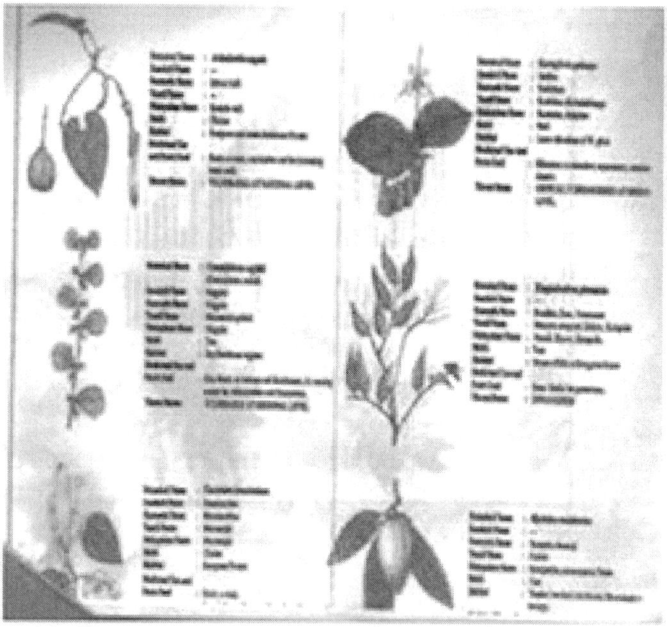

Activity 4: Draw a graph to show how many students below five years of age die of malnutrition in India. Students are asked to observe the graphical data and critically analyse the issue.

Activity 5: A drama is enacted on the impact of chemicals, e.g. Endosulfan. It is followed by a poster presentation about the impact of using such chemicals.

Activity 6: A debate is conducted on the topic—Genetically engineered crops—a boon or a bane.

Relief eludes many endosulfan victims

Activity 7: Teacher initiates a discussion on how organic farming is better than chemical farming.

Activity 8: A collage is developed on the topic malnutrition and excess and wastage of food. Develop awareness about the various causes of malnutrition and wastage of food.

Activity 9: Pupil is asked to act upon the nutritional mode in human beings. They will enact as from where we get food, who produces it, how it is prepared etc. From this activity the concept of Heterotrophs is brought in. They are asked about the nutrition in other animals too. They are asked about the following questions:

- What do lion eat as food?
- What is the food of hen?
- What is taken as food by cow?

From these questions they come to the conclusion that animals depend on others for food and these are called as Heterotrophs.

Activity 10: Pupils are asked to perform an experiment to demonstrate Photosynthesis in plants that is as follows: "Take two potted plants of the same kind. Keep one in dark (or in a dark box) for 72 hours and other in sunlight. Perform iodine test with the leaves of both the plants and record the results. Leave the pot which was earlier kept in dark in the sunlight for 3-4 days and perform the iodine test again on its leaves and record the observations".

Activity 11: Pupil is asked to discuss on water scarcity in different places. They also discuss on the various causes for water scarcity and how it affects life forms especially plants. They are also asked to reflect upon different ways of preserving or conserving groundwater. They are asked to visit some people in their village (locality) and collect data regarding water depletion occurred in their locality. They are also asked to collect newspaper cuttings regarding the various methods to conserve rainwater and rainwater harvesting. They are asked to reflect upon the following questions.

- Is water a renewable or non-renewable resource?
- What are the reasons for water depletion in the country?
- What are the various ways to conserve rainwater?

Activity 12: Pupil is asked to find out the various gases present in our atmosphere. They are asked to present a chart showing the graphical representation of concentration of various gases in the atmosphere (e.g. of year 1997 and 2007). They are asked to compare the amount of various gases and they are asked to discuss on the changes in the concentration of various gases. Pupil collects information about the impact of increase in CO_2, CO etc. in the atmosphere with special reference to the environment.

Activity 13: Pupil is asked to explore into the different uses of solar energy. They are also asked about different household items that work by using sunlight as a source of energy and how it is important in saving energy. They are asked to have a discussion on the importance using different sources of energy in order to prevent the unplanned utilisation of non-renewable resources. The concept of sustainable development is brought in this aspect.

Activity 14: Pupil is asked to enumerate the importance of O_2 to living things. They are also asked about how O_2 is produced and how can its decreasing amount affect the life and climate of a place. It is linked to the importance of plants and the impacts of deforestation.

Activity 15: Pupil is asked about the organisms they have seen in dead and decaying matter. They are asked to list few organisms seen on dead and decaying matter. They are shown some examples of fungus that are saprotrophs. They are asked to find out how microbes are useful in various industries like paper industries, beverages etc.

Activity 16: Pupil is asked to enact a role play on symbiotic relationship seen in few organisms like Lichens. They are asked on how it is mutually benefited, how it is able to survive etc. They are asked to quote few examples from their surroundings showing symbiotic relationship. The Rhizobium bacteria in the root nodules are observed by the students. They are asked about the type of relationship they exhibit and how are they benefited from each other. The importance of it in farming is also brought in.

Activity 17: The pupil is asked to visit a nearby paddy field and find out the type of vegetation they follow in a year. They also visit few farmers and enquire about:

- What are the fertilizers they use?
- What are its use and harm of using these fertilizers?
- What is the eco-friendly way of agriculture?
- What are the natural manures that can be used?
- What is the importance of crop rotation? etc.

Pupil is also asked to explore other Nitrogen fixing bacteria which are Free-living and which are living symbiotically. The pupil is asked to find out solutions for avoiding the depletion of soil nutrients in a natural way and protection of soil.

Activity 18: Take a piece of bread and moisten it with water. Leave it in a moist warm place for 2-3 days or until fluffy patches appear in them. Observe the patches under a microscope or a magnifying glass. Write down their observations in their book.

Project

Take a potted plant with broad leaves. Take two strips of black paper and cut out a small square in the centres. Cover a part of two leaves with these papers and secure them with paper clips. Keep the plant in the sunlight for 2-5 days. Observe the difference in the colour of the covered and the uncovered portions on the one leaf. Perform iodine test on this leaf. Now take another leaf, remove the strip and expose the covered part to the sunlight for 2-3 days and do the iodine test again. Describe the observation (NCERT VII standard Science textbook).

UNIT 2: FIBRE TO FABRIC

Scope

The unit deals with the various fibres obtained from different animals like sheep, goat and silkworm. The unit focuses on the different ways of rearing these animals and the processing of fibres and also the importance and ways of sustaining them without harming its population.

Focus points

- Why do we prefer selective breeding in domestic animals? How is it helpful?
- Role of rearing animals in eradicating poverty and also helping in growth of the economy.
- Sericulture and its prospects in India.
- Sericulture and sustainable development.

Issues to be raised

1. Where is wool obtained from?
2. Which part of the world mostly uses woolen clothes?
3. Which are the animals other than sheep that produce wool?
4. Why do sheep have hairy skin?
5. What are the two types of fibres present in the hairy skin of sheep?
6. What is selective breeding? How is it important?
7. How does rearing of sheep help in eradicating poverty and growth of economy?
8. List out few varieties of sheep.
9. Name some of the breed of sheep that are reared in our country.
10. Explain the different steps in processing of wool.
11. Where is silk obtained from? What is rearing of silkworm called as?
12. Explain the life history of silkworm.
13. What is the importance of sericulture industry in India?
14. What are the new technologies in sericulture?
15. What are the steps involved in rearing of silkworm?
16. Reflect upon the killing of pupa inside the cocoon of silkworm.
17. How can sericulture play its role in sustainable development?
18. How do we process silk?
19. What is heeling of silk?
20. What are the uses of silk?

Learning objectives

The pupil

1. Recalls that wool is obtained from hair (fleece) of sheep or yak.
2. Recalls that silk fibres come from cocoon of silk moth.
3. Recognizes that both wool and silk are animal fibres.
4. Identifies that wool comes from sheep, goat, yak and some other animals.
5. Hypothizes that the wool yielding animals bear hair on their body and hair traps a lot of air. Since air is a poor conductor of heat, it keeps them warmer.
6. Understands that hairy skin of sheep has two types of fibres i.e. Coarse beard hair and fine soft under-hair.
7. Infer that selective breeding is done for producing offsprings of special characteristics.
8. Identifies the place from where Angor wool is obtained.
9. Identifies where Llama and Alpaca species are found.
10. Recalls that fur of camel is also used as wool.
11. Communicates the uses of wool in colder parts of the world.
12. Infer the importance of growing farm animals and its importance in eradicating poverty and growth of economy.
13. List out the names of some breeds of sheep reared in our country, which are selectively bred.
14. Observes the various steps involved in processing the fibres into wool.
15. Recalls that sericulture is the rearing of silkworm for obtaining silk.
16. Discusses the different stages in the life cycle/life history of silkmoth.
17. List few examples of different varieties of silkworm.
18. Enumerate the importance of producing silk on commercial scale.
19. Discusses the importance of sericulture industry and its potential in India.
20. Discusses the importance of sericulture industry in the economy of a country.
21. Predict the importance and disadvantages of new technologies in sericulture.
22. Recognizes the most common silkmoth.
23. Identifies the different steps and processes in rearing of silkworm.
24. Reflect on the rearing of silkworm resulting in killing of pupa inside the cocoon.
25. Predict the importance of conserving the genetic resources of silkworm.
26. Discusses on the importance of sustainable development in sericulture and progressive increase of its productivity.
27. Explain the processing of silk.
28. Define what is reeling of silk.
29. List out the importance of silk.

Resources

Pictures of sheep, goat, camel, yak, silkworm, woolen thread, silk, Multimedia presentation of the different steps involved in the processing of wool, Multimedia presentation on processing of silk, visit to a sericulture department, cocoon, outline map of India, pure silk piece, artificial silk.

Activities

Activity 1: Pupil is shown pictures of sheep, goat, camel, yak, silkworm and asked how are they important to human beings and why do we rear these animals. They are asked to reflect upon the season in which we use woolen clothes and which part of the country uses woolen clothes more and how do woolen clothes keep us warm. They are also asked about places where sheep are found and how does the hairy skin of these animals help in keeping them warm.

Activity 2: Pupil is asked to find out the characters that are inherited from their parents and also those characteristics that are not inherited from parents. The same way they are asked to observe their pets to identify the characteristics which are similar to its parents and which are dissimilar. They then compare it with selective breeding in sheep to inherit the desired characters like disease resistant varieties, high yielding varieties etc. Pupil make five groups and discusses on the importance of rearing farm animals and its importance in eradicating poverty and how it help in the growth of the economy of a country.

Activity 3: Students are asked to feel the hair on their body and arms and those on their head. They are asked whether they find any difference. Which one seems to be coarse and which one is soft? (NCERT VII standard Science textbook). They are then asked to compare the hairy skin of the sheep with these two types, which form the fleece of sheep: (i) the coarse beard hair, and (ii) the fine soft under-hair close to the skin.

Activity 4: Students are shown a multimedia presentation of the different steps involved in the processing of wool. The different steps involved like shearing, scouring, sorting etc. are shown to pupil in a series. They are also asked to bring their observations regarding,

- The cruelty shown to animals.
- Is rearing of sheep for wool a cruelty against animals? If so how?
- Will the population of sheep be affected by rearing of sheep?

Activity 5: The students are shown a multimedia on a sericulture department and asked to find out the processes involved in rearing of silkworm. They are also asked to reflect on the life cycle of a silkworm moth and compare it with the life cycle of a butterfly.

Pupil also identifies a cocoon and its nature, colour etc. The processing of silk from cocoon is shown through a multimedia presentation. They also reflect on the cruelty shown to the pupa inside the cocoon and compare it with the rearing of sheep for wool. They are asked to collect more information regarding the recent technologies involved in the rearing of silkworm and processing of silk and also asked to reflect on their idea of bringing out an appropriate technology (which they feel) in silkworm rearing and egg production. A discussion is also initiated on the sustainable development of sericulture and steps to be adopted for a progressive increase in its production.

Activity 6: To find out when the cocoon stage is reached in the life history of the silk moth, the following activity is carried out. Cut out pictures of the stages of the life history of the silk moth, and paste them on the pieces of cardboard or chart paper. Jumble them. Now students are asked to try and arrange the stages in the correct sequence. Whoever does it fastest wins the game. They are insisted to describe the life history in their own words and write it down in their scrapbook.

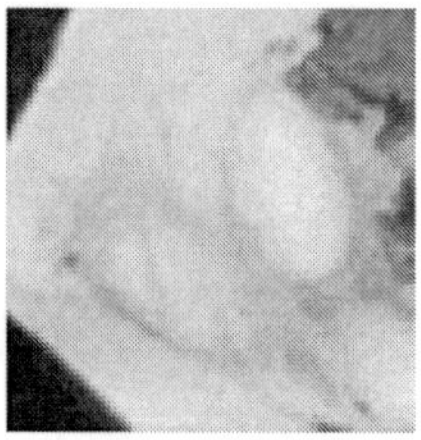

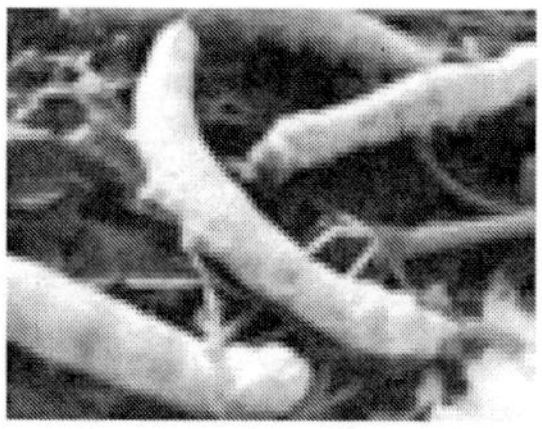

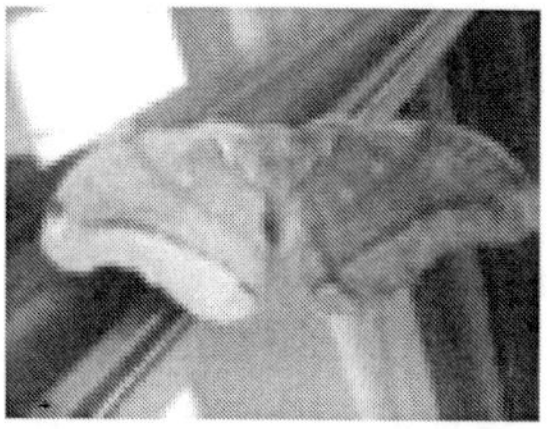

Activity 7: Students are asked to collect pictures of animals whose hair is used as wool and stick them in their scrapbook. If you are unable to get pictures, try and draw them from the ones given in the book. Find out words for sheep, goat, camel and yak in your local language and also in other languages of our country.

Yak

Alpaca

Angora goat

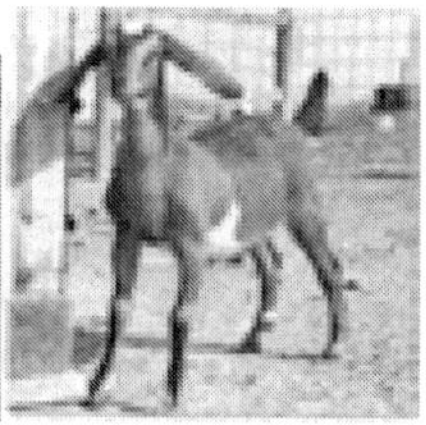

Goat

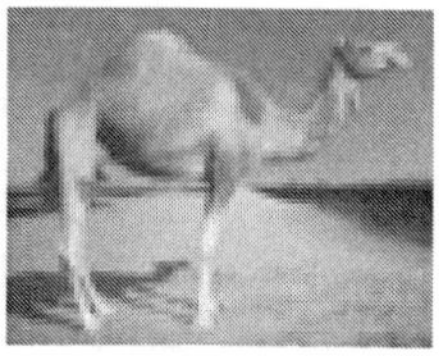

Camel

Activity 8: Procure an outline map of India and the world. Find out and mark the places on the map where we find animals that provide wool. Use different colours to denote the location for different wool yielding animals (NCERT VII standard Science textbook).

Activity 9: Debate amongst your classmates whether it is fair on the part of humans to rear sheep and then chop off their hair for getting wool (NCERT VII standard Science textbook).

Activity 10: Pupil is asked to discuss on the various importance of silk, how is it used and why is it more costly. They are also asked to visit a nearby textile shop and collect information regarding the names of different silks and also find out the price of each type. They are also asked to gather information regarding the quality of the material and what are the indications to identify pure silk. They also collect information regarding the mixing of different types of other materials in the silk.

Activity 11: Students are asked to collect pieces of silk cloth of various types and samples of woolen cloth pieces from their homes or neighborhood or tailor shops and paste them in their scrapbook. They may be insisted to visit a tailor's shop where they can find a heap of waste cut pieces. They can take help of others like aunt or teacher and identify the types of silk such as mulberry silk, tassar silk, eri silk, mooga silk, etc. Compare the texture of these silks with that of the artificial silk pieces, which contain synthetic fibres (NCERT VII standard Science textbook).

Activity 12: Students are asked to take an artificial (synthetic) silk thread and a pure silk thread and asked to burn these threads carefully. Ask them to notice any difference in the smell while burning? This is followed by burning a woolen fibre carefully and students are asked to find out whether it smell like burning of artificial silk or that of pure silk? They are asked to explain the reason (NCERT VII standard Science textbook).

Extended activity

Look for eggs of any moth or butterfly in your garden or park or any other place full of plants. They look like tiny specks (dots) laid in a cluster on the leaves. Pull out the leaves containing eggs and place them in a cardboard box. Take some leaves of the same plant or another plant of the same variety, chop them and put them in the box. Eggs will hatch into caterpillars, which are busy eating day and night. Add leaves everyday for them to feed upon. Sometimes you may be able to collect the caterpillars. But be careful. Use a paper napkin or a paper to hold a caterpillar. Observe every day. Note the (i) number of days taken for eggs to hatch, (ii) number of days taken to reach the cocoon stage, and (iii) number of days to complete life cycle. Record your observations in your notebook (NCERT VII standard Science textbook).

UNIT 3: HEAT

Scope

The unit deals with the hot and cold nature of objects and the dresses one wears during summer and winter. It also deals with the devices, unit etc. for measuring temperature and also how transfer of heat occurs.

Focus points

- Impact of heat on climatic change.
- Impact of heat on human health.
- Why the usage of non-conventional power plants should be increased?
- How solar energy can be used for domestic purpose?
- Why global temperature is increasing?

Issues to be raised

1. What clothes do one prefer to wear during summer and winter?
2. What is the reliable measure of hotness?
3. Name the device used to measure hotness.
4. What is a clinical thermometer and name its parts?
5. What is the scale we use in clinical thermometer?
6. What is the normal temperature of human body?
7. What do you mean by normal temperature of a human body?
8. What is a laboratory thermometer and what precautions should be taken while using a laboratory thermometer?
9. What is conduction?
10. What are conductors and insulators?
11. What is convection?

12. Differentiate between sea breeze and land breeze.
13. What is radiation?
14. Why do we feel comfortable in wearing dark coloured clothes during winter and light coloured clothes in summer?
15. How do woollen clothes keep us warm during winter?
16. How does climatic change cause change in temperature?
17. What are the changes that you have observed in your body temperature when you are not well or having fever?
18. What are non-conventional power plants?
19. How can we make use of solar energy in various domestic purposes?

Learning objectives

The pupil

- Interprets the importance of wearing different types of dresses during different seasons.
- Observes the device used for measuring temperature and its scale.
- Observes and differentiates between a clinical thermometer and a laboratory thermometer.
- Conduct experiments to find out the normal temperature of a human body.
- Identifies and differentiates between conductors and insulators.
- Understands the concept of convection.
- Interprets what is sea breeze and land breeze.
- Describes radiation.
- Analyse which type of dress keeps one comfortable during summer and winter.
- Interpret how and why woollen clothes keep us warm during winter.
- Infer the climatic changes due to change in temperature.
- Recalls the temperature changes they experienced when they had fever.
- Reflect on the importance of non-conventional power plants.
- Infer the use of solar energy as an alternative source of energy for various domestic purposes.

Resources

Newspaper cuttings on changes in climatic patterns followed by poster presentation, Mug, hot and cold water, Clinical thermometer, laboratory thermometer, plastic scale, iron rod, steel spoon, pencil, knife, beaker, tripod, flask, pictures of some articles that work with the help of solar energy, wool, cotton, tin can.

Activities

Activity 1: Students are asked to discuss about the clothes they prefer to wear during summer and during winter. They are also asked to discuss on what colour makes them comfortable during summer and winter. They can also collect information from their parents, relatives etc. regarding the same.

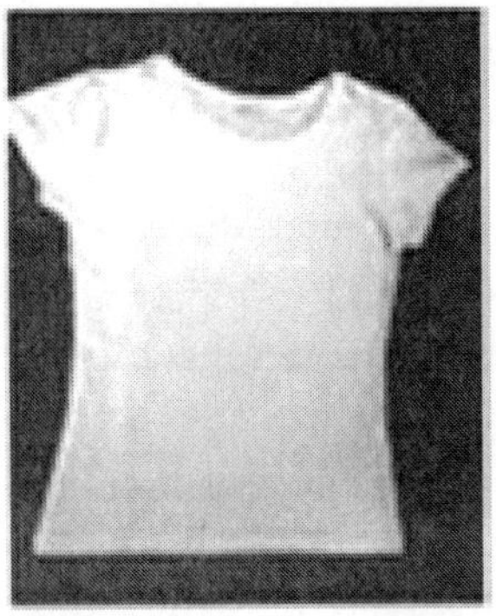

Activity 2: Students are made into groups and asked to collect few newspaper cuttings regarding changes in the temperature and how it can cause changes in climatic patterns. They are also asked to discuss on the impact of such rise in temperature on the various life forms on earth. The discussion can be followed by a poster presentation, which can be exhibited.

Activity 3: Students are given a list of items and are asked to classify them into hot, cold and neither hot nor cold. It can be marked as a tick mark (√) in the following table.

Object	Cold/Cool	Warm/hot	Neither hot nor cold
Ice cream			
Spoon in a teacup			
Fruit juice			
Water			
Handle of a frying pan			
Book			
Clothes			

Activity 4: Students are asked whether they got fever any time and how do doctors measure their temperature and the device needed for measuring the human temperature. They are asked to bring a thermometer and observe it carefully to find out the scale used for measuring temperature, how to measure and how to take the readings, precautions to be taken while taking measurement etc. A discussion is initiated on the importance of having a thermometer at home and how can it be helpful in having a health consciousness.

Activity 5: Students are asked to demonstrate how to measure the temperature of a human body. One of the students takes a thermometer and washes it with an antiseptic solution and firmly gives few jerks to bring the mercury level down below 35°C. The student is asked to place the bulb of the thermometer under their tongue. After a minute, take the thermometer out and note the readings. Find out your body temperature in the same way.

Activity 6: Measure the body temperature of some of your friends (at least 10) with a clinical thermometer. Record the observations and find out the normal body temperature of a human body (NCERT VII standard Science textbook).

Activity 7: Take a laboratory thermometer and observe it closely to find out its highest and lowest temperature it can measure, how much smaller divisions are there, how to measure using a laboratory thermometer, how to take the readings etc. They are also given a clinical thermometer and asked to compare it finding out the differences and similarities in both.

Activity 8: Students are asked to perform an experiment to demonstrate that transfer of heat occurs from hotter to colder part. An Iron rod is taken and fix few small wax pieces on the rod. These pieces should be at nearly equal distance. Now heat the rod on one end and observe the changes. The students are also asked to find out answers for the following questions.

- Wax on which part of the iron rod melts first and which melts late?

Why all the wax is not melting at the same time? (NCERT VII standard Science textbook).

Activity 9: Heat water in a small pan or a beaker. Collect some articles such as a steel spoon, plastic scale, pencil and divider. Dip one end of each of these articles in hot water. Wait for a few minutes. Touch the other end. Enter your observation in the below table.

Articles	Materials with which the article is made of	Does the other end get hot. Yes/No
Steel spoon		
Pencil		
Knife		
Glass		

Activity 10: One of the students is asked to demonstrate the following experiment. Take a round bottom flask (if flask is not available, a beaker can be used). Fill it two-thirds with water. Place it on a tripod, or make some arrangement to place the flask in such a way that you can heat it by placing a candle below it. Wait till the water in the flask is still. Place a crystal of potassium permanganate at the bottom of the flask gently using a straw. Now, heat the water by placing the candle just below the crystal. The students are asked to write their observations in the notebook and also draw a picture of what they observed. The students are also asked to observe what happens to the water when it is heated, what happens to the water near the flame, which water rises up, which water moves down towards the source of heat etc. (NCERT VII standard Science textbook).

Activity 11: Take some tap water in a beaker A and hot water in beaker B. Dip the laboratory thermometer in water so that the bulb is immersed in water but does not touch the bottom or sides of the container. Hold the thermometer vertically and observe the movement of mercury in the thermometer. Wait till the mercury thread becomes steady. Note the readings. Compare the temperature of water recorded by each student in the class. Are there any variations? Discuss the possible reasons. Also take the temperature of water in beaker B and observe the thermometer after taking it out of the beaker. They are also asked to compare how to take the readings using a clinical thermometer and a laboratory thermometer.

Activity 12: Students are asked to collect a list of metals that can conduct heat (conductors), and also a list of metals that do not conduct heat (insulators). They are asked to observe a copper wire and find out which part conducts electricity and which part does not. They are also asked to reflect on the impact of using the non-renewable sources of energy and how these can be overcome by using various non-conventional power plants that are helpful in order to save energy. They are also asked to reflect upon the impact of using cables through underground and how one can develop environmentally friendly cables.

Activity 13: Few students who stays nearby sea is asked to narrate about the climatic changes they have noticed during day-time and night-time. They are also asked about the direction in which the wind blows during day and that which blows during night. They are also asked to discuss on the differences they have experienced during a sea breeze and land breeze.

Activity 14: Students are asked to narrate on their experiences they had on a hot sunny day while moving out. They are also asked about why one should use an umbrella during hot sunny day and what are the impacts in moving out in the hot sun and they are asked about how can radiation have an influence on human body.

Activity 15: Students are shown pictures of some equipment that are run with the help of solar energy, e.g. solar heater, solar cooker etc. They are also asked about the importance of using these types of things for household purposes. A discussion is also followed which focuses on the importance of using solar energy in place of utilizing other resources as a source of energy. They are also asked to reflect on how they can increase the use of renewable energy for various purposes so that we can limit the consumption of non-renewable energy resources.

Activity 16: Take two identical tin cans. Paint the outer surface of one black and of the other white. Pour equal amounts of water in each and leave them in the mid-day sun for about an hour. Measure the temperature of water in both the cans. Students are asked to find out if there is any difference in the temperatures? In which can is the water warmer etc. They are then asked to compare their findings with the colour of dress they prefer to wear during summer and also during winter.

Fill the two cans with the same amount of hot water at the same temperature. Leave the cans in a room or in a shade. Note the temperature of water after 10-15 minutes. Students are asked to find out:

- Whether the temperature of water in both the cans fall by the same amount?
- What type of dresses do they wear on summer and winters?

How do woollen clothes keep us warm? (NCERT VII standard Science textbook).

UNIT 4: WEATHER, CLIMATE AND ADAPTATIONS OF ANIMALS TO CLIMATE

Scope

The unit deals with the meaning and differences between weather and climate. It also emphasize on the different climates and adaptations shown by different organisms, like those living in Polar Regions and tropical rainforests.

Focus points

- What are the reasons for the changing weather patterns?
- Why the adverse weather conditions occur in some parts of the world?
- Why the impact of Greenhouse effect is considered to be very serious?
- Impact of climatic change on the polar ice caps.
- Impact of melting of polar ice caps on the different life forms.
- Impact of deforestation.
- Impact of endangered species—its causes, effects and ways of conserving them.
- Climatic change and impact on life forms.

Issues to be raised

1. What do you mean by weather of a place?
2. What are the elements of weather?
3. How can you measure the maximum and minimum temperature in a day?
4. What are the causes for changes in weather patterns of the world?
5. Why do adverse weather conditions like drought, flood etc. occur in some places?
6. What is greenhouse effect and what are their impacts?
7. Why days are shorter in winter than summer?
8. What do you mean by climate of a place?
9. What are the climatic changes occurring in the world? What are its causes and how can one solve it?
10. Differentiate between hot, hot and wet and wet climate and name few places that experience it.
11. What do you mean by adaptations?
12. How can climatic changes bring about changes in polar ice cap?
13. What are the characteristic features of Polar Regions?
14. What are the special features seen in polar animals like polar beer and penguin?
15. How can the melting of polar ice caps affect the life forms in Polar Regions?
16. Why do tropical region have a hot temperature?

17. Name some places that are located in Polar Regions.
18. Name some places, which have tropical rainforests.
19. What is deforestation and how it can affect the life of various species?
20. How do some species become endangered?
21. What are the characteristic features of tropical rainforest?
22. What are the major types of animals that are seen in tropical rainforest?
23. What are the characteristic features of animals that live in tropical rainforest?
24. How do the various species in tropical rainforest get affected due to deforestation?
25. How can the changes in the climatic conditions influence the life forms in tropical rainforest?

Learning objectives

The pupil

- Understands the meaning of weather and the different elements that contribute weather.
- Conducts experiments to find out the maximum and minimum temperature in a day.
- Explore the causes for changes in weather patterns of the world.
- Discusses on the various adverse conditions like drought and flood occurring in some places.
- Explore the causes for greenhouse effect and its impact on the earth.
- Analyses why days are shorter in winter than in summer.
- Explore the meaning of climate.
- Observes and interprets the climatic changes occurring in the world.
- Infers the causes of climatic changes and solutions to solve the same.
- Differentiates between hot, hot and wet, and wet climate.
- Identifies the places that have hot, hot and wet, and wet climate.
- Observes and explains the meaning of adaptation.
- Infer the impact of climatic changes on the changes in polar ice caps.
- Observes the characteristic features of polar regions.
- Identifies the special features seen in polar animals like polar beer and penguin.
- Interpret the impact of melting of polar ice caps on the life forms in polar regions.
- Observes and explains the reason for having hot temperature in the tropical region.
- Identifies the places located in polar regions.
- Observes and list out the names of places that are located in the polar region.
- Observes and list out the names of places that have tropical rainforests.
- Recalls the meaning of deforestation and interpret how it can affect the life of various species.

- Interprets the reasons for some species becoming extinct.
- Identifies the characteristic features of tropical rainforests.
- Observes and lists out the major type of animals that are seen in tropical rainforests.
- Identifies the characteristic features of animals that live in tropical rainforests.
- Interprets how the various species in tropical rainforests get affected due to deforestation.
- Interprets how the changes in climatic conditions influences the life forms of tropical rainforests.

Resources

Newspaper cuttings on weather forecast, Pictures of floods, tsunami, drought, Thermometer, Multimedia presentation of various lives (in extreme climatic areas, tropical rainforest and Polar Regions), on graph paper.

Activities

Activity 1: Pupil reads a newspaper cutting regarding the weather forecast and find out the maximum and minimum temperature of a place, humidity and rainfall. They also bring the news regarding weather forecast of different days and read it in classroom. The pupil is asked about how they can define weather and to find out the various elements that constitute weather.

Activity 2: Pupil are asked about various situations like planning for a family function, a cricket match etc. where one has to look into the weather. They are also asked to reflect upon a recent cricket match which they have observed in Television and analyze on what are the factors of weather that are dealt with in such type of games and whether the weather of that place have a profound effect on the games.

Activity 3: Cut out the weather reports of last week from any newspaper. Record the information from the weather reports and fill in the following table.

Sl. No.	Date	Max. Temp. (°C)	Min. Temp. (°C)	Min. Humidity (%)	Max. Humidity (%)	Rainfall

Pupil is then asked to find out which day they have recorded has the maximum temperature and which one has minimum temperature and also which day has maximum humidity and minimum humidity (NCERT VII standard Science textbook).

Activity 4: Students are shown various pictures and news cuttings of the changes in weather patterns like drought, flood, cyclones, tsunami etc. The students are made into groups and asked to discuss on:

- The various reasons for such drastic changes in the atmosphere.
- What are the roles of man in causing such disaster?
- How can you prevent such disasters in future?
- What are the impacts of such changes in life?

Activity 5: Students are asked about the time in a day during which there occurs maximum temperature and the time in a day when there is minimum temperature. They are also asked to share their experiences they had during a summer afternoon and early morning in winter. They are then shown a maximum and minimum thermometer and explain its function and how to measure the maximum and minimum temperature.

Activity 6: Pupil is asked to collect about the weather patterns in different parts of the world, say, U.S., U.K., India, Australia, Africa, etc. and find out the variations they have observed in the weather. They are also shown a world map of these places showing the climatic patterns in these regions and asked to define what is climate?

Activity 7: Pupil is asked to conduct an interview with their grandparents and some old people in their village to collect information regarding the changes in climate they experience in their locality today with that of their younger days. They also collect the opinion regarding the reasons for these changes and how to solve the climatic problems.

Activity 8: Students are asked about how they protect themselves during extreme cold and extreme hot. They are also asked to spot some places in the globe where they have these extreme climate. They are also shown a multimedia presentation of various lives in these places. The pupil is asked to list the name of animals they have observed in these areas in the slide. The climatic patterns and changes in these places are observed. They are also shown an animated picture of earth, which rotates and revolves around sun. This is used to come to a conclusion that in Polar Regions the sun does not rise for 6 months and does not set for another 6 months. From the life forms the pupil is asked to find out the following:

- Observe the polar bear and identify its habit, adaptations and other characteristics.
- Observe the penguin and identify its habit, adaptations and other characteristics.

Activity 9: Pupil is shown an experiment to demonstrate the impact of melting of ice to the low-lying areas using some ice—cubes and a simulated situation. They are also asked about what are the reasons of these melting of ice and how it can influence the life forms in low-lying and coastal areas. They are also asked to reflect on the impact of melting of polar ice caps on the life in Polar Regions also.

Activity 10: Pupil is shown a globe and asked about which part of the globe has maximum temperature and why. They are also asked to identify the areas in these places where there are forest and asked them to suggest the name for such forests. They are asked about the places where they find tropical rainforests. A multimedia presentation is shown to demonstrate the life in tropical rainforests and the pupil is asked to list down the names of animals they found in tropical rainforests. They are also asked to identify the habit, adaptations and other characteristic features of few animals of tropical rainforests, e.g. lion-tailed macaque, elephant, touchan (bird) etc.

Activity 11: Students are asked whether they have seen trees cut down on either sides of road (e.g. in Mysore—Bengaluru highway), for widening the roads. They are also asked whether they have seen trees being cut down for constructing dams, buildings, houses etc. and they are asked to reflect on the various life forms that have lost from the earth or animals that are getting reduced in number (e.g. sparrow, frogs etc.) and analyze the reasons for such changes.

Activity 12: Students are asked to make groups and discuss on 'the relationship between endangered species and deforestation'. Their findings are being presented.

Activity 13: A debate is conducted on 'whether development can be attained without causing harm to earth'.

Activity 14: The temperature analysis of different years is collected and pupil is asked to discuss on the impact of rise in temperature on the earth and also on life forms.

Activity 15: Pupil is asked to collect weather reports of seven successive days in the winter months (preferably December). Collect similar reports of summer months (preferably June). Now prepare a table for sunset and sunrise times in the table and answer the following questions:

JUNE			DECEMBER		
Date	Sunrise	Sunset	Date	Sunrise	Sunset

- Is there any difference in the time of sunrise during summer and winter?
- When do you find that the sun rises earlier?
- Do you find any difference in the time of sunset during the month of June and December?
- When are the days longer?
- When are the nights longer?
- Why are the days sometimes longer and sometimes shorter?
- Plot the length of the day against the days chosen in June and December (NCERT VII standard Science textbook).

Project

Pupil is asked to collect a list of endangered species and find out the causes and effects of species getting endangered. The project should be concluded with a discussion on how to prevent the species from becoming extinct and endangered.

UNIT 5: WINDS, STORMS AND CYCLONES

Scope

The unit focuses on the movement of wind and wind currents. It also gives emphasis on thunderstorms and cyclones and how a thunderstorm becomes a cyclone. The chapter also deals with the various destructions caused by cyclones and also what effective safety measures one should take during a cyclone and how far technology is helping in predicting and escaping from such natural disasters.

Focus points

- How wind energy can be used as an alternative source of energy?
- Mention the way by which one can harvest wind energy.
- How the earth gets heated up due to the pollutants? What are the different ways by which we can minimize the pollution?
- What is the impact of heat on polar regions?
- What are the reasons for the occurrence of hurricanes like typhoon, tornado, flood and drought?
- What are the precautions one should take during these timely warnings?
- Epidemics and cyclones—Elaborate.
- Types of houses in cyclone prone areas.
- Science and technology for a sustainable society—Discuss.

Issues to be raised

1. What is wind?
2. What is the relationship between the direction of wind and air pressure?
3. How are wind currents being generated?
4. How can you utilize wind energy for domestic purposes?
5. What changes in temperature one can experience near equator and near poles?
6. Explain the movement of wind in relation to polar and equatorial regions.
7. Which part of the earth (land or water) near the equator warms up faster in summer and why?
8. How can different pollutants raise the temperature of earth?
9. What is greenhouse effect and global warming and what are its impact?
10. What is the impact of heat on Polar Regions and on low-lying and coastal areas?
11. How changes in wind patterns can causes difference in climate?

12. What are the directions of wind in summer and in winter?
13. Which is the wind that carries water and brings rain?
14. What is thunderstorm and how does it develop?
15. What are the ill effects brought about by hurricanes like typhoon, tornado, flood, drought etc.?
16. How can one make use of timely warnings given by meteorological agencies during such hurricanes?
17. How does a thunderstorm become a cyclone?
18. What are the factors that contribute towards the development of cyclones?
19. What are the various destructions caused by cyclones?
20. What is a tornado?
21. What is the relationship between weather, climate and water resources towards the economic development and well-being of humans?
22. What are the impact of cyclones and tornadoes on earth and life forms?
23. What are the measures to be taken in a cyclone-hit area?
24. What types of houses are suitable in places, which are prone to cyclonic attack?
25. How far technology has helped in giving warning during a natural calamity?
26. What are the steps (measures) to be taken when one receives a warning from meteorological department about a hurricane like cyclone, tornado etc.?
27. What is the role of science and technology in providing warnings about any natural hurricanes like cyclone and tornado?

Learning objectives

The pupil

- Understands the meaning of wind.
- Explains the relationship between the direction of wind and air pressure.
- Infers how the wind currents are being generated.
- Hypothesize on how wind energy can be utilized for various domestic purposes.
- Infer the changes in temperature one can experience near the equator and at poles.
- Explains the direction of movement of wind in relation to polar and equatorial regions.
- Hypothesize and justify which part of earth (land or water) near the equator warms up faster in summer.
- Reasons out how can different pollutants raise the temperature of earth.
- Discuss what is greenhouse effect and global warming and its impact.
- Predict the impact of heat on Polar Regions and on low-lying and coastal areas.
- Interpret how changes in wind patterns cause difference in climate.
- Analyse the direction of wind in summer and winter.
- List out the name of the wind that carry water and brings rain.

- Explain how a thunderstorm develops.
- Discuss and predict the ill effects brought about by hurricanes like typhoon, tornado, flood, drought etc.
- Extrapolate on how one can make use of timely warnings given by meteorological agencies during hurricanes.
- Explain how a thunderstorm becomes a cyclone.
- Analyse the different factors that contribute towards the development of cyclones.
- Discusses the various destructions caused by cyclones.
- Explain the meaning of a tornado.
- Compare what is weather and climate.
- Analyses the relationship between weather, climate and water resources towards the economic development and well-being of humans.
- Interpret the impact of cyclones and tornadoes on earth and life forms.
- Reasons out the measures to be taken in a cyclone-hit area.
- Hypothesize on the type of houses that are suitable to places that are prone to cyclonic attack.
- Justify the role of technology in giving warnings during a natural calamity.
- Discusses the steps (measures) to be taken when one receives warning from meteorological department about hurricanes like cyclone, tornado etc.
- Analyses the role of science and technology in providing warning about any natural hurricanes like cyclone or tornado.

Resources

A tin can, candle, plastic bottle, balloon, paper strips, water, cold water, hot water.

Activities

Activity 1: Take a tin can with a lid. Fill it approximately half with water. Heat the can on a candle flame till the water boils. Let the water boil for a few minutes. Blow out the candle. Pour out the water and immediately put the lid tightly on the can. Be careful in handling the hot can. Put the can carefully in a shallow metallic vessel or a washbasin. Pour freshwater over the can. What happens to the shape of the can? Can you guess why the shape of the can gets distorted? If you cannot get a tin can, take a soft plastic bottle. Fill it with hot water. Empty the bottle and immediately cap it tightly. Place the bottle under running water (NCERT VII standard Science textbook).

Activity 2: Crumple a small piece of paper into a ball of size smaller than the mouth of an empty bottle. Hold the empty bottle on its side and place the paper ball just inside its mouth. Now try to blow on the ball to force it into the bottle. Try the activity with bottles of different sizes (NCERT VII standard Science textbook).

Activity 3: Take two balloons of approximately equal size. Put a little water into the balloons. Blow up both the balloons and tie each one to a string. Hang the balloons 8-10 cm apart on a cycle spoke or a stick. Blow in the space between the balloons. What did you expect? What happens? Try different ways of blowing on the balloons to see what happens (NCERT VII standard Science textbook).

Activity 4: Hold a strip of paper, 20 cm long and 3 cm wide, between your thumb and forefinger. Now blow over the paper. What do you think will happen to the paper? (NCERT VII standard Science textbook).

Activity 5: Take a boiling tube. Stretch a balloon tightly over the neck of the tube. You can use a tape to make it tight. Pour some hot water in a beaker. Insert the boiling tube with the balloon in the hot water. Observe for 2-3 minutes for any change in shape of the balloon. Take the tube out, let it cool down to the room temperature. Take some ice-cold water in another beaker and place the tube with the balloon in cold water for 2-3 minutes. Observe the change in the shape of the balloon (NCERT VII standard Science textbook).

Activity 6: Take two paper bags or empty paper cups of the same size. Hang the two bags in the inverted position on the two ends of a metal or wooden stick. Tie a piece of thread in the middle of the stick. Hold the stick by the thread as in a balance. Put a burning candle below one of the bags. Observe what happens. Why is the balance of the bags disturbed? (NCERT VII standard Science textbook).

Activity 7: Visit places, factories and houses to see the uses of different kinds of energy and make a list of their utilities.

Sl. No.	Energy	Uses
1.	Electricity	Heating, light
2.	Coal	

Note down the cost of each fuel being used. Also find the relative cost of energy obtained from different sources such as electricity, coal, kerosene, petroleum gas and firewood. If this identical job (say boiling two litres of water) would be done using different fields, the cost should be estimated. Thus the relative cost of using different fuels could be calculated.

Energy used to boil two litres of water.

Energy/Fuel	Amount	Cost (₹)
Firewood	(kg)	
Electricity	(Units)	

Survey at least 25 families in different localities and note down the total amount of different kinds of energy used by them in a week/month. From this calculate the average amount of fuel used by one person per day. Estimate the total amount of different fuels consumed over during a month by the village/city.

Activity 8: Collect the data about the consumption of coal, electricity and petroleum products in India over the last couple of decades and extrapolate its demand for the future.

Activity 9: Arrange a visit for the students to an area nearby the school. Let them look for an area of bare soil or trails of sand or earth after a storm and also look for dust accumulated on broad leaves of nearby plants. This helps in understanding the concept that soil erosion occurs by air.

Activity 10: The pupil is shown a working model of a windmill where it is used in generating electricity and also for grinding flour. The working of the windmill is demonstrated and the production of a cheaper source of energy is also explained. A discussion is also followed to discuss on the importance of conserving non-renewable resources and how one can make use of renewable sources of energy in various household activities.

Activity 11: A multimedia presentation is shown about the polar and equatorial regions and asks the pupil to identify the characteristic features of these two areas. They are also shown a global representation of the movement of wind in these areas. Pupil explains the direction of movement of wind in relation to polar and equatorial regions.

Activity 12: Pupil is shown a globe and asked to find out the location of India on the globe. They are asked to find out whether it is near the equator or not. They are asked about which part of the earth (land or water) near the equator warms up faster in summer and why.

Activity 13: Pupil is asked to list the common sources of air pollution. From their past experiences and from surveying the locality note down the major sources that pollute air. Also conduct an interview with an elderly person in your locality on the temperature changes they have experienced from their childhood and how different pollutants have contributed for the increase in temperature of their locality.

Pupil is asked to collect leaves of plants from different localities (near the road, near a forest, away from the road, near a bazaar etc.) and examine the dust particles settled on them. Discuss its source and its ill-effects. The pupil is asked to come to a conclusion for the following questions:

- Which places have more polluted air (bazaar, near a road, near a forest etc.)?
- What are the sources of suspended particles in the air?
- At what time of the day, the air is more polluted?

Activity 14: Refer various literatures to find out which are the common air-polluting gases. Make a list of such gases, their sources and their effect on human beings and the environment. Ask pupils to collect newspaper cuttings regarding news on specific gases that cause pollution and its effect on human beings and environment. They are also asked to collect information from various literatures regarding greenhouse effect and global warming. They are also taken to a nearby nursery (where plants are cultivated) where there is a greenhouse for the germination of different plants. They are also asked to discuss on the impact of global warming on the low-lying or coastal areas and Polar Regions.

Activity 15: Pupil is asked to find out the direction of wind during summer and winter seasons, which can be done by conducting an interview with their neighbours or family members. They are also asked to collect the names of different wind that carry water and bring rain.

Activity 16: A multimedia presentation of the formation of thunderstorm is shown to the students. They are also shown about how a thunderstorm becomes a cyclone. They are asked to discuss and predict on the ill-effects brought about by hurricanes like typhoon, tornado, flood, drought etc.

Activity 17: The pupils observe the latest paper cuttings and photos about a recent natural calamity like cyclone, flood, drought etc. and read out the various destruction happened to life and property. They also discuss the various safety measures taken during such natural calamities and the agencies that provide timely warnings about such disasters. The discussion will also focus on the importance of science and technology during different natural calamities.

UNIT 6: SOIL

Scope

The unit focuses on the soil properties, types, soil profile and how it is important to different life forms. The unit also gives importance to how the soil gets depleted due to various human activities and how can one protect the soil from deterioration. There is also focus on water percolation into the soil and how to increase the percolation of water by rainwater harvesting and also the relationship between soil management and water management.

Focus points

- Why soil depletion is considered to be more severe problem now-a-days?
- What are the causes, effects and preventive measures of soil erosion?
- What are the human activities that lead to loss of humus soil?
- How do mining affect the soil profile?
- What is the relationship between water and weathering?
- How do soil erosion affect the transport of minerals?
- Why do we need to preserve soil?
- How percolation of water is related to various chemicals in the soil?
- How is soil water content related to infiltration rates?
- How drainage gets affected by runoff and flood?
- How is soil moisture and agriculture related?
- What are the main reasons for maintaining a better reservoir?
- Why is it necessary to maintain a better water quality?
- How is soil management related to crop management?

- How is soil fertility related to crop nutrition/crop productivity?
- What are soil borne diseases and how can we reduce it by eco-friendly means?
- What are the advantages and disadvantages of using chemical fertilizers in the soil?
- Why is it important to use natural (organic) fertilizers and what are its advantages?

Issues to be raised

1. What is soil?
2. What are the importances of soil?
3. What is soil erosion?
4. How is soil formed?
5. What is soil profile?
6. What are the different soil layers?
7. How does the humus get depleted?
8. How does mining affect the soil profile?
9. What are the different types of soil?
10. How do lichens help in weathering of soil?
11. What is chemical weathering and mechanical weathering?
12. How can you preserve the soil and why?
13. What is percolation rate of water?
14. What are the agents that affect the percolation rate of water?
15. What is soil moisture?
16. How does soil moisture influence the agriculture?
17. What are the agents that affect the soil?
18. Which are the different types of soil present in different parts of India?
19. Which are the types of soil suitable for different agricultural crops?
20. How does the weather and climate of a place influence the soil?
21. What is run off potential?
22. What is the relationship between soil management and crop management?
23. What is the relationship between soil fertility and crop nutrition?
24. What are soil borne diseases?
25. What is salinity, soil pH and the nutrient requirements?
26. What are organic fertilizers and what are their importances?

Learning objectives

The pupil

- Defines what is soil.
- Discusses the importance of soil.

- Interpret the impacts of soil erosion.
- Discusses the process of soil formation.
- Explains what is soil profile.
- Identifies the different layers of soil.
- Interpret the different ways of depleting the humus in the soil.
- Extrapolate the impact of mining on the soil profile.
- Identifies the different types of soil.
- Understands the importance of lichens in weathering of rocks.
- Differentiates between chemical weathering and mechanical weathering.
- Analyse the different ways of preserving soil and its need.
- Defines what is percolation of water.
- Identifies the different agents that affect the percolation of water.
- Defines what is soil moisture.
- Explains the relationship between soil moisture and the type of agriculture.
- Identify the various agents that affect the soil.
- Lists out the different types of soil found in different parts of India.
- Describes the types of soil suitable for different agricultural crops.
- Interpret how the weather and climate of a place influence the soil.
- Defines what is run off potential.
- Identifies the relationship between soil management and crop management.
- Identifies the relationship between soil fertility and crop nutrition.
- Defines soil borne diseases.
- Differentiates salinity, soil pH and the nutrient requirements.
- Explains what are organic fertilizers and its importance.

Learning resources

Soil samples from different places, slide shows showing the impact of soil erosion, glass tumbler, pictures on mining, slide shows on weathering of rocks, samples of clayey, loamy and sandy soils, hollow cylinder or a pipe, boiling tube, visits a water body, funnel, filer paper, paper cuttings regarding heavy floods, measuring cylinder, dropper, pictures of Dams, water from different sources.

Activities

Activity 1: Collect some soil samples from different places and ask the students to observe it carefully. From their observations of the soil sample and also their previous experience, let them complete the following table:

Sl. No.	Soil source	Plants found	Animals found	Any other observations
1.	Soil near a pond			
2.	Soil from roadside			

(NCERT VII standard Science textbook)

Activity 2: Pupil is asked to collect information from their parents and grandparents about the various soil deterioration that has occurred in their locality. They are also asked to find out how those landscapes looked like in their younger age and what changes has happened to them.

Activity 3: Pupil is shown some slide shows showing the impact of soil erosion. They are also asked to reflect on the various causes for soil erosion and how does it affect the plants, animals and other living organisms of the area? The pupil is made into groups and asked to discuss on the preventive measures that can be taken to prevent this soil erosion.

Activity 4: Take a little soil. Break the clumps with your hand to powder it. Now take a glass tumbler, three quarters filled with water, and then add a handful of soil to it. Stir it well with a stick to dissolve the soil. Now let it stand undisturbed for some time. Afterwards, observe it and answer the following questions:

- Do you see layers of particles of different sizes in the glass tumbler?
- Draw a diagram showing these layers.
- Are there some dead rotting leaves or animal remains floating on water?

(NCERT VII standard Science textbook)

Activity 5: Pupil is shown soil sample from a fertile land and asked them what makes the soil fertile. They are introduced the concept of humus. They are shown some paper cuttings on different ways of soil being deteriorated. They are asked to discuss in groups about the various ways by which the humus in the soil gets depleted. They also suggest ways of preventing such depletion.

Activity 6: Pupil is shown some pictures on mining being occurring in different places. The pictures showing some quarries are also shown. The pupil is asked to reflect on what would be the place look like if it was not used in mining. They are asked to reflect on its impact on soil profile, and what is the alternative to prevent such massive destruction.

Activity 7: Pupil discusses about the various agents that are responsible for causing weathering of soil. They are asked to reflect on the relationship between water and weathering and also between lichens and weathering. To justify the findings they are shown slide shows on weathering of rocks with the help of water and lichens.

Activity 8: Collect samples of clayey, loamy and sandy soils. Take a fistful of soil from one of the samples. Remove any pebbles, rocks or grass blades from it. Now add water drop by drop and knead the soil. Add just enough water so that a ball can be made from it, but at the same time it should not be sticky. Try to make a ball from this soil. On a flat surface, roll this ball into a cylinder. Try to make a ring from this cylinder. Repeat this activity with other samples also. Does the extent to which a soil can be shaped indicate its type? Can you suggest which type of soil would be the best for making pots, toys and statues? (NCERT VII standard Science textbook).

Activity 9: For this activity divide yourself into three teams. Name the teams A, B and C. You will be finding out how fast the water passes down the soil. You will need a hollow cylinder or a pipe. Ensure that each team uses pipes of the same diameter. Some suggestions for obtaining such a pipe are given below:

1. If possible, get a small tin can and cut off its bottom.
2. If PVC pipe (approx. diameter 5 cm) is available, cut it into 20 cm long pieces and use them.

At the place where you collect the soil, place the pipe about 2 cm deep in the ground. Pour 200 mL water in the pipe slowly. For measuring 200 mL water you can use any empty 200 mL bottle. Note the time when you start pouring water. When all the water has percolated leaving the pipe empty, note the time again. Be careful not to let the water spill over or run down on the outside of the pipe while pouring. Calculate the rate of percolation by using the following formula:

$$\text{Percolation rate} = \frac{\text{Amount of water (mL)}}{\text{Percolation time (min)}}$$

Calculate the rate of percolation in your soil sample. Compare your findings with others and arrange the soil samples in the increasing order of the rate of percolation.

Activity 10: Take a boiling tube. Put two spoonful of a soil sample in it. Heat it on a flame and observe it. Let us find out what happens upon heating. Do you see water drops any where? If yes, where did you find them? (NCERT VII standard Science textbook).

Activity 11: Pupil visits a water body nearby and collects some water. They are asked to find out the impurities present in it. They are asked the reason why it is not safe to drink such water. They are also asked to find out the soil content in it. They are asked to reflect on how did the soil reach the water bodies and how soil erosion leads to transportation of such impurities to water bodies.

Activity 12: Pupil is shown a power point presentation illustrating the relationship between percolation of water and the amount of various chemicals in the soil. It also demonstrates the relation between soil water content and infiltration rates.

Activity 13: Take a plastic funnel. Take a filter paper (or a piece of newspaper sheet), fold and place it as shown in the figure. Weigh 50g of dry, powdered soil and pour it into the funnel. Measure a certain amount of water in a measuring cylinder and pour it drop by drop on the soil. You can use a dropper for this purpose. Do not let all the water fall at one spot. Pour water all over the soil. Keep pouring water till it starts dripping. Subtract the amount of water left in the measuring cylinder from the amount you started with. This is the amount of water retained by the soil. Record your results in your notebook (NCERT VII standard Science textbook).

Activity 14: Pupil is shown some paper cuttings regarding heavy floods that occurred in the recent times in a city. They were asked about the outbreak of various diseases in that locality and they were asked to focus on the drainages there and how can it affect the areas that are flooded. They are also asked to discuss on the impact of such drainage and floods on the life, and the steps to be taken to prevent such disasters.

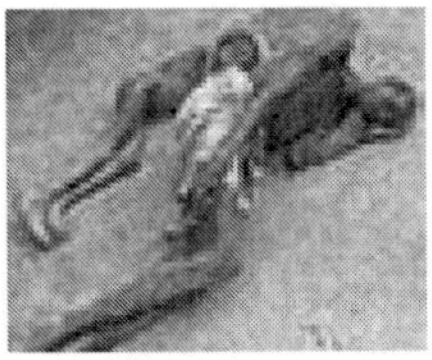

Activity 15: Take 100g soil. (Take help from any shopkeepers to weigh the soil.) Place it on a newspaper in the sun and allow it to dry for two hours. This activity is best done in the afternoon. Take care that the soil does not spill outside the newspaper. After drying it, weigh the soil again. The difference in the weight of the soil before and after drying gives you the amount of moisture contained in 100g of soil. This is called the percentage moisture content (NCERT VII standard Science textbook).

Activity 16: Pupil is asked to collect information regarding the different types of soil along with their moisture content, and find out the type of vegetation that is being seen in such areas. They are asked to reflect on how the moisture content of soil determines the vegetation of the place.

Activity 17: Pupil is asked about the temperature of the day, whether it was hot, cold or average. They are also asked about the seasons that they experience in a year. They are also asked about what is climate and how to differentiate between weather and climate. They also explain the relationship between weather and climate and how they are mutually dependent.

Activity 18: Crops such as wheat are grown in the fine clayey soils, because they are rich in humus and are very fertile. Find from your teachers, parents and farmers the type of soils and crops grown in your area. Enter the data in the following table (NCERT VII standard Science textbook).

Sl. No.	Soil type	Crops grown
1.	Clayey soil	Wheat...

Activity 19: Pupil is shown some pictures of Dams that are about to collapse due to several reasons. A discussion is initiated on the various reasons for dams being in such a dangerous condition. The conclusions are listed on the black board. The pupil is asked to reflect upon these and find out some suggestions for the safety and security of dams.

Activity 20: The pupil is asked to bring water from different sources. They are asked to categorize into two groups as the water which one can take in and the one which we cannot take in. They are asked about the reason for not using certain water and how can one detect the quality of drinking water.

Activity 21: The pupil is taken to a nearby field where crops are grown. They are asked to find out how the crops have been grown and how the soil management is been done in those areas. They are also asked to find out the relationship between soil management and crop management.

Activity 22: Pupil is asked to visit some farmers in their nearby areas and collect information regarding some of the soil borne diseases that usually attack their crops in the field. The pupil asks their parents, friends, grandparents and so on for collecting the relevant information. Each student makes a presentation on their collected material.

They are also asked to collect information regarding the relationship between soil fertility and crop productivity.

Activity 23: The pupil is asked to collect information regarding organic fertilizers that are being produced. The different ways of producing organic fertilizers are also being explored. They are asked to list out how these fertilizers are produced at home and its usage. They also find out the different materials from which organic fertilizers can be produced.

Project

- Pupil makes a compost pit in the school so that they can dispose all the degradable wastes into it and can be used as a manure or if possible as a biogas plant.
- Pupil also prepares a vermicompost in their school campus, so that natural fertilizers can be obtained from it.

UNIT 7: FORESTS—OUR LIFELINE

Scope

The unit focuses on forest as a natural resource and its importance. The unit also emphasizes the role of forest as an important component in the life cycle and food chain.

Focus points

- Why fossils are considered as an important natural resource? Why should we give more importance in protecting it?
- How the ecological balance disturbed when the forests and wildlife are disturbed?
- What are the chief forest products and why is it important to conserve them?
- What are the main reasons for the tropical and sub-tropical forests getting disturbed?
- What are the main causes for the destruction of forests and how can it influence the life on earth?
- How is Desertification, Deforestation and Afforestation related?
- How is soil fertility related to growth of plants?
- How is forest helpful in improving the economy of a country?
- How does an increase in CO_2 in the atmosphere affect the globe?
- What are the advantages of eco-tourism to the environment and economy of a nation?

Issues to be raised

1. Why are forests called as green lungs?
2. Why do you say that forests are an important renewable resource?
3. What is top canopy of a forest?
4. What are creepers and climbers?

5. Name some animals that depend on forest for living.
6. What are decomposers?
7. What is transpiration?
8. What is the relationship between tribes and forests?
9. Name some animals that help in seed dispersal.
10. Why do you say that forest is a natural absorber of rainwater?
11. What is the role of forests in controlling floods, soil erosion, noise pollution and bringing rainfall?
12. How can you substantiate that forests and wildlife help in maintaining ecological balance?
13. Which are the chief forest products?
14. What are the main reason for the tropical and sub-tropical forests being disturbed?
15. What are the reasons for destruction of forests?
16. What is the role of forests in maintaining the ecological balance?
17. What is Desertification, Deforestation and Afforestation?
18. What are the impacts of increase in CO_2 in the atmosphere?
19. What is the relationship between forest and economy?
20. What is eco-tourism?
21. Comment on the aesthetic value of forest.

Learning objectives

The pupil

- Give reasons for forests been called as green lungs.
- Explains the reasons why forests are called as renewable resources.
- Describes what is top canopy of a forest.
- Differentiates between creepers and climbers.
- List out the names of some animals that depend on forests for their life.
- Defines what are decomposers.
- Explains transpiration.
- Explores the relationship between tribes and forests.
- List out the names of animals that helps in seed dispersal.
- Predict the reason why forest is a natural absorber of rainwater.
- Justify how forests help in controlling floods, noise pollution and soil erosion.
- Predicts how forests can help in bringing rainfall.
- Reasons out how forests and wildlife help in bringing ecological balance.
- List out the chief forest products.
- Explore into the reasons for the tropical and sub-tropical forests being disturbed.
- Predicts the reason for destruction of forests.

- Explains the role of forests in maintaining the ecological balance.
- Compare Desertification, Deforestation and Afforestation.
- Predicts the impacts of increase in CO_2 in the atmosphere.
- Analyse relationship between forest and economy.
- Defines eco-tourism.
- Reflects on the aesthetic value of forest.

Activities

Activity 1: Observe the various things in your home and make a list of those which are made from material which may have been obtained from the forest (NCERT VII standard Science textbook).

Activity 2: Visit a forest or a park in your neighbourhood. Observe the trees and try to identify them. You can take the help of some elders or books on trees. List the characteristics of the trees that you observe, such as the height, shape of leaves, crown, flowers, and fruits. Also draw the crowns of some trees (NCERT VII standard Science textbook).

This can be followed by the asking few questions like:

- What is the colour of the forest?
- What are its uses?
- Why are plants called as green lungs?
- Why forests are called as renewable resources?
- What do you mean by top canopy in a forest?

Activity 3: Few creepers and climbers are brought to the classroom. The pupil is asked to differentiate between the two, based on their habit, nature etc. They are also asked to discuss on their role in a forest.

Activity 4: Pupil is asked to list out the names of animals that are found in a forest. They are also asked about the role of decomposers in a food chain; the animals that helps in seed dispersal; and also what makes it possible.

Activity 5: Take a potted plant. Select any leaf and cover it using a polythene cover. Cover it properly to see that no air space is left out. Keep in this manner for one day and observe the plant leaf on the next day. The observation is noted down, and the pupil explains how transpiration occurs in plants.

Activity 6: Pupil is shown some pictures of people who depend on forests for their living (Tribes). They are also asked about the different modes of dependence of these people on the forest. They are asked to discuss on what would be the impact on these people if the forest gets destroyed.

Activity 7: Dig a small pit. Put vegetable waste and leaves in it. Cover them with soil. Add some water. After three days, remove the upper layer of the soil. Does the pit feel warm inside? (NCERT VII standard Science textbook).

Few dried leaves are spread on the soil and pour some water on it. Leave it as such for few days. The leaves are removed after few days and observe the moisture inside. From this the importance of forests in conserving rainwater is brought into. This finally leading to water conservation is also dealt here. They are also shown a water cycle so that they reflect on how rainwater is formed and also the role of forests in bringing about rainfall.

Activity 8: Pupil is taken to a garden nearby where there are lot of trees. One of the students is asked to call his friends name from behind a tree. Repeat it without the cover of a tree. The pupil is asked to recognize which made more noise and which had less noise. The conclusion will help in inferring that trees help in controlling noise pollution.

Activity 9: Pupil is made into groups and different groups are given different forest products and they are asked to discuss on its origin and economic use. They are also asked to find out other forest products and list out their origin and economic value of them and list them on the black board.

Activity 10: Pupil is asked about the nearby places that are facing destruction of forests. They are asked about the impacts of destruction of forest on different life forms.

Activity 11: A film regarding the impact of increase in CO_2 on the earth and life forms are screened.

Activity 12: Pupil is shown a picture of a plant with roots. They are asked to discuss on the importance of roots and how it helps in soil conservation. They also discuss how a large number of trees in a forest can help in preventing soil erosion.

Activity 13: The whole class is engaged in playing the following game. Different crowns are made out of paper on which are written names of different animals (Lion, frog, deer, cow...), plants, birds and other living organisms found in the forest. Each student is asked to select a crown and they wear it. A long thread is taken and it is linked to one student to another according to their dependence on food which finally forms a food web.

One of the students (say Frog) completely leaves the thread and the pupil identifies the imbalance happening in that ecosystem. In this way they reach the conclusion of how forests and wildlife help in maintaining an ecological balance.

Activity 14: In Fig. the artist has forgotten to put the labels and directions on the arrows. Mark the directions on the arrows and label the diagram using the following labels: Clouds, Rain, Atmosphere, Carbon dioxide, Oxygen, Plants, Animals, Soil, Roots, Water table (NCERT VII standard Science textbook).

UNIT 8: WASTE WATER STORY

Scope

The unit focuses on the harmful effects of waste water from different sources and waste water treatment. It also gives importance for the need of safe drinking water. The unit also focuses on the meaning of sewage and proper sewage disposal, sanitation and outbreak of various diseases and also the importance of being an active citizen.

Focus points

- How does stagnant water result in spreading of contagious diseases?
- What are the ill-effects of stagnant water?

- What are the reasons for contamination of water?
- What are the steps to be taken for bringing about awareness among public about the importance of maintaining safe drinking water?
- How do overexploitation lead to water pollution?
- What are the different ways for the proper disposal of wastes (from hospitals, industries etc.).
- What will happen if we mix degradable and non-degradable wastes and what are its consequences?
- What is the safe way for disposing sewage in highly polluted and populated places?
- How can you maintain a sewage pit properly?
- What are the different ways by which we make useful products from sewage?
- How can you make use of technology in waste water treatment?
- How can citizens help in maintaining a sewage free environment?
- How is sanitation of a place and spread of diseases related? What are the diseases spread through water?
- What are the different eco-friendly ways of sewage disposal?
- What practices can one adopt for maintaining sanitation in public places?
- What are some of the individual and collective actions that can be undertaken for better sanitation practices?

Issues to be raised

- What is waste water?
- What are the impact of stagnant water to life forms?
- What are the reasons for increasing scarcity of freshwater?
- When is the International Decade for action on "Water for life"?
- What is sewage treatment?
- What are chemical and microbial contamination of water?
- What are the steps to be taken for maintaining safe drinking water?
- What are the reasons for water pollution?
- What do you mean by sewage and what are the organic and inorganic impurities in the sewage?
- Which are the sources from which wastes are added to different water sources?
- How can you dispose degradable and non-degradable wastes?
- How will you dispose sewage in highly polluted places and also at places of human settlements?
- What are sewage pits and how can you maintain it properly?
- What is waste water treatment plant?
- How can you make useful products from sewage?

- What is the role of technology in waste water treatment?
- What are the roles of citizens in maintaining a sewage free environment?
- What is the relation between sanitation and diseases?
- What are the diseases that can be affected due to unhygienic waste disposal and stagnant water?
- What are the alternative arrangements for sewage disposal?
- How can you assure sanitation at public places?
- What are the individual and collective actions that can be undertaken for better sanitation practices?

Learning objectives

- Explain the meaning of waste water.
- Explains the impact of stagnant water to life forms.
- Give reasons for increasing scarcity of freshwater.
- Identifies the International Decade for action on "Water for life".
- Defines what is sewage treatment.
- Identifies which are the chemical and microbial contaminants of water.
- Identifies the steps to be taken for maintaining safe drinking water.
- Predicts the reasons of water pollution.
- Explains what sewage is and identifies the organic and inorganic impurities in it.
- Identifies the sources from which wastes are added to different water sources.
- Explain the ways of disposing degradable and non-degradable wastes.
- Explain the different ways of sewage disposal in highly polluted places and also at places of human settlements.
- Explains what are sewage pits and how can you maintain it properly.
- Explain what is waste water treatment plant.
- Mention different ways of making useful products from sewage.
- Explore the role of technology in waste water treatment.
- Discusses the roles of citizens in maintaining a sewage free environment.
- Analyse the relation between sanitation and diseases.
- List out the diseases that can be affected due to unhygienic waste disposal and stagnant water.
- Discusses on the alternative arrangements for sewage disposal.
- Explore the different ways to assure sanitation at public places.
- Analyse the individual and collective actions that can be undertaken for better sanitation practices.

Learning resources

Activities

Activity 1: Pupil is asked about the water they drink. They are asked about what type of water they take for drinking and what makes the water suitable for drinking?

They are asked about the waste water from kitchen, bathroom etc. They are shown paper cuttings of several diseases that are spreading in the recent years and its ill effects. It is followed by asking the following questions:

- What makes water impure?
- What are the ill effects brought about by stagnant wastewater?
- How can you keep your surroundings neat and clean?
- How can you reduce the spreading of mosquitoes?
- What are the diseases that have started spreading in the recent years?

Activity 2: Pupil is shown a slide show on scarcity of freshwater in different places. They are asked to discuss on the causes for water scarcity. A debate is conducted on the topic—United Nations International Decade for action on "Water for life". They are also asked to reflect on the various steps to be taken for maintaining safe drinking water.

Activity 3: Pupil is asked to prepare two dustbins outside the classroom. They are asked to dispose all the degradable wastes in one dustbin and non-degradable ones in the other. The pupil is asked about the reasons for separating them. They are also asked to reflect on the following:

- How will you dispose sewage in highly polluted places?
- How will you dispose sewage places of human settlements?
- How wastes can be made into some useful products on economical value?

Activity 4: Pupil is shown pictures of waste treatment plant and asked to explain the functioning of it. They are also asked about how we can protect sewage pits from the outbreak of some contagious diseases.

Activity 5: Pupil is shown a slide show about the role of various technologies in wastewater treatment. They are asked about how one can protect water bodies by not making it polluted from any sources.

Activity 6: Locate an open drain near your home, school or on the roadside and inspect water flowing through it. Record colour, odour and any other observation. Discuss with your friends and your teacher and fill up the following table:

Sl. No.	Type of sewage	Point of origin	Substances which contaminate	Any other remarks
1.	Sullage water	Kitchen		
2.	Foul waste	Toilets		
3.	Trade waste	Industrial and commercial organisations		

(NCERT VII standard Science textbook)

Activity 7: Pupil is asked to list out the names of few diseases that are usually spread among Human beings. They are asked to categorise into different groups based on their mode of transmit.

Diseases spread through air	Diseases spread through water

They also list the names of some diseases that are spread by mosquitoes.

Activity 8: Study the sewage route in your-home/school/building. Do the following:

- Make a line diagram of the sewage route.
- Walk down the street or survey the campus to find the number of manholes.
- Follow an open drain and find out where it ends and which living organisms are found in and around it.

In case you do not have a sewerage system in your locality, find out how sewage is being disposed off.

Activity 9: Divide yourself into groups to perform the activity. Record observations at each stage:

- Fill a large glass jar 3/4 full of water. Add some dirty organic matter such as grass pieces or orange peels, a small amount of detergent, and a few drops of an ink or any colour.
- Cap the jar, shake it well and let the mixture stand in the sun for two days.
- After two days, shake the mixture and pour a small sample into test tube. Label this test tube "Before treatment; Sample 1". How does it smell?
- Use an aerator from an aquarium to bubble air through the sample in the glass jar. Allow several hours for aeration; leave the aerator attached overnight. If you do not have an aerator, use a mechanical stirrer or a mixer. You may have to stir it several times.
- The next day when aeration is complete, pour another sample into a second test tube. Label it as "After aeration; Sample 2".
- Fold a piece of filter paper to form a cone. Wet the paper with tap water and then insert the cone in a funnel. Mount the funnel on a support (as you have learnt in Class VI).
- Place layers of sand, fine gravel and finally medium gravel in the funnel (An actual filtration plant does not use filter paper, but the sand filter is several metres deep).
- Pour the remaining aerated liquid through the filter into the beakers. Do not allow the liquid to spill over the filter. If the filtered liquid is not clear, filter it a few times till you get clear water.
- Pour a sample of the filtered water into a third test tube labelled "Filtered; Sample 3".
- Pour another sample of the filtered water into a fourth test tube. Add a small piece of a chlorine tablet. Mix well until the water is clear. Label the test tube "Chlorinated; Sample 4". Observe carefully the samples in all the test tubes. Do not taste! Just smell them!

Now answer the following questions:

(a) What changes did you observe in the appearance of the liquid after aeration?

(b) Did aeration change the odour?

(c) What was removed by the sand filter?

(d) Did chlorine remove the colour?

(e) Did chlorine have an odour? Was it worse than that of the wastewater? (NCERT VII standard Science textbook)

Activity 10: Here is a crossword puzzle: Good luck!

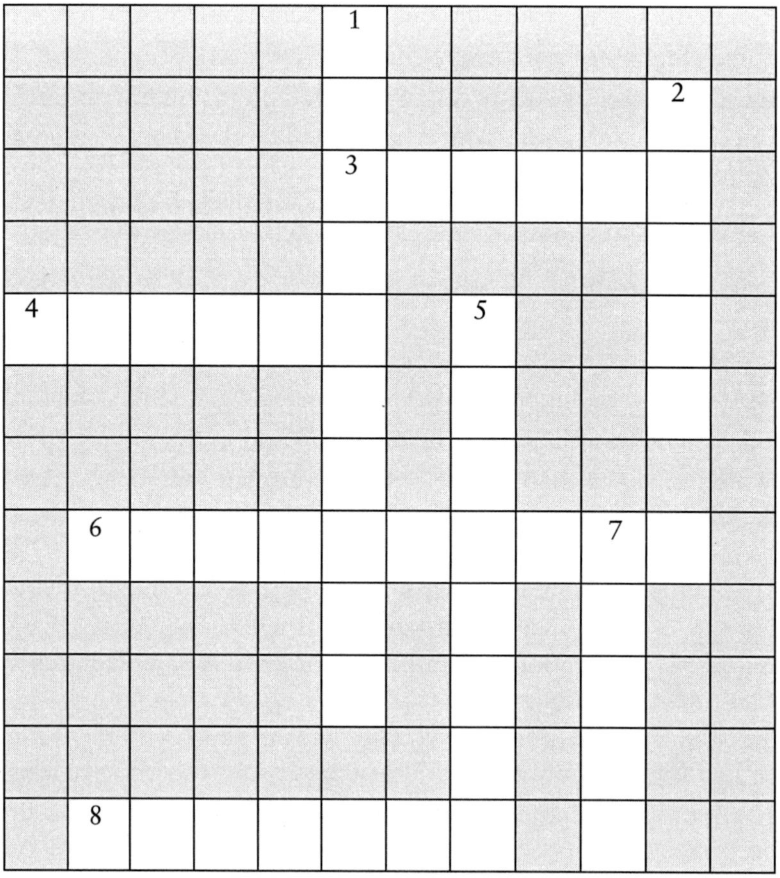

Across

3. Liquid waste products
4. Solid waste extracted in sewage treatment
6. A word related to hygiene
8. Waste matter discharged from human body

Down

1. Used water
2. A pipe carrying sewage
5. Micro-organisms which causes cholera
7. A chemical to disinfect water

(NCERT VII standard Science textbook)

Activity 11: Pupil is asked to discuss on what can be done as an active citizen for protecting water bodies and what the better housekeeping practices are. Pupil is also asked to make a table and find out what can one do at individual and collective level for conserving water.

Individual level	Collective level
1. 2. 3. 4.	

Activity 12: Collect from different books/reviews about the alternative arrangements for sewage disposal with special reference to disposal of wastes in Railway stations, Bus depot, airport etc.

UNIT 9: WATER—A PRECIOUS RESOURCE

Scope

The unit deals with the amount water recommended per person per day, how much water is available, forms of water with special reference to groundwater as an important source of water. The unit also focus on the Depletion of water table, Distribution of water and water management. The unit emphasize on what role can one play in conserving water and also the effect of water scarcity on plants.

Focus points

- How much water is been utilised per person per day?
- Why does water scarcity occur in the modern world?
- What are the ways by which we can have a better way of managing water?
- How can individual play a major role in water management?
- Why is the amount of usable water on the earth getting reduced? What are the alternative measures?
- How does water depletion has an impact on the environment?
- Why do we need to nationalise the rivers?
- What are the reasons for water becoming a political issue? How can such issues be solved?

- Why are different projects being given importance for protecting and conserving water?
- What are the various ways by which water get polluted in places of human settlements and how can we minimise such pollution?
- How is industrialisation related to water pollution? What are the steps to be taken in order to prevent water pollution by industries?
- Why is it important to reutilise and recycle wastewater? How can you do it?
- Why is rainwater harvesting considered to be a solution to water problems?
- What are the steps that one can adopt for proper water management in kitchen and garden?
- What roles can one play towards conserving water?
- What are the main reasons for the depletion of water table?
- How is population increase and level of groundwater related?
- How is agriculture and groundwater related?
- How does the percolation of water into the soil get reduced?
- How do changing climatic patterns influence water?
- What human activities are responsible for the occurrence of flood and drought? How can we minimise such activities?
- How can we make use of wastewater so that we can reduce the pressure on freshwater?
- What are the different ways of rainwater harvesting which we can practice at home?
- How can each individual help in reducing water scarcity?
- What roles can you play at home and school to reduce water scarcity?

Issues to be raised

1. When is the world water day celebrated?
2. What is the amount of water recommended per person per day?
3. What are the causes and effects of water scarcity in the modern world?
4. What are the different methods of managing water?
5. What are the duties of an individual in managing water?
6. What is the amount of water present on the earth?
7. Which is the water that can be used by human beings?
8. What do you mean by freshwater?
9. What are the reasons for decreasing amount of usable water on earth?
10. What are the impacts of water depletion?
11. How water gets polluted?
12. What is eutrophication?
13. How many rivers are there in your state?
14. What is the importance of nationalising rivers?

15. Why water is becoming a political issue?
16. What is water cycle?
17. What are the different forms of water?
18. What are the various projects to protect water?
19. How do human settlements pollute water?
20. What is the relationship between industrialisation and water pollution?
21. How can you reutilise and recycle water?
22. What are the laws in India to control water pollution?
23. How can you assess the water quality?
24. What are the techniques for cleaning polluted water?
25. What are water table, infiltration and aquifer?
26. What is acid rain?
27. What do you mean by rainwater harvesting?
28. How can you have proper water management in kitchen and garden?
29. How can an individual help in conserving water?
30. How do the water table get depleted?
31. What is the relationship between increasing population and groundwater?
32. What is the relationship between agriculture and groundwater?
33. What are the different reasons for reducing the percolation of water into the soil?
34. How do changing climatic patterns influence water?
35. What are the causes of floods and drought?
36. How do wastage of water happens?
37. What are the different ways of rainwater harvesting?
38. What is Bawri and drip irrigation?
39. How can you ensure a sustainable water usage?
40. What are the effects of water scarcity on plants?
41. What role can you play in reducing water scarcity?
42. What are your roles at home and school to reduce water scarcity?

Learning objectives

- Recalls when is world water day celebrated.
- Understands the amount of water recommended per person per day.
- Interprets the causes and effects of water scarcity in the modern world.
- Analyse the different methods of managing water.
- Identifies the duties of an individual in managing water.
- Explores the amount of water present on the earth.

- Recalls which is the water that can be used by human beings.
- Defines what is freshwater.
- Explore the reasons for decreasing amount of usable water on earth.
- Reflects on the impacts of water depletion.
- Explains how water gets polluted.
- Defines eutrophication.
- List out the names of river in your state.
- Analyse the importance of nationalising rivers.
- Reasons out why water is becoming a political issue.
- Defines water cycle.
- Communicates the different forms of water.
- Mention the various projects to protect water.
- Reflects on how human settlements pollute water.
- Analyse the relationship between industrialisation and water pollution.
- Hypotheses on reutilising and recycling of water.
- What are the laws in India to control water pollution.
- Explore the different ways of assessing the water quality.
- Analyse the various techniques for cleaning polluted water.
- Define what are water table, infiltration and aquifer.
- Defines acid rain.
- Communicates what is rainwater harvesting.
- Explains the different ways of water management in kitchen and garden.
- Analyse the roles of different individuals in conserving water.
- Explains how water table get depleted.
- Analyse the relationship between increasing population and groundwater.
- Analyse the relationship between agriculture and groundwater.
- Infer the different causes for reducing the percolation of water into the soil.
- Reflect on the how the changing climatic patterns influence water.
- Analyse the causes of floods and drought.
- Explains how the wastage of water occurs.
- Mention the different ways of rainwater harvesting.
- Explains what is Bawri and drip irrigation.
- Explain different ways to ensure sustainable water usage.
- Explore the effects of water scarcity on plants.
- Discuss on different roles you can play in reducing water scarcity.
- Discuss on different roles one can play at home and school to reduce water scarcity.

Activities

Activity 1: The pupil is asked to refer few books and find out when is the world water day and why is it celebrated. They are asked to share their findings in the classroom. They are also asked about the amount of water is recommended per person per day. The students are asked to find out whether they are taking in the required amount of water daily and what is the importance of taking enough water each day.

Activity 2: Pupil is asked to share their experience about summer seasons. They are also asked about the water problem they experienced during summer. They are asked to discuss on the reasons for such water problem being experienced and the possible solutions to solve such water problems in the future.

Activity 3: The pupil is shown a multimedia presentation, chart or newspaper cutting on different ways of managing water and they are asked to discuss on the importance of such water management.

Activity 4: Pupil read certain issues on water between states, countries etc. in the class. They are then asked about why there are water issues between states, countries and nations? Why there is water scarcity? What can one do at the individual level/community level for conserving water? Why bloodshed has occurred in the name of water?

Activity 5: Students observe the pictures of different lakes and rivers getting dried off. They are asked about the reason for such disaster. The discussion is focused on the following points:

- What are the impacts of water depletion?
- How water gets polluted?
- What do you mean by nationalizing rivers? What are its advantages?
- How many rivers are there in your state?

Activity 6: Refer few journals and find out the nature of various projects to protect water.

Activity 7: Pupil is asked to divide into two groups and each group is asked to have a presentation on:

- Group A—Human settlement and water pollution.
- Group B—Industrialisation and water pollution.

Activity 8: An elocution competition is been conducted in the classroom on the topics:

- Reutilisation and recycling of waste water.
- Water pollution control through law.

Activity 9: Data on the present groundwater level is shown and pupil is asked to compare it with that of previous years. They are also asked to analyse on the risk of groundwater depletion on the life forms and to the environment. The following are the areas to be discussed:

- What are the different ways of increasing the groundwater level?
- What are the various reasons for reducing the percolation of water?
- What is rainwater harvesting?
- What is the advantages of constructing pits/bunds in water management?

- How can one have a proper water management in the kitchen?
- How can one have a proper water management in the garden?

Activity 10: Pupil is asked about the changes in the colour of rainwater, acid rain that occurred in different parts of the country. They are asked about the possible causes for such happenings.

Activity 11: A film is screened on the changing climatic patterns.

Activity 12: Pupil is given a description of Green revolution and they are asked to discuss on:

- Meaning of sustainable agriculture.
- Meaning of sustainable water use.

Activity 13: Pupil is asked to develop some strategies for creating awareness about water conservation at different areas like:

- Plan activities for water conservation at community level.
- Plan activities for water conservation at school, home and society.

Activity 14: Collect clippings from newspapers and magazines on the news items, articles and pictures related to water shortage. Paste them in your scrapbook and share it with your friends. List some problems faced by the people and discuss them in the class.

Activity 15: Most of us assume water to be a limitless resource. From this activity can you appreciate the actual amount of water available for human use? Does the finding worry you? Discuss this in your class.

Steps	Figure	Remarks
Take a medium-sized bucket and fill it up with water. It contains about twenty litres of water.		Assume that this water represents all the water present on the earth.
Take a tea spoon of about 5mL capacity and transfer 100 spoons of water from the bucket to a small container, like a bath mug.		This represents total freshwater on the earth.
From the bath mug transfer thirty spoons of water to a glass tumbler.	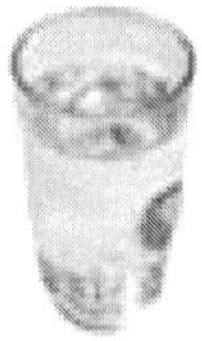	This gives a measure of usable water present as groundwater.

<table>
<tr><td>Finally take out a quarter (1/4th) spoonful of water from the mug.</td><td></td><td>It represents all the water present in all the lakes and rivers of the world.</td></tr>
<tr><td colspan="3">• The water left in the bucket represents the saline water present in the seas, oceans and partly as groundwater. This water iş not fit for human use.
• The water left in the bath mug represents the water, which is present in the frozen form in glaciers, ice caps and permanent snow; again not available readily.</td></tr>
</table>

(NCERT VII standard Science textbook)

Activity 16: The following figure shows the processes involved in the water cycle. Mark the following processes given below in the figure:

1. Groundwater
2. Evaporation
3. Condensation
4. Clouds
5. Transpiration
6. Infiltration
7. Precipitation

(NCERT VII standard Science textbook)

Activity 17: Name some industries familiar to you. Make a list of the products obtained from these and used in our daily life. Discuss with your teacher and parents how the growing industrial activity is responsible for the depletion of water table.

Activity 18: Given here is the rainfall map of India. It gives the average annual rainfall in different regions of our country.

- Locate on the map the place you live in.
- Are you blessed with sufficient rainfall?
- Is there sufficient water available in your area throughout the year?

It may be possible that we are living in an area where there is sufficient rainfall yet there is shortage of water. Can we attribute this to mismanagement of water resources?

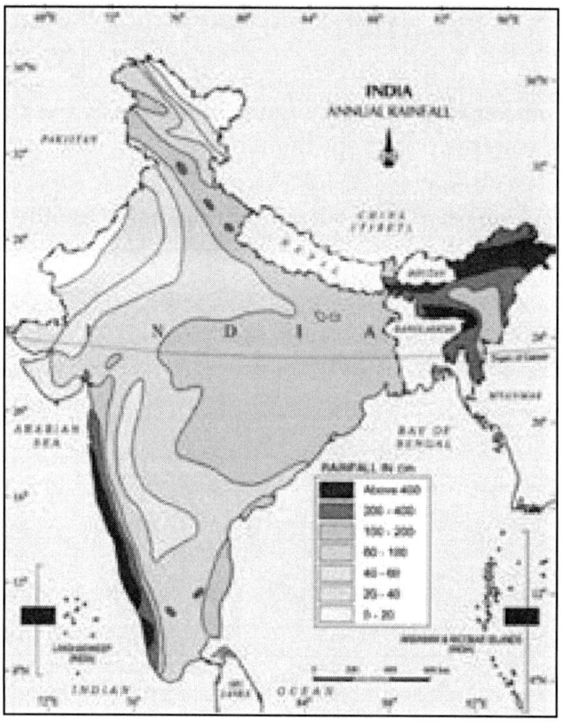

Rain map of India

1. Government of India, Copyright 2007.
2. Based upon Survey of India map with the permission of the Surveyor General of India.
3. The territorial waters of India extend into the sea to a distance of twelve nautical miles measured from the appropriate baseline.
4. The external boundaries and coastlines of India agree with the Record/Master Copy certified by Survey of India. (NCERT VII standard Science textbook)

Activity 19: You can have the following role play enacted in your classroom.

You are a water detective in your school. You have a team of six members. Survey the campus and make a note of the following:

(a) Total number of taps
(b) Number of taps leaking
(c) Amount of water wasted due to leakage
(d) Reasons of leakage
(e) Corrective measures taken (NCERT VII standard Science textbook).

Project

Form groups of 4 to 5 students in the class and prepare a report on the various traditional ways of water harvesting. If possible, use the following web link: www.rainwaterharvesting.org

UNIT 10: ENVIRONMENT

Scope

The unit deals with the meaning of environment, natural and man-made environment, human influence on natural environment. The unit also deals with the nature of lithosphere, hydrosphere, atmosphere and biosphere along with its inter-relationships. The unit focuses on how climatic changes influence the earth's atmosphere and the life forms on earth. The unit also give emphasis on the meaning and deterioration of ecosystem, human environment and their influence on nature.

Focus points

- What are the human activities that can disturb the natural environment? How can we reduce such human activities or reduce the impact of human activities on the environment?
- What are the human activities that can cause the topsoil of lithosphere to be washed away?
- What are the human activities that cause changes in climatic conditions and how does it influence the various life forms on earth?
- What steps can we take for conserving natural vegetation and wildlife? Why is it necessary?
- How can we minimise those activities that lead to the vanishing, pollution and destruction of ecosystem?
- How was the environment considered as in the ancient world and how far it has changed in the modern world and what are its impact?
- How do modern human settlements, transport and communication cause hindrance to natural environment? How can we reduce its impacts?
- What are the human activities that can be a cause for global warming, greenhouse effect, and ozone depletion? How can we reduce such activities for minimizing such climatic changes?
- What are the changes in the world due to globalisation, commercialisation, urbanisation etc. and how it can influence the life forms.
- What are the measures to control industrialisation, urbanisation etc.

Issues to be raised

1. What is environment?
2. What is natural environment?
3. What is man-made environment?
4. What do you mean by human environment?
5. How do the natural environment get disturbed by human influence?
6. How do human activities influence the land, climate, vegetation and wildlife?

7. What are the components of natural environment?
8. What is the nature of lithosphere, hydrosphere, atmosphere and biosphere?
9. How the topsoil of the lithosphere get washed away?
10. What are the major landforms of earth?
11. How are lithosphere, hydrosphere, atmosphere and biosphere interrelated?
12. How climate changes influences the earth's atmosphere and its life forms?
13. What is the need for conserving natural vegetation and wildlife?
14. What is ecosystem?
15. How an ecosystem gets vanished, polluted and destroyed?
16. What are the changes in the human environment of the ancient and modern world?
17. How human settlement, transport and communication causes hindrance to natural environment?
18. What are the impact of global warming, greenhouse effect, ozone depletion etc. on the environment?
19. What are the changes in the world due to globalisation, commercialisation, urbanisation etc. and how it can influence the life forms?
20. What are the measures to control industrialisation, urbanisation etc.?
21. Why do we need to sustain the natural environment?

Learning objectives

- Recalls the meaning of environment.
- Explains what is natural environment.
- Explains what is man-made environment.
- Explains the meaning of human environment.
- Interprets how the natural environment get disturbed by human influence.
- Interprets how do human activities influence the land, climate, vegetation and wildlife.
- Analyse the different components of natural environment.
- Explains the nature of lithosphere, hydrosphere, atmosphere and biosphere.
- Explains how the topsoil of the lithosphere get washed away.
- Describes the major landforms of earth.
- Analyse how the lithosphere, hydrosphere, atmosphere and biosphere inter-related.
- Interprets how climate changes influences the earth's atmosphere and its life forms.
- Analyse the need for conserving natural vegetation and wildlife.
- Explains what is ecosystem.
- Infer how an ecosystem gets vanished, polluted and destroyed.
- Explore the changes in the human environment of the ancient and modern world.
- Explains how human settlement, transport and communication causes hindrance to natural environment.

- Predict the impact of global warming, greenhouse effect, ozone depletion etc. on the environment.
- Analyse the changes in the world due to globalisation, commercialisation, urbanisation etc. and how it can influence the life forms.
- Explore the measures to control industrialisation, urbanisation etc.
- Reflect on the need to sustain the natural environment.

Activities

Activity 1: Look at your surroundings. Make a list of uses that the land in your neighbourhood is being put to.

Activity 2: Recollect any development that has happened in your area recently. It may be construction of a building, shopping mall, road etc. The pupil is asked to recollect what are the ill effects of such developments? They are asked to discuss on similar situations where human activities influences the land, climate, vegetation and wildlife.

Activity 3: A role play is enacted to show the inter-relationship between the various realms of earth.

Activity 4: Pupil is asked to collect the information regarding rainfall from their grandparents and how it was in their childhood days. They are asked to find out the difference in rainfall during olden days and present days. They are asked about the consequences on the topsoil if such heavy rains prevail. They are asked about different ways by which the topsoil gets washed away.

Activity 5: Through a drama students act the importance of natural vegetation and wildlife and also the need for conserving them and also how an ecosystem gets vanished, polluted and destroyed.

Activity 6: How some pictures of different developments from ancient to modern world in the areas of transport, human settlement and communication and pupil is asked to discuss on how these developments can cause hindrance to natural environment.

Activity 7: Pupil is made into groups and each group is asked to collect information regarding the following and they are asked to present in the classroom:

- Global warming and its influence on life.
- Ozone depletion and its influence on life.
- Globalisation and its influence on life.
- Urbanisation and its influence on life.

Activity 8: Where does the water you use in your home and school come from? Make a list of different uses of water in our daily life. Have you seen anyone wasting water? How?

Activity 9: Observe the sky while coming to school. Make a note whether the day is cloudy, rainy, sunny, foggy etc. (NCERT VII standard Social Science textbook).

Activity 10: Sketch or bring photographs of your place (NCERT VII standard Social science textbook).

Activity 11: Talk to some elderly person in your neighbourhood and collect information about:

- The trees in his/her neighbourhood when he/she were your age.
- The indoor games he/she played.
- His/her favourite fruit at your age.
- How did they make themselves comfortable during hot summers and cold winters? Display your answers on a wall/bulletin board.

Activity 12: Imagine an ideal environment where you would love to live. Draw the picture of your ideal environment (NCERT VII standard Social Science textbook).

UNIT 11: INSIDE OUR EARTH

Scope

The unit deals with why our earth is called a dynamic planet, the interior of our earth, nature of crust, core and mantle and its impact on mining. The unit also give emphasis on the different types of rocks and minerals, rocks and groundwater conservation, quarrying and impact on environment, depletion of different types of rocks, rock cycle and over-exploitation of minerals.

Focus points

- Is there a relationship between rocks and groundwater conservation?
- How does quarrying has an impact on environment?
- What are the ways by which we can assure a sustainable development of mineral resources?
- How do the exploitation of minerals influence the nature and life forms?

Issues to be raised

1. Why is earth known as a dynamic planet?
2. Describe the interior of earth.
3. What is the nature of crust, core and mantle?
4. What is rock?
5. What are the different types of rocks?
6. What is the relationship between rocks and groundwater conservation?
7. What is the relationship between quarrying and its impact on environment?
8. How do the different types of rocks get depleted?
9. What do you mean by sustainable development of mineral resources?
10. What is rock cycle?
11. How do the exploitation of minerals influence the nature and life forms?

Learning objectives

- Infer why earth is known as a dynamic planet.
- Describe the interior of earth.
- Analyse the nature of crust, core and mantle.
- Defines what is rock.

- Lists the different types of rocks.
- Analyse the relationship between rocks and groundwater conservation.
- Analyse the relationship between quarrying and its impact on environment.
- Interprets how the different types of rocks get depleted.
- Reflect on sustainable development of mineral resources.
- Explains what is rock cycle.
- Analyse how the exploitation of minerals influence the nature and life forms.

Activities

Activity 1: Pupil is shown a globe and asked about what they know about the planet earth. Their conclusions are written on the black board.

Activity 2: Pupil is shown a transverse section of an onion and a boiled egg to explain the interior structure of earth, which is followed by a discussion on the impact of mining on different layers of earth.

Activity 3: Pupil is shown a piece of rock and they are asked to discuss on what are rocks, and the different types of rocks followed by rock cycle. A chart showing the rock cycle is also exhibited in the classroom.

Activity 4: Pupil is made into 4 groups and each group is given one topic for making a presentation in the class.

- Group 1: Rocks and groundwater conservation.
- Group 2: Phosphate rocks for sustainable agriculture.
- Group 3: Quarrying and its impact on the environment.
- Group 4: Over-exploitation of minerals and its influence on environment and life.

Activity 5: Pupil is asked to visit a petrol pump near their area and asked to list down the amount of petrol and diesel that is been sold in a day. They are asked to find out the market rate of petrol and diesel and analyse on the amount that is spend on these per day. They are asked to find out how much is spend per month and per year on these non-renewable resources and discuss on the impact of it if it continues for several years.

Activity 6: A discussion is been initiated in the classroom to discuss on the various alternative sources that can be utilised to reduce the pressure on non-renewable sources.

Activity 7: From the above discussion pupil is asked to come out with some suggestions on sustainable development of mineral resources.

Activity 8: What are the minerals found in your state? Collect some samples to show in your class.

Activity 9:

(i) What are the minerals most commonly used in the following objects?

(ii) Identify some more objects made up of different minerals.

Pan/Tava

Hammer

Bell

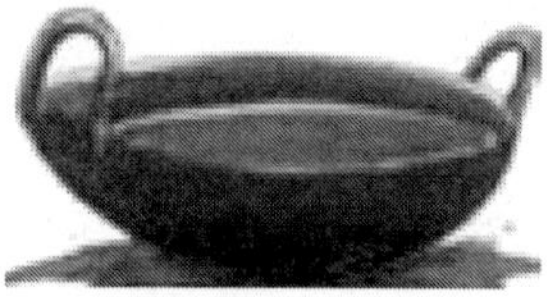

Karhai

Ornaments

Lamp

(NCERT VII standard Social Science textbook)

Project

Collect pictures of some monuments and find out which are the rocks used to build them. Two pictures have been collected for you.

The Red Fort is made of red sandstone

The Taj Mahal is made of white marble

(NCERT VII standard Social Science textbook)

UNIT 12: OUR CHANGING EARTH

Scope

The unit deals with what are lithospheric plates, its movement, endogenic and exogenic forces, volcano, earthquake, focus and epicentre. The unit also focus on how man's activity affect the earth, tsunami as a natural calamity, volcanic gases and how technology helps in predicting natural calamities. The unit also emphasize on weathering, soil erosion with its causes and effects, working of a river, sea waves, ice and wind, with focus on how human activities have led to the drastic environmental changes.

Focus points

- How and what are the human activities that affects the earth?
- Tsunami—why it occurs and what are the precautionary measures?
- The impact of various gases emitted during a volcanic eruption and how it harms the environment?
- How can technology be utilised for predicting natural calamities?
- What are the causes for soil erosion and how can we prevent them?
- What are the human activities that cause water pollution?
- What are the impact of flood on life and environment?
- What are the present condition of glaciers and glacial moraines?
- How do greenhouse effect has an impact on glaciers and coastal areas?
- Do wind help in erosion? Is it a climatic change?

Issues to be raised

1. What are lithospheric plates and their movement?
2. What are endogenic and exogenic forces?
3. What are volcanoes and earthquake?
4. What is focus and epicentre?
5. What are the activities of human beings that affect the earth?
6. What are the causes of Tsunami?
7. What are the gases that are emitted during a volcanic eruption and how it harms our environment?
8. What is the importance of technology on predicting natural calamities?
9. What are weathering and soil erosion and what are its causes and effects?
10. What is a waterfall?
11. What are Meanders, oxbow lake, delta, levees, flood plain and distributaries?
12. What is the relation between human activities and water pollution?
13. What is flood and what are its importance and impact on life and nature?
14. What are sea caves, arches, stacks and sea cliff?

15. What are tsunami waves and what are its causes, effects and how can one prevent such natural calamities?
16. What are glaciers and glacial moraines?
17. What is greenhouse effect and what are its impact on glaciers and coastal areas?
18. How do wind help in erosion?
19. What are mushroom rocks, sand dunes and loess?

Learning objectives

The pupil

- Explains what are lithospheric plates and their movement.
- Differentiates between endogenic and exogenic forces.
- Describes what are volcanoes and earthquake.
- Differentiates between focus and epicentre.
- Hypothesize the activities of human beings that affect the earth.
- Analyse the causes of Tsunami.
- Recognize the gases that are emitted during a volcanic eruption and how it harms our environment.
- Analyse the importance of technology on predicting natural calamities.
- Explains what are weathering and soil erosion and what are its causes and effects.
- Defines what is a waterfall.
- Explains what are Meanders, oxbow lake, delta, levees, flood plain and distributaries.
- Analyse the relation between human activities and water pollution.
- Discuss what is flood and its importance and impact on life and nature.
- Explains sea caves, arches, stacks and sea cliff.
- Analyse what are tsunami waves and what are its causes, effects and how can one prevent such natural calamities.
- Explains glaciers and glacial moraines.
- Defines greenhouse effect and interprets its impact on glaciers and coastal areas.
- Justify how do wind help in erosion.
- Defines what are mushroom rocks, sand dunes and loess.

Activities

Activity 1: Pupil is asked about what are lithospheric plates, explain with an experiment the meaning of endogenic and exogenic forces.

Activity 2: Take a small coloured paper pellet and put it in a beaker half filled with water. Place the beaker on a tripod stand and heat it. As the water warms up, you will observe that the paper pellet is moving upward along with the warm layers of water and then sinks back along with the cooler layers of water. The molten magma inside the earth moves in a similar manner.

Activity 3: A demonstration is done to show the formation of a volcano and earthquake with special reference on focus and epicentre. Newspaper cutting on the recent earthquake is asked to read out in the class and also asked to discuss on how the gases that are emitted during a volcano can harm the environment.

Activity 4: Take a container, fill it with water and close it with a lid. Put the water to boil. Now put some peas, spoon and beads on top on the lid. What do you notice? As the water boils the lid begins to shake. The things which you have put on the lid also vibrate. The beads roll down and the spoon vibrates to make a sound. In the same manner, the earth vibrates when an earthquake occurs.

Activity 5:

Earthquake – A Case Study

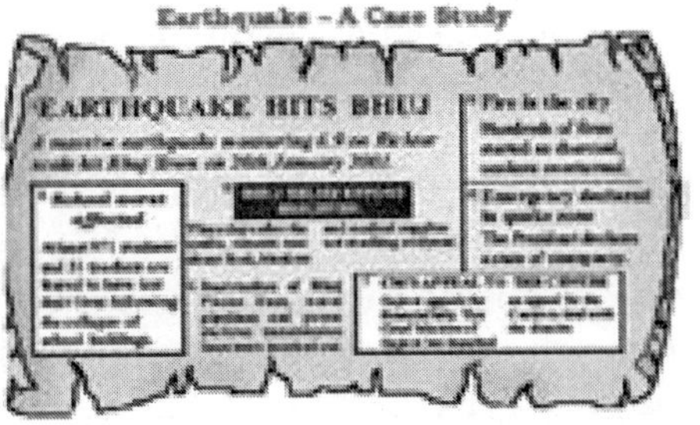

1. Read the 'Earthquake—A case study' given in the form of headlines that appeared in the newspapers after the quake. Arrange the events in the right sequence of their happening.
2. Imagine if a quake suddenly shook in the middle of the school day, where would you go for safety? (NCERT VII standard Social Science textbook).

Activity 6: A video is shown about the Tsunami attack that happened in December 26, 2004. Followed by it a presentation is made on the causes for such natural disaster and man's role in causing danger to earth.

Activity 7: Pupil is shown a model of volcanic eruption and also a multimedia presentation on the emission of various gases during a volcanic eruption. They are asked to discuss on how it harms the environment.

Activity 8: Pupil is asked about the importance of technology in predicting natural calamities and how it can be harmful.

Activity 9: Pupil is asked to discuss on weathering and some photographs are shown on soil erosion and different agents that cause soil erosion with special reference on wind as an agent of soil erosion.

Activity 10: Pupils are shown a photograph of any waterfall and ask them to define what a waterfall is.

Activity 11: Teacher explains what are meanders, oxbow lake, delta, levees, flood plains and distributaries.

Activity 12: Pupil is made into two groups and each group is asked to make a presentation on any one of the following:

- Human activities and water pollution.
- Flood—its importance and impact on life forms.

Activity 13: Pupil is shown pictures of sea caves, arches, stacks, sea cliffs, glaciers, glacial moraines, mushroom rocks, sand dunes and loess and asked to define each.

Activity 14: Can you find out names of some rivers of the world that forms a delta?

UNIT 13: AIR

Scope

The unit deals with the meaning of atmosphere, its importance and air being considered as one of the five elements. The unit also deals with the composition of atmosphere, maintaining its balance, how atmosphere gets polluted, need for planting more trees, impact of increase in the concentration of CO_2. The unit also focus on the structure of atmosphere and how troposphere, stratosphere, mesosphere, thermosphere and exosphere get affected by human activities. The unit highlights the meaning of weather and climate, air pressure, wind (permanent wind, seasonal wind and local winds), moisture, loo, temperature, insolation, trapping of solar energy, monitoring the impact of climatic change, deforestation and various forms of pollution, how industrialisation, modernisation, globalisation bring changes in temperature. The unit also emphasize on the rains that are not seasonal and its impact on environment.

Focus points

- What is the importance of maintaining a balance of atmospheric gases? What are the impacts if their balances get disturbed?
- What is the need for planting more trees?
- How do the increase in the concentration of CO_2 effect the environment?
- How do the different layers of atmosphere get affected by human activities?
- Climatic changes, deforestation and pollution affects the life and environment—How?
- How can you make use of solar energy for domestic activities by not using any highly expensive devices?
- Industrialisation, modernisation and globalisation lead to increase in temperature—analyse.
- What could be the cause for occurrence of non-seasonal rains in some areas of the world? What are its impact?

Issues to be raised

1. What is atmosphere and what is its importance?
2. How was water considered as in the ancient days?
3. What is the importance of maintaining a balance of atmospheric gases?
4. Why do you need to plant more trees?
5. What are the impacts on atmosphere due to increase in the concentration of CO_2?
6. What are troposphere, stratosphere, mesosphere, thermosphere and exosphere and how it get affected due to human activities?

7. Differentiate between weather and climate.
8. What are the impacts of climate change, deforestation and pollution on life and environment?
9. What is temperature and insolation?
10. How can you make use of solar energy for domestic purpose?
11. How do industrialisation, modernisation and globalisation lead to increase in temperature?
12. What is air pressure?
13. What are cyclones and its impact?
14. What is wind?
15. Differentiate between permanent wind, seasonal wind and local winds.
16. What is loo?
17. Why do non-seasonal rains occur in some areas?
18. What is atmospheric moisture?
19. How is rain formed?

Learning objectives

- Explains what is atmosphere and its importance.
- Analyse how was water considered in the ancient days.
- Discuss the importance of maintaining a balance of atmospheric gases.
- Predicts the importance of planting more trees.
- Analyse the impacts on atmosphere due to increase in the concentration of CO_2.
- Explain what are troposphere, stratosphere, mesosphere, thermosphere and exosphere and how it get affected due to human activities.
- Differentiates between weather and climate.
- Reflect on the impacts of climate change, deforestation and pollution on life and environment.
- Explains what is temperature and insolation.
- Explores on how can you make use of solar energy for domestic purpose.
- Analyse on how industrialisation, modernisation and globalisation lead to increase in temperature.
- Explains the meaning of air pressure.
- Describes what is cyclone and its impact.
- Defines wind.
- Differentiate between permanent wind, seasonal wind and local winds.
- Explains what is loo.
- Reflect on the reasons why non-seasonal rains occur in some areas.
- Defines what is atmospheric moisture.
- Explains how rain is formed.

Activities

Activity 1: The teacher narrates a sloka in Sanskrit

"Madhuvata Rtayate, Madhu ksharanti Sindhavah
Madhvirana Santosodhih
Madhunaktamutososih Madhumat Parthivam rajah
Madhurdourastunah pita Madhuvan me vanaspathi
Madhvinam astusuryah, madhurgabobnabantu nah". (Rigveda 1-90, 6-8)

The above wish occurring in the Rigveda means the following:

"For us who are governed by the great cosmic order,
May the breeze blow sweet and pleasant,
May the river flow sweet and pleasant,
May the plants be sweet and pleasant,
May the night and dawn be sweet and pleasant.
May the dust of earth be sweet and pleasant.
May the upper regions, our father, be sweet and pleasant
May the tree be sweet and pleasant
May the sun be sweet and pleasant
And may our cattle, wealth and speech be sweet and pleasant."

It designates the five elements of the universe: earth, fire, air, space and water. Pupil is then asked to explain on the importance given to air in the ancient days. From this pupil is asked to define what is atmosphere.

Activity 2: Pupil is shown a chart showing the composition of various gases in the atmosphere. They are asked to discuss on the impact if some of these gases get increased. They are asked to discuss on the impact of increase in concentration of CO_2 in the atmosphere, followed by the ways to prevent the accumulation of CO_2 in the atmosphere.

Activity 3: Pupil is shown a slide show on the impact of greenhouse effect and global warming on the environment and life.

Activity 4: Pupil is shown a chart on the different structure of atmosphere. A debate is initiated on the

- Effect of human activities on the troposphere, stratosphere, mesosphere, thermosphere and exosphere.

Activity 5: Pupil is asked to collect about the weather patterns in different parts of the world, say, U.S., U.K., India, Australia, Africa etc. and find out the variations they have observed in the weather. They are also shown a world map of these places showing the climatic patterns in these regions and asked to define what is climate?

Activity 6: Pupil is asked to collect information from their elders on the climatic changes that have occurred in their earlier years and asked to find out the various pollution that have occurred from their younger days to the present day.

Activity 7:

Read and Ponder: Is global warming a serious issue in today's world? They are also asked to discuss on temperature and insolation. (NCERT VII standard Social Science textbook).

Activity 8: For ten days note down weather report from a local newspaper and observe the changes occurring in the weather (NCERT VII standard Social Science textbook).

Activity 9: Pupil is shown pictures of solar panels, solar cooker etc. and they are asked to discuss on how these renewable resources can be made use in order to have a sustainable development and also to reduce the pressure over non-renewable resources.

Activity 10: Class is made into three groups and each group is asked to collect information regarding any one of the following and present in the classroom.

- Industrialisation and temperature.
- Modernisation and temperature.
- Globalisation and temperature.

The discussion is followed by a poster presentation on its impacts.

Activity 11: Pupil is asked to discuss on the formation of cyclones and its impact with its relationship on air pressure. They are also asked to discuss on the various non-seasonal changes occurring like heavy rains during monsoon, rains during summer, lack of rain, rain in desert etc. Pupil is asked to come out with possible reasons and its impact on life and environment.

Activity 12: Pupil is shown the paper cuttings about the cyclones and heavy rains in some parts of India. Pupil is asked to discuss on the impact of these non-seasonal rains over the environment.

Activity 13: Pupil is asked about the various names of wind that have occurred in the recent times. They are asked to discuss about its formation and the various impacts.

Activity 14: Pupil is shown a glass containing ice cubes. After some time they are asked to observe the outside of the glass and find out what they observe and how these water droplets are formed on the glass. Students are also asked about how the wet clothes dry after it is kept for drying. From these discussions they come to a conclusion on the meaning of moisture, water vapour and how rain is formed.

UNIT 14: WATER

Scope

The unit deals with the meaning of water cycle, the importance given to water in the ancient days, developments in water management and how the water shortage can lead to epidemics, hunger, despair and death. The unit also focus on the distribution of water bodies with watershed projects, rainwater harvesting, activities to prevent runoff water and the importance of avoiding concretizing the floor. The unit give emphasis on ocean circulation, waves, tides and currents, tsunami, human activities leading natural disasters.

Focus points

- How is water being considered in ancient days?
- How can we reduce the mismanagement of water due to different developmental activities?
- What could be the various disasters that can arouse due to shortage of water?
- What are the importance of various water shed projects?
- What are the importance of rainwater harvesting?
- What are the different ways of conserving water?
- Tsunami—and its varied impacts on life.
- Impact of earthquake and volcanic eruptions.

Issues to be raised

1. What is water cycle?
2. What is the importance given to water in the ancient days?
3. What are the developments that have led to mismanagement of water?
4. What are the disasters that can be faced due to shortage of water?
5. What do you mean by watershed projects?
6. What is rainwater harvesting?
7. How can you conserve water?
8. What are waves, tides and currents?
9. What is Tsunami and its impact on life?
10. What are the cause of earthquake and volcanic eruptions?
11. What is high tide, low tide, spring tide and neap tides?
12. What are ocean currents?

Learning objectives

- Explains what is water cycle.
- Analyse the importance given to water in the ancient days.
- Describes the developments that have led to mismanagement of water.
- Interprets the disasters that can be faced due to shortage of water.
- Analyse the meaning of watershed projects and its importance.

- Explains what is rainwater harvesting.
- Identifies different ways of conserving water.
- Compare waves, tides and currents.
- Explains what is Tsunami and its impact on life.
- Analyse the cause of earthquake and volcanic eruptions.
- Defines what is high tide, low tide, spring tide and neap tides.
- Explains what are ocean currents.

Activities

Activity 1: The teacher narrates a sloka in Sanskrit

"Madhuvata Rtayate, Madhu ksharanti Sindhavah
Madhvirana Santosodhih
Madhunaktamutososih Madhumat Parthivam rajah
Madhurdourastunah pita Madhuvan me vanaspathi
Madhvinam astusuryah, madhurgabobnabantu nah". (Rigveda 1-90, 6-8)

The above wish occurring in the Rigveda means the following:

"For us who are governed by the great cosmic order,
May the breeze blow sweet and pleasant,
May the river flow sweet and pleasant,
May the plants be sweet and pleasant,
May the night and dawn be sweet and pleasant.
May the dust of earth be sweet and pleasant.
May the upper regions, our father, be sweet and pleasant
May the tree be sweet and pleasant
May the sun be sweet and pleasant
And may our cattle, wealth and speech be sweet and pleasant."

It designates the five elements of the universe: earth, fire, air, space and water. Pupil is then asked to explain on the importance given to water in the ancient days.

Activity 2: Make your own Terrarium—Fill one-fourth of a big jar with soil and press it well. Put a thin layer of humus on top of it. Plant the largest plants first and then arrange the smaller area around them. Spray the arrangement with water and close the jar. The water that evaporates from the leaves and soil condenses and falls back as forms of water drops (NCERT VII standard Social Science textbook).

Activity 3: Pupil is asked to discuss on the various developments that led to the mismanagement of water and also the impact of water shortage like, epidemics, hunger, despair and death.

Activity 4: Take 2 litres of water. Let it represent the total water on the surface of the earth. Measure out 12 spoons of water from this vessel into another bowl. The water that is left behind in the vessel represents the salty water found in oceans and seas. This water is obviously not fit for consuming. It is saline (contains salts). The 12 spoons of water that was taken in a bowl is the total amount of freshwater on earth. See for yourself how much water can actually be used by you (NCERT VII standard Social Science textbook).

Activity 5: Pupil is demonstrated an experiment. Two glass jars are taken and both are filled with soil. One plant is planted in each pot. One of the jars is concretized on the top of soil. Keep it for drying. Everyday teacher asks the pupil to pour water and observe both jars. They are asked to identify the fate of plant in the concretized jar and they are to compare it with concretizing their floors and its impact on soil and life.

Activity 6: Pupil is asked whether their parents or grandparents say about the tides i.e., it is high tide, it is low tide etc. From their explanations, pupil is asked to find out the meaning of tide, waves and current. A chart showing high tide and low tide, when it occurs are shown to the students. Another chart to explain spring tide and neap tide is also shown in the class.

Activity 7: Pupil is shown a video on tsunami waves that happened in 2004, December 26. Pupil is asked to recall the consequences of it and also on the reasons/causes for the occurrence of tsunami.

Activity 8: Pupil is asked about waves and how the energy from waves can be utilized for producing energy which are renewable sources of energy.

Activity 9: A paper cutting on the news and photo of mining of oil from the sea beds e.g. in Mumbai is shown to the classroom. Pupil is asked to reflect on the consequence of it. Their conclusions are presented in the classroom.

Activity 10: Take a mug of water and add some oil in it. Ask the pupil to observe the changes. They are asked to discuss on what are the reasons for oil spills entering the sea and how does this affect the life forms in the oceans and seas.

Activity 11: A debate is conducted on the topic ‘Oceans are the main waste disposal area of the world’.

Activity 12: Fill three-fourths of a bucket with tap water. Heat the water by putting an immersion road on one side of the bucket. On the other side introduce an ice tray just removed from the freezer. Add a drop of red ink to observe the path of current by the process of convection (NCERT VII standard Social Science textbook).

Activity 13:

- Why water is important for us?
- Suggest some ways in which water can be conserved in your home and in your school (NCERT VII standard Social Science textbook).

Activity 14: A collage is made on the pathetic condition of the various beaches in India, and pupil is asked to discuss on the various measures that can be taken to keep our beaches neat and clean.

Activity 15: Following is an international law relating to the high seas. Read them carefully and the pupil is asked to discuss on the pros and cons of such law with special reference to the present disastrous condition of some seas.

> Desiring to codify the rules of international law relating to the high seas, recognizing that the United Nations Conference on the Law of the Sea, held at Geneva from 24 February to 27 April 1958, adopted the following provisions as generally declaratory of established principles of international law,
>
> Article 2
>
> The high seas being open to all nations, no State may validly purport to subject any part of them to its sovereignty. Freedom of the high seas is exercised under the conditions laid down by these articles and by the other rules of international law. It comprises, inter alia, both for coastal and non-coastal States:
>
> (1) Freedom of navigation;
> (2) Freedom of fishing;
> (3) Freedom to lay submarine cables and pipelines;
> (4) Freedom to fly over the high seas.
>
> These freedoms, and others which are recognized by the general principles of international law, shall be exercised by all States with reasonable regard to the interests of other States in their exercise of the freedom of the high seas.

Activity 16: Following is a passage regarding cruelty that man sometimes shows towards animals. Pupil is asked to read them and observe the following photographs. They are asked to discuss on the topic and asked to come out with some suggestions by which one can prevent such cruelty to animals.

Denmark is a big shame.

The sea in the following photographs is seen to be stained in red and it's not because of the climate effects of nature. It's because of the cruelty that the human beings (civilised human) do to animals by killing hundreds of the famous and intelligent Calderon dolphins. This happens every year in Feroe Island in Denmark. In this slaughter the main participants are young teens. It is to show that they are adults and mature.... In this big celebration, nothing is missing for the fun. Everyone is participating in one way or the other, killing or looking at the cruelty "supporting like a spectator". Is it necessary to mention that the dolphin Calderon, like all the other species of dolphins, get near men to play and interact, in a way of pure friendship. They don't die instantly; they are cut 1, 2 or 3 times with thick hocks. And at that time the dolphins produce a grim extremely compatible with the cry of a new born child. But he suffers and there's no compassion till this sweet being slowly dies in its own blood.

Activity 17: The pupil is shown some of the photos and paper cuttings about the oil spills that are given out by the vessels that move about in the oceans and seas. The pupil is asked to discuss on the consequence of such oil spills and how can it have an impact on various life forms. The pupil is asked to come out with some solutions for preventing such oil spills.

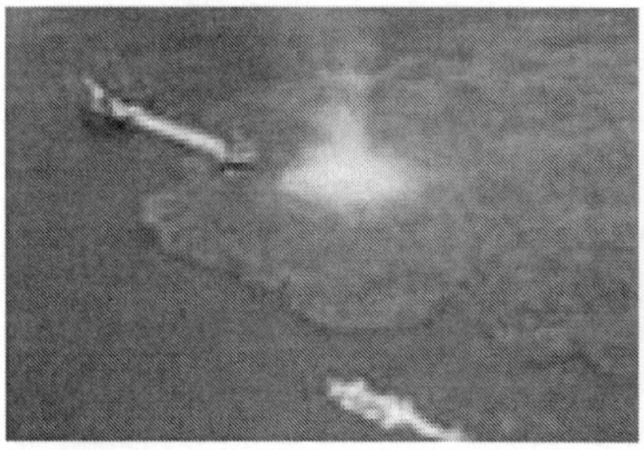

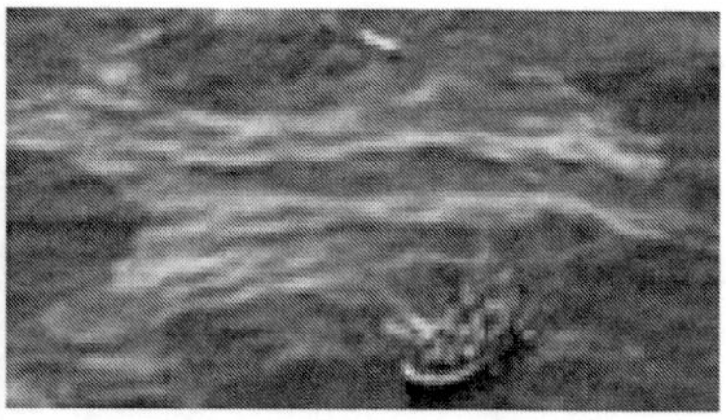

Project

Pupil is asked to make rainwater harvesting pits in their school with the help of staff and teachers of the school.

UNIT 15: NATURAL VEGETATION AND WILDLIFE

Scope

The unit deals with the meaning of biodiversity, distribution of species. The unit also deals with the vegetation and wildlife seen in tropical evergreen forest, tropical deciduous forest, temperate evergreen forest, temperate deciduous forests, Mediterranean vegetation, coniferous forests, tropical and temperate grasslands, thorny bushes.

Focus points

- What is the importance of protecting biodiversity?
- What are the declarations and legal provisions for protecting biodiversity? Why is it been given more priority?
- What are the species distributed in Polar Regions and how are they being affected by human activities?
- How do the human activities affect the various forest types and how can you restore the biodiversity.

Issues to be raised

- What are the major types of classification of natural vegetation?
- What is biodiversity and why it should be protected?
- What are the declarations and legal provisions for protecting biodiversity? Why is it been given more priority?
- What are the species distributed in Polar Regions and how are they being affected by human activities?
- What are flora and fauna seen in the following types of forests and how they are getting affected due to human activities and how can you restore the biodiversity.
    * tropical evergreen forest
    * tropical deciduous forest
    * temperate evergreen forest
    * temperate deciduous forests
    * Mediterranean vegetation
    * coniferous forests
    * tropical grasslands
    * temperate grasslands
    * thorny bushes.

Learning objectives

- Discuss about the major types of classification of natural vegetation.
- Explains what is biodiversity and why it should be protected.
- Communicates the declarations and legal provisions for protecting biodiversity and why is it been given more priority.
- Explore species distributed in Polar Regions and how are they being affected by human activities.
- Analyse the flora and fauna seen in the following types of forests and how they are getting affected due to human activities and how can we restore the biodiversity.

* tropical evergreen forest
* tropical deciduous forest
* temperate evergreen forest
* temperate deciduous forests
* Mediterranean vegetation
* coniferous forests
* tropical grasslands
* temperate grasslands
* thorny bushes.

Activities

Activity 1: Pupil is shown a globe and asked to identify the different regions on the globe. They are also asked to list out the different types of vegetation that are on the earth.

Activity 2: A field visit is conducted to know about the plants and animals found in tropical evergreen forest.

Activity 3: When you go to visit any new place, notice the type of natural vegetation occurring there and try to think of factors responsible for the growth of such vegetation in that habitat.

- Note down if any human interference has taken place in that area in terms of deforestation, grazing, cultivation of cash crops, constructional activities etc.

Activity 4: Pupil is asked about the meaning of biodiversity and what are the hotspot areas.

Activity 5: Where in India do tropical evergreen and tropical deciduous forests occur? Name the states.

- Which type of forest dominates most part of India?

Activity 6: A multimedia presentation is done on the flora and fauna of the following:

- tropical evergreen forest
- tropical deciduous forest
- temperate evergreen forest
- temperate deciduous forests
- Mediterranean vegetation
- coniferous forests
- tropical grasslands
- temperate grasslands
- thorny bushes.

It is followed by a discussion on and how these forests are getting affected due to human activities and how can we restore the biodiversity.

Activity 7: Look around in your surroundings and find out the articles made of hard wood and soft wood. Find out and learn few names of trees of your locality (NCERT VII standard Social Science textbook).

Activity 8: A talk by an eminent environmentalist/naturalist is arranged to know the importance of protecting biodiversity.

Activity 9: Pupil is given paper cuttings on different measures taken in India for protecting wildlife and natural vegetation and also the various national and international declarations, conferences etc. and followed by a discussion on why natural vegetation and wildlife is been given priority in the modern world.

Activity 10:

In the crossword table given below, some words are hidden. They are all about vegetation and wildlife and are to be found horizontally and vertically. Work in pairs with a friend.

M	T	N	L	P	L	M	E	H	R	T	B	A	M	B	O	O	P	N	A
B	E	A	R	A	I	X	S	E	E	R	C	M	W	H	A	L	E	D	C
T	L	P	F	L	O	R	A	N	L	E	O	P	A	R	D	C	E	E	M
A	E	I	A	M	N	L	I	C	H	E	N	S	L	P	O	A	P	E	S
N	P	O	U	D	O	O	S	T	Z	X	E	D	R	H	X	M	A	R	J
A	H	T	N	H	R	D	P	I	N	E	S	C	U	I	V	E	L	D	K
C	A	C	A	M	P	O	S	G	V	N	N	A	S	E	A	L	M	Q	U
O	N	A	C	F	O	W	L	E	E	E	A	C	D	E	O	D	A	R	M
N	T	C	H	I	R	N	G	R	V	E	K	T	M	O	S	S	E	S	O
D	O	T	E	A	K	S	R	S	E	M	E	U	S	A	P	C	O	A	N
A	X	U	R	M	A	A	N	G	R	A	S	S	W	K	A	R	Q	V	K
P	S	S	U	H	F	T	A	I	G	A	T	U	L	B	I	U	Y	A	E
O	H	F	I	R	P	R	A	I	R	I	E	S	A	B	E	B	O	N	Y
B	R	B	H	G	O	A	T	D	E	C	I	D	U	O	U	S	W	N	A
T	U	N	D	R	A	X	Z	E	D	R	A	H	O	R	S	E	L	A	K
C	H	E	E	A	X	L	L	A	N	O	S	A	T	P	A	M	P	A	S

(NCERT VII standard Social Science textbook)

Activity 11:

(i) Collect pictures and photographs of forests and grasslands of different parts of world. Write one sentence below each picture.

(ii) Make a collage of rainforest, grassland and coniferous forests (NCERT VII standard Social Science textbook).

UNIT 16: HUMAN ENVIRONMENT—SETTLEMENT, TRANSPORT AND COMMUNICATION

Scope

The unit deals with the meaning of human settlement, different types of settlement, problems faced by the modern settlements. The unit also give emphasis on the different modes of transport and how these are causing pollution to the environment and also the different ways of communication.

Focus points

- How do the different types of settlements affect the environment?
- How exploiting of nature by man started? What are its impacts?

- Why do rural areas need development and which are the areas that need developments?
- Explain how the changes in urban cities have brought about changes in culture, environment, and morality? What are the various ways to minimise it?
- What are the different modes of transport in the modern world and how does it affect the environment?
- How can we attain a sustainable way of communication?

Issues to be raised

1. What are the different types of human settlement?
2. What are temporary, permanent, rural, compact and scattered settlements and what are its impact on environment?
3. How exploiting of nature by man started?
4. Why do rural areas need development and which are the areas that need developments?
5. Explain how the changes in urban cities have brought about changes in culture, environment, and morality?
6. Explain what are the ancient and modern modes of transport and how does it cause exploitation of natural resources?
7. What are the different modes of transport in the modern world and how does it affect the environment?
8. What are the different ways of communication and how it can be used for a sustainable mode of life?

Learning objectives

- Identify the different types of human settlement.
- Explain temporary, permanent, rural, compact and scattered settlements and how do they affect environment.
- Analyse how the exploiting of nature by man started.
- Hypothesize why the rural areas need development and which are the areas that need developments.
- Explain how the changes in urban cities have brought about changes in culture, environment, and morality.
- Explain what are the ancient and modern modes of transport and how does it cause exploitation of natural resources.
- Observes the different modes of transport in the modern world and analyse how they affect the environment.
- Identify the different ways of communication and interpret on how it can be used for a sustainable mode of life.

Activities

Activity 1: Pupil is asked about what you mean by settlements and the different types of settlements like temporary, permanent, rural, compact and scattered settlements. They are asked to discuss on how early man has lived a life in accordance with nature and how man started to exploit the nature.

They are asked to discuss on how compact and urban settlements are polluting the environment and 'what are the developments that should be introduced to the rural areas'.

Activity 2: Pupil is asked about the various means of transport and how transportation was done in olden days and how it is different from modern times. They are also asked about how modern transport is causing pollution and exploiting our natural resources.

Activity 3: Gradually in cities and towns transportation becoming unmanageable due to increasing number of cars and private vehicles. Ask the students do they think, improving public transport system may solve the problem? Allow them to discuss in groups and make their suggestions.

(*The Hindu*, November 25, 2009)

Activity 4: The increasing population in urban areas lead to greater pressure to transportation, where poor public transport facility leads to chaos. The two picture shows the risk of travelling in public transport. Consider yourself as a expert team who is planning for improvement of public transport system and through discussion, observation and interviews with public, concerned authorities make a plan to suggest the government.

(*The Hindu*, Feb. 24, 2010) and (*The Indian Express*, November 25, 2009).

Activity 5: List the different modes of transport used by the students of your class while coming to school.

Activity 6: Find out the names of some newspapers and TV news channels in English, Hindi and a regional language.

Activity 7: What if the cities have special roads for cyclists? What are the implications of it in urban transport? What will be the difficulties in implementing it?

Activity 8: Brainstorm on the issue.

Population and sustainability—Do we learn from nature?

Activity 9: Provide a situation as given here. A house has 3 rooms and a family of 4 members are comfortably living in the house. Suppose another family of 4 members join them to live in the house, the space need to be shared. The house gets over-crowded or congested. Allow the students to imagine such a situation and let them discuss the advantages and disadvantages of having to live with more people sharing the house and resources.

Lastly pose the question if you are head of the original family living in the house and to take a decision, what decision would you take? Why?

Which solution is acceptable to you to meet this challenge?

(a) Allow the new family to live in.

(b) Refuse to share the house and resources with this new family.

(c) Accommodate only 2 members to live in with your family.

Allow the students to vote.

Activity 10: Encourage the students to collect statistical information on the population size, land area and density of population of different states of India as well as the whole country, make a comparison of density of population of different states and infer.

Some states have high density of population—Why?

Pose the questions and allow them to gather more information on the geographical, social, economic and cultural factors which were responsible for the high density of population in those states. Allow the groups to make presentations.

Activity 11: Some multinational companies are allowed to set up industries in Karnataka. Allow students to discuss what would happen to the density of population of the region/state? What associated challenges have to be addressed by the government to meet the requirements of the population? List the major items. Is overcrowding a challenge to sustainability?

Activity 12: Let the students in groups critically examine the lifestyle of an affluent family and compare it with the lifestyle of an economically deprived family (or the family living in a multi-storey building and another one living in slums). Write the merits and demerits of their lifestyle giving reasons (If possible by interviewing them). If you think that their lifestyle is not of a good quality, suggest measures for improving the same.

Activity 13: Encourage the students to play the role of rural illiterate farmer (man/woman) having many children justifying his/her choice to have many children having at conversation with an urban literate employed person (man/woman) with one or two children justifying the choice for a small family. Allow the students to critically think about the issue and debate.

Activity 14: Pupil is made into 4 groups and each group is assigned to collect information on any one of the following topics and asked to make a presentation:

- Roadways and different types of roads.
- Railways-its invention and different types of railways.
- Waterways—Types, oil leakage from ships and how is it harmful.
- Airways.

Activity 15: Conduct a survey in your locality and find out how people commute to their respective workplaces using:

(a) More than two modes of transport.

(b) More than three modes of transport.

(c) Stay within walking distance.

Activity 16: Mention which mode of communication you will prefer most in the following situations:

(a) Your grandfather has suddenly fallen ill. How will you inform the doctor?

(b) Your mother wants to sell the old house. How will she spread this news?

(c) You are going to attend the marriage of your cousin for which you will be absent from the school for the next two days. How will you inform the teacher?

(d) Your friend has moved out with his/her family to New York. How will you keep in touch on a daily basis? (NCERT VII standard Social Science textbook).

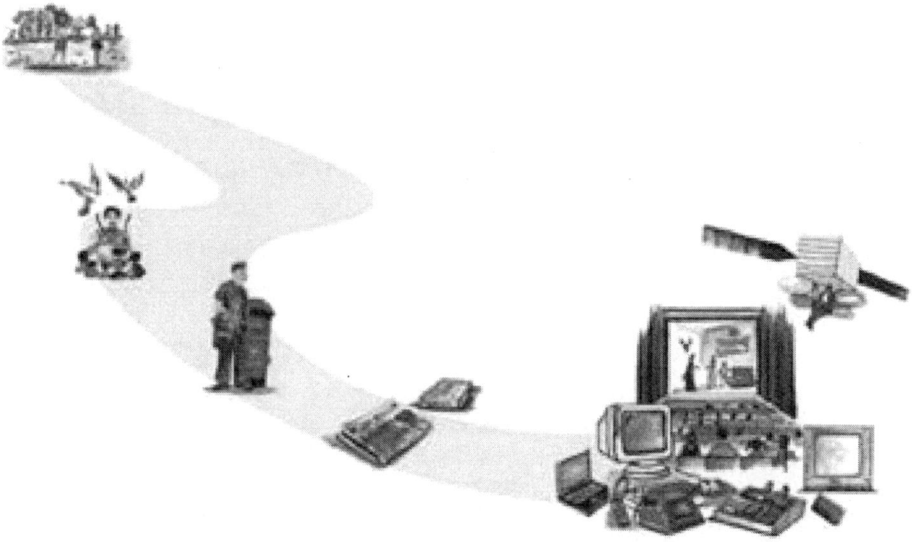

Activity 17: Pupil is asked to exhibit the pictures of different modes of communication on the notice board of their classroom.

Activity 18: Arrange any one of the competitions/extracurricular activities on population, transport and sustainability.

- Poster with slogan contest.
- Quiz.
- Essay writing.
- Debate.
- Short skit.

UNIT 17: HUMAN ENVIRONMENT INTERACTIONS—THE TROPICAL AND THE SUB-TROPICAL REGION

Scope

The unit deals with the human environment interaction in the tropical and sub-tropical region, with the type of vegetation, climate and the people. The unit also focuses on how we can sustain these forests.

Focus points

- Why it is very important to preserve the Amazon basin. What are the disasters that are faced by Amazon basin?
- What are the main reasons for deforestation of rainforests?
- How technology like remote sensing is helping in conserving Amazon forest?
- What is the need for adopting the culture and lifestyle that suits ones environment?
- What are the causes for different multinational companies and corporate sectors causing threat to forests and how can we prevent them?
- What are the impacts on the environment due to the deforestation in Amazon area?
- Water resource management in Ganga-Brahmaputra basin—why is it important?
- What are the solution for the international conflicts on water?
- How can we reduce the environmental factors that affect the quality and quantity of water?
- Why is national water policy given more priority?
- What are the geomorphic importance of floods?

Issues to be raised

1. What is meant by the mouth of a river?
2. Which are the countries through which the river basin of Amazon drains?
3. What are the climatic features of Amazon basin?
4. What are the characteristic features of Amazon rainforests and what are the flora and fauna found here?
5. What are the impacts of deforestation in rainforests?
6. How do remote sensing technology help in conservation of Amazon forests?
7. What are the main occupation of people in living in Amazon area and what are the crops grown here?
8. What are the threats to Amazon basin?
9. What are the characteristics of life in Ganga-Brahmaputra basin?
10. What are the flora and fauna in Ganga-Brahmaputra basin?
11. What are the vegetation seen in Ganga-Brahmaputra basin?
12. Which are the places located in Ganga-Brahmaputra region?
13. How is transportation and tourism linked in these area?

14. How is water resource managed in Ganga-Brahmaputra basin—why is it important?
15. What are the solution for the international conflicts on water?
16. How can we reduce the environmental factors that affect the quality and quantity of water?
17. Why is national water policy given more priority in the modern world?
18. What are the geomorphic importance of floods?

Learning objectives

- Recall what is meant by the mouth of a river.
- Identifies the countries through which the river basin of Amazon drains.
- Discuss the climatic features of Amazon basin.
- Explains the characteristic features of Amazon rainforests and what are the flora and fauna found here.
- Predicts the impacts of deforestation in rainforests.
- How do remote sensing technology help in conservation of Amazon forests?
- What are the main occupation of people in living in Amazon area and what are the crops grown here?
- What are the threats to Amazon basin?
- What are the characteristics of life in Ganga-Brahmaputra basin?
- What are the flora and fauna in Ganga-Brahmaputra basin?
- What are the vegetation seen in Ganga-Brahmaputra basin?
- Which are the places located in Ganga-Brahmaputra region?
- How is transportation and tourism linked in these area?
- How is water resource managed in Ganga-Brahmaputra basin—why is it important?
- What are the solution for the international conflicts on water?
- How can we reduce the environmental factors that affect the quality and quantity of water?
- Why is national water policy given more priority in the modern world?
- What are the geomorphic importance of floods?

Activities

Activity 1: Pupil is shown a map showing the vegetation in Amazon forest and pupil is asked to discuss on the climate prevailing in these areas along with the plants and animals that are found here.

It is followed by a discussion on how these Amazon forests get destroyed.

Activity 2: Some TV channels broadcast documentaries on the wildlife of the world. Try to watch some of the films and share your experience with the class.

Activity 3: Ashok is the son of a farm labourer from interior rural village which is 5 km away from the main road. He is studying in a school in the nearby village which is 1 km away from his home. Sunil is from a metro city, his parents working as government officers and studies in a public school. Manoj is the son of a rickshaw-puller living in a urban slum and he study in municipal school. Neeraj is from a village which is close the town and his father is working as a teacher. All the four are 7th standard students and meet in tourists spot. They share where they come from and their experiences. Ask your students to do a role play on these four characters and express what they aspire for the following dimensions.

Dimension	Ashok	Sunil	Manoj	Neeraj
What you want to become?				
What kind of place do you want to live?				
What kind of facilities required in your home?				
What kind of facilities required for your transportation?				
What kind of clothes do you want to wear?				

Activity 4: Photographs of people living in Amazon forests are shown to the people and find out their different agricultural practices and discuss on the disasters that are happening to the Amazon forest.

Activity 5: Pupil is shown a map on Ganga-Brahmaputra basin and find out the types of climate, vegetation, wildlife and tourism confined to the area.

Activity 6: River Brahmaputra is known by different names in difference places. Find the other names of the river.

Activity 7: One of the pupils is asked to read out some articles regarding some of the projects for protecting wildlife such as tiger project, elephant project etc. They are asked to reflect on why these animals are being protected and how can we prevent the killing of such animals. What are the laws prevalent that are aiming at protection of wildlife?

> **Project Tiger,** launched in 1972 has been proclaimed as a successful intervention for conserving the tiger population. There were 1827 tigers in 1972 the same has gone up to 3642 in 2001-02 when the tiger census was last conducted.
>
> **Project Elephant,** launched in 1992 helps protect wild elephants from pahing and scientific management of elephant habitats. There are 24 elephant reserves in the country as on 31-03-2004. A programme called 'Monitoring of Illegal Killing of Elephants (MIKE)' launched in 2003-04 for effective prevention of poaching.

Activity 8: Pupil is asked to discuss on the floods that occur in Ganga-Brahmaputra basin, environmental and geomorphic importance of floods, water resource management and International conflicts in the name of water and the need of co-operation in solving such problems.

Activity 9: Collect some handicrafts made from jute, bamboo and silk. Display them in the class. Find out in which area they were made in?

Activity 10: Make a collage to show places of attractions in India. You can divide the class in different groups to show attractions based on mountain landscapes, coastal beaches, wildlife sanctuaries and places of historical importance.

Activity 11: The teacher asks the children to discuss on topic Deforestation and its pro's and con's with focus on Habitat loss leads species decline and also on the Expected correlation between Human population Growth and species Decline.

- Each year an estimated 27,000 species of animals, plants, fungi, and microorganisms become extinct.
- Human migrations lead to pollution, deplete the atmospheric ozone shield, and leads species extinction, UV radiation which can change the DNA of any organism etc.
- The steady increases in human populations have an adverse effect on forest, which is natural resources; leads to extinction of some species which are widely consumed by mankind.

Activity 12: A video clipping about Mangrove is shown in the classroom. The pupil is asked to discuss on the impact of loss of mangrove. A video clipping on the Tsunami in 2004 is also shown and the pupils reflect on how can mangroves help in preventing such natural disasters?

Mangroves: Mangroves protect the shoreline from sea erosion, minimizes the destruction caused by cyclones and acts as hatching place for thousands of fish species. Destruction of mangroves can expose the shoreline to the dangers of erosion and also reduce the availability of fishes in the sea.

Activity 13: The pupil is asked to read the following article in the classroom. They are asked to reflect on which are the countries that are using large amount of papers and also on how the papers are made. They are asked to find out some alternative sources from which the paper can be produced without causing harm to either the forest cover or the biodiversity. They are also asked to give some suggestions to reduce the usage of paper.

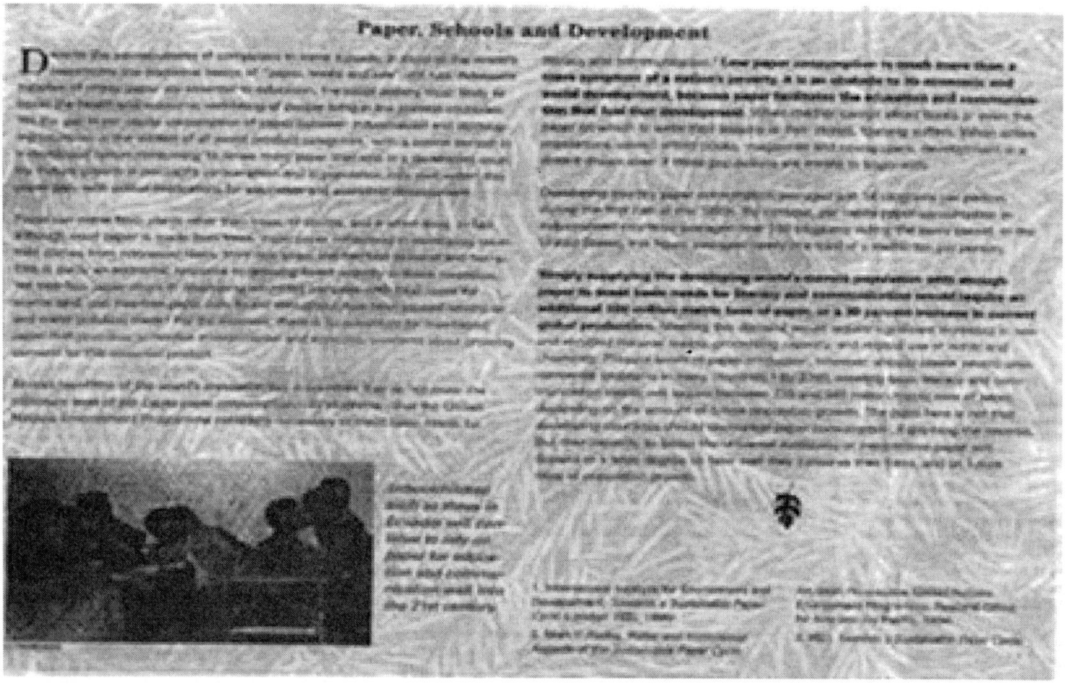
Paper, Schools and Development

Case study 1

In the state of Madhya Pradesh forests, the tribal's major economy is based on the Beedi leaf collection (Tendu leaves) (Botanical name—*Diospyrus melanoxylon-Ebenaceae*). If we do not protect the plant species, it not only cause imbalance to the ecology, but also the economy of the community. [Similarly Teak wood (*Tectona grandis-Verbanaceae*) for further information refer to Population and Environment-Impacts in the developing world, an information kit containing questions and answers, abstracts of recent scientific papers, charts, official statements and a resource kit.]

- Followed by this, the teacher can initiate a discussion on Biological species pressure/ species exploitation.
- What are the ways to restore such plants from getting depleted?
- Suggest some ecofriendly ways by which one can improve the economy as well as the environmental diversity.

Case study 2

In 1973, a scientist (naturalist) discovered that all the trees of a particular kind in Mauritius were over 300 years old. About 13 in number, they were all dying. Though they bore fruits and nuts, none of their nuts were germinating. The scientist then happened to recall that about 300 years ago the last dodo was killed there. The scientist deduced that the nuts would not germinate unless they were first eaten by a dodo and had passed through its gut. Stones in the dodo's crop (a pouch in its gut) may have helped grind up the nuts, softening the seed-coat, so that the seedling could grow. The dodos were extinct, and no other bird on Mauritius was able to crush the hard nuts of what the scientist called the dodonut tree. The scientist knew that turkey, a kind of bird found in the American continent had a crop (gut) similar to that of the dodo. When turkeys were brought from America, and they were fed the nuts from the dodonut tree, the seeds in the turkeys' droppings were seen to germinate. Thus, turkeys had to be introduced in Mauritius for the dodonut trees to be saved from extinction.

- What does this story warn you about?
- What adaptive advantage might the tree have in bearing nuts with hard seed-coats? You may do some 'research' on the climate, soil, flora and fauna of Mauritius to make up a realistic story about the possible advantages.
- Many Indian trees have hard seeds. The Indian Laburnum amaltas, is one such tree. Find out the conditions under which it grows best and the time taken for its seeds to germinate. Do you know of any other tree with a hard seed-coat?
- The dodo and the tree were 'made for each other' species; one was a plant and the other an animal. Do you know of any such plants and animals in India? List them and discuss the species in class.
- Turkeys were introduced to Mauritius Island. The island's flora and fauna had not evolved to deal with these birds. What new problems may the turkeys introduce into Mauritius?

Case study 3

In 1813, bird expert John James saw a single flock of passenger pigeon that he estimated was 16 kilometer (10 miles) wide and hundreds of kilometer long and contained perhaps a billion birds. The flock took three days to fly past him and was so dense that it darkened the skies. By 1914, the passenger pigeon had disappeared forever. How could a species that was once the most common bird in North America (and probably the world) becomes extinct in only a few decades? The extinction of this species largely resulted from uncontrolled commercial hunting and loss of bird's habitat and food supply as forests were cleared to make room for farms and cities. Beginning in 1858, passenger pigeon hunting became a big business. In 1878, one professional pigeon trapper made $60,000 by killing 3 million birds at their nesting grounds near Petoskey, Michigan. On early 1880's few thousand birds remained. At that point, recovery of the species was doomed because the female laid only one egg per nest each year. On March 1900, a young boy in Ohio shot the last known wild passenger pigeon. The last passenger pigeon on earth, a hen named Martha died in Cincinnati zoo in 1914. Her stuffed body is now at the National Museum of natural history in Washington, D.C. (Miller).

Questions

- Why should we care about protecting wild species?
- Which human activities endanger wildlife?
- How can we help prevent premature extinction of species?
- Discuss your reaction to the following statement: "Eventually all species become extinct. Thus, it does not really matter that the passenger pigeon is extinct and that the whooping crane and the world's remaining tigers are endangered mostly because of human activities."

Case study 4

A Disturbing message from the birds

Human activities are causing serious declines in the populations of many bird species. Approximately 70% of the world's 9,800 known bird species are declining in numbers, and roughly one of every six bird species is threatened with extinction, mostly because of habitat loss and fragmentation. Birds are excellent environmental indicators because they live in every climate and biome, respond quickly to environmental changes in their habitats and are easy to track and count. They also play important ecological roles—control of rodents and insects, pollinate variety of flowering plants, spread plants throughout their habitat, scavenge dead animals etc. (Miller)

- What can one do to the environment to prevent pollution thereby protect the endangered species?
- What will you do if you observe that some of the bird species in your locality is getting reduced in number?

Case study 5

The non-native Kudzu vine has spread throughout much of the southern United States and is almost impossible to control. In 1930s the Kudzu vine was imported from Japan and planted in the Southeastern United States in an attempt to control soil erosion. It is so prolific and difficult to kill that it engulfs hillsides, gardens, trees, abandoned houses and cars, stream banks, patches of forest and everything else in its path. (Miller)

- Is it right to plant some imported variety of plants in your garden. Why?

UNIT 18: ON EQUALITY

Scope

The unit deals with the meaning of equality and inequality, universal adult franchise, inequality and nation's progress, impact of casteism in India, Provisions on equality in Indian constitution and civil rights movement.

Focus point

- Meaning of equality and inequality.
- Importance of universal adult franchise.
- Inequalities in our country.
- Casteism in India.
- Constitutional provisions on equality.
- Civil rights movement in America.

Issues to be raised

- What is equality and inequality?
- How do inequalities hinder the progress of a country?
- Give some examples of inequality from daily life and its impact.

- What is universal franchise and how does it help in the proper functioning of the country?
- What are the impacts of casteism in India?
- Why are there certain provisions on equality in the Indian constitution?
- Are there laws and provisions in the constitution that are being benefitted by all equally?
- How civil rights movement emerged in America and what are its consequences?
- What are the agitations in India that were for equality?

Learning objectives

- Explains what is equality and inequality.
- Analyse the relationship between inequality and the progress of a country.
- Give some examples of inequality from daily life and its impact.
- Understands the importance of universal adult franchise and how does it help in the proper functioning of the country?
- Reflect on the impacts of casteism in India.
- Identifies and reflects on the provisions on equality in the Indian constitution.
- Analyse whether the laws and provisions in the constitution that are being benefited by all equally.
- Civil rights movement emerged in America and what are its consequences.
- What are the agitations in India that were for equality?

Activities

Activity 1: Teacher tells a story on the equality of people in casting their votes and inequalities shown in choosing education, hospitals etc. Pupil is asked to give few more examples of inequalities they have seen around.

Activity 2: Pupil is made into groups and each group is asked to discuss on some of the inequalities we find in our society and discuss on how such practices can hinder the progress of the country.

Activity 3: Students are asked to collect some news cuttings or pictures on inequality seen in our society and paste them in the science diary.

Activity 4: One of the students reads out few advertisements of various matrimonial advertisements that appear in newspapers. They are asked to list down the cases where it gave reference to caste. One of the student is asked to read out the two stories (in the textbook)—one of Omprakash Valmiki and another of Mr. and Mrs. Ansari. Pupil is asked to write 4 lines on how would they feel if they were in the place of Omprakash or Mr./Mrs. Ansari. They are also asked to discuss on the impact of Casteism in India and narrate any incidence where they came across caste discrimination.

Activity 5: Pupil is shown some photographs on inequality. They are asked about the various laws that prevent inequality. They are also asked to discuss on the various provisions in the Indian constitution that helps in preventing inequality among caste, religion, race etc. and also the importance of such laws.

Activity 6: Pupil is made into groups and they are asked to discuss on the story of Rosa Parks an African-American woman who was the cause of Civil Rights Movement. They are also asked to name few personalities who fought for bringing equality and few agitations in India that were for equality.

Project

Collect the photographs of some personalities who fought for equality and paste in science diary.

UNIT 19: ROLE OF GOVERNMENT ON HEALTH

Scope

The unit deals with meaning of health, how food was considered as in olden days, causes for poor health, condition of health in India, public and private health centres, health programmes being conducted and the Costa Rican approach.

Focus point

- Meaning of health.
- Food as medicine in olden days.
- Causes for poor health and precautions to be taken.
- Medical status and health care situations in India.
- Condition of public hospitals.
- Inequalities in providing treatments.
- Public and private health care facilities/hospitals.
- Facilities and expenses in a private hospital.
- Health programmes in Kerala.
- Costa Rican approach.

Issues to be raised

- What is meant by health?
- What is the quality of food we had in olden days?
- What are the causes for poor health and what are the precautions to be taken?
- What is the present medical status and health care situations in India?
- What is the condition of public hospitals?
- What are the inequalities we see in providing treatments?
- Differentiate between public and private health care facilities/hospitals.
- What are the facilities and expenses in a private hospital?
- How the Health programmes in Kerala can set an example for healthy living?
- What is Costa Rican approach?

Learning objectives

- Recalls the meaning of health.
- Analyse the nature of food in olden days.
- Analyse the causes for poor health and precautions to be taken.
- Analyse and explains the medical status and health care situations in India.
- Identify the conditions of public hospitals.
- Recall the incidences of inequalities in providing treatments.
- Distinguish between public and private health care facilities/hospitals.
- Distinguish the facilities and expenses in a private and public hospital.
- Analyse the Health programmes in Kerala.
- Infer the advantages of Costa Rican approach.

Activities

Activity 1: Teacher asks about the food they had taken in the afternoon. They are also asked about the need for taking food and how it helps in maintaining proper health. Pupil is asked to explain the meaning of health.

Activity 2: One of the students is asked to read out news cutting from the newspaper entitled as "Food as medicine" in the olden days and also among tribals. The pupil finds out the importance of food in those days.

Activity 3: Pupil is given a worksheet to analyse the different factors that are responsible for improper health among the modern people. It also has a discussion on the logging of water on health, precautions to be taken during rainy season and community programmes on maintaining a healthy environment.

Activity 4: Pupil is given few statements on the positive developments and negative aspects of health care in India. They are asked to read each statement and they are asked to formulate a title for each one. Each group forms the title for all the statements. The pupil is asked to compare the positive and negative aspects in the healthcare of India and each group is asked to give few suggestions to reduce the negative aspects of healthcare facilities in India.

Activity 5: One of the students is asked to read out the story of Hakim Sheik (from textbook). All the other students are asked to be judge and asked to give out their verdict. Each student gives their verdict.

Activity 6: A role play is enacted in the class about the 'cost of a cure' where two students one from a rich family and another from a poor family had to go for treatment for a viral fever (from textbook). The pupil is asked to discuss on the impact of such discrimination and they are asked to discuss on how it lead to an unequal society and how it can affect sustainable development of the society.

Activity 7: Students are asked about the different public and private health centres in their locality. They are made into groups and each group is given a concept map on the public and private health care services. It is followed by some points on which they should discuss. The discussion is initiated on the difference between public and private health facilities, discrimination among people in selecting public and private health centres and suggestions to improve the condition of public health centres.

Activity 8: Students are asked about the private hospitals in their area. They are also asked about their functioning. They are asked to discuss about the various facilities and the expenses in a private hospital. They are also asked to share any of their experience of visiting a private hospital and asked to compare it with a public hospital facilities and expenses.

Activity 9: Students are asked to list any health centres in their locality. They are also asked to list out some health related programmes (like polio drops, distributing iron tablets to pregnant women, distribution of bleaching powder to all houses having wells etc.) and its importance. They are also asked to discuss on how Kerala has set an example on health programmes.

Activity 10: One of the students is asked to read out the story of Costa Rica (in the textbook) and how Costa Rica has become a rich country. The pupil discusses on the impact of war and how does a country progress if they spend money on health and education instead of spending on Army.

UNIT 1: NUTRITION IN PLANTS

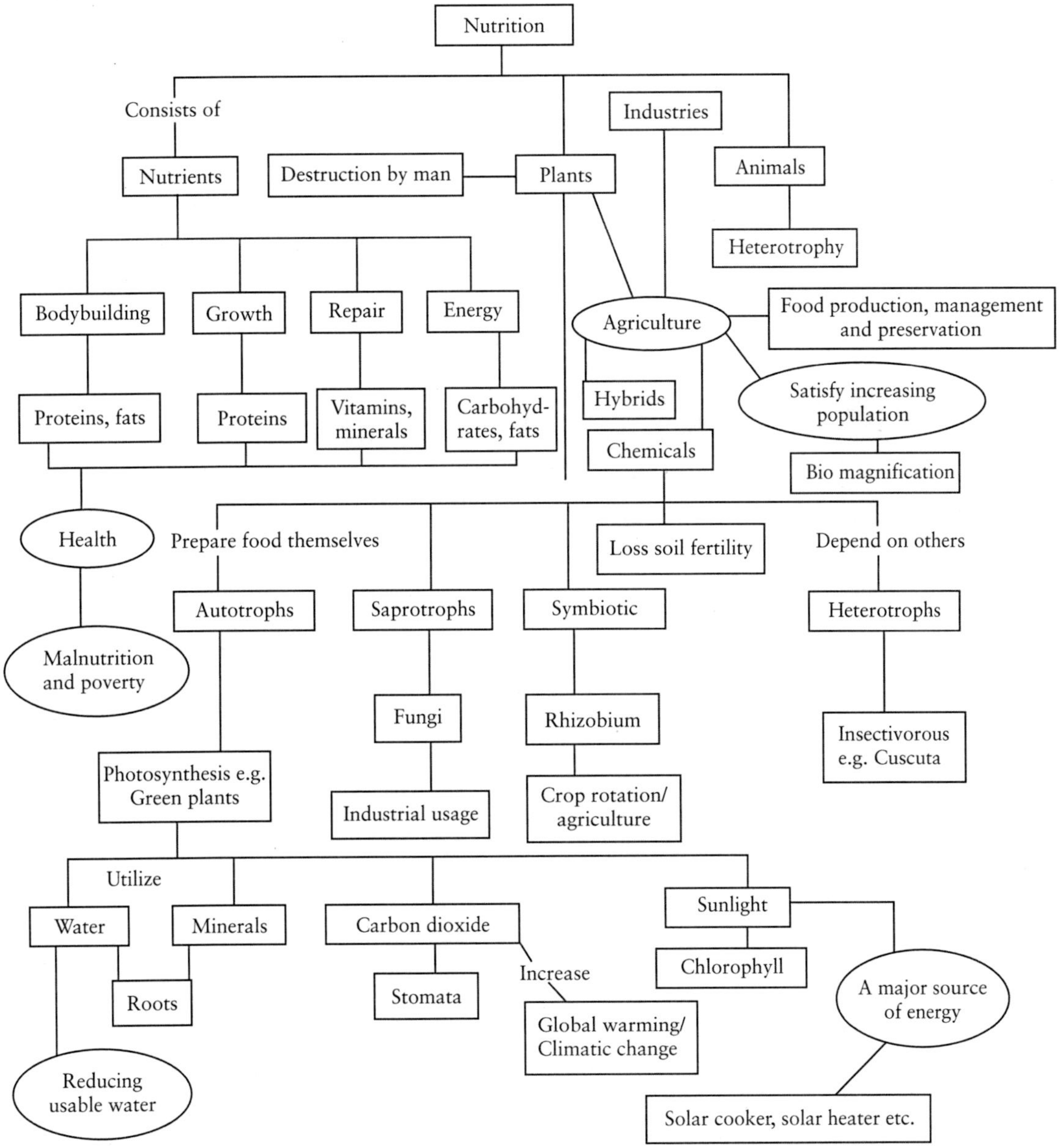

UNIT 2: FIBRE TO FABRIC

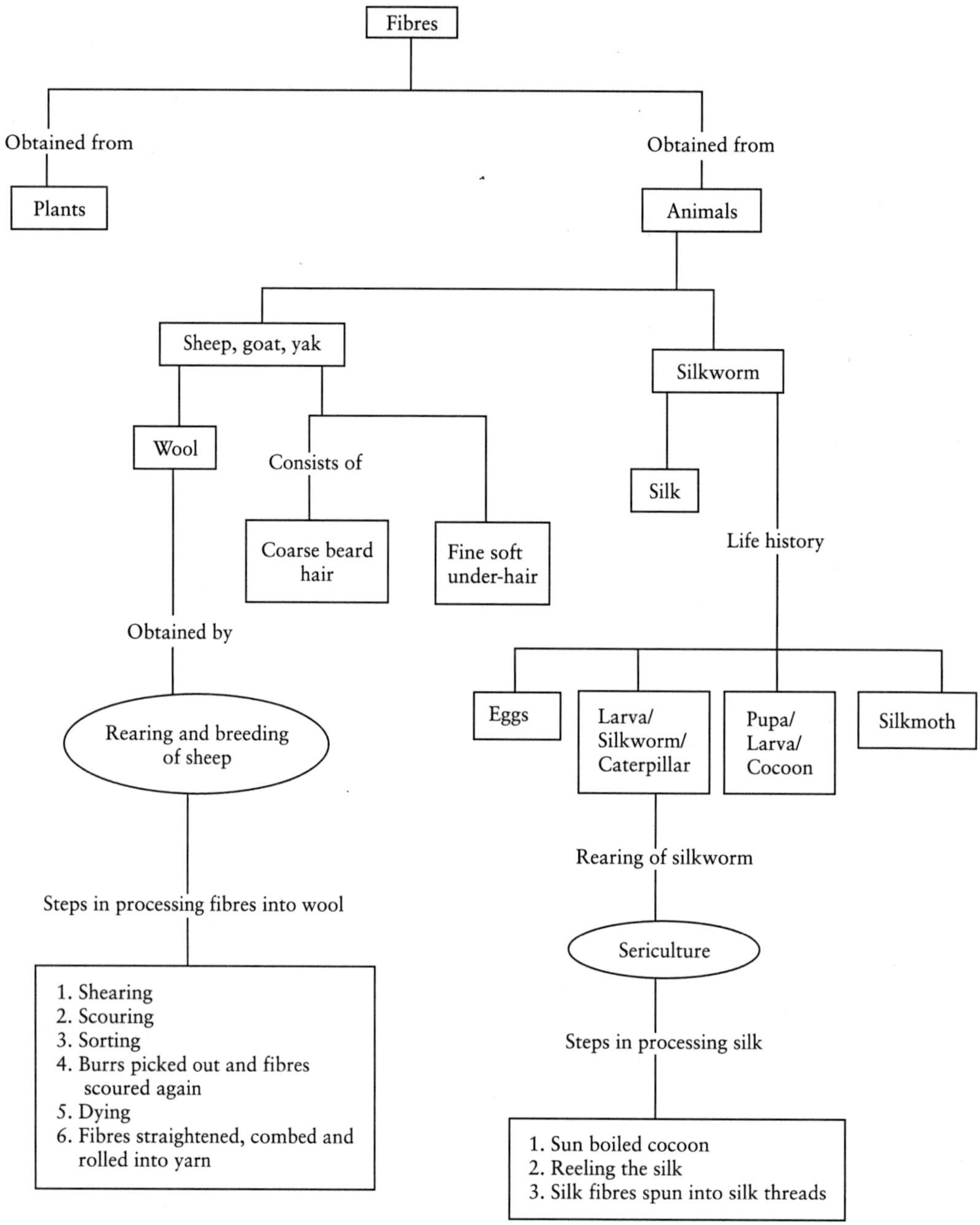

UNIT 4: WEATHER, CLIMATE AND ADAPTATIONS OF ANIMALS TO CLIMATE

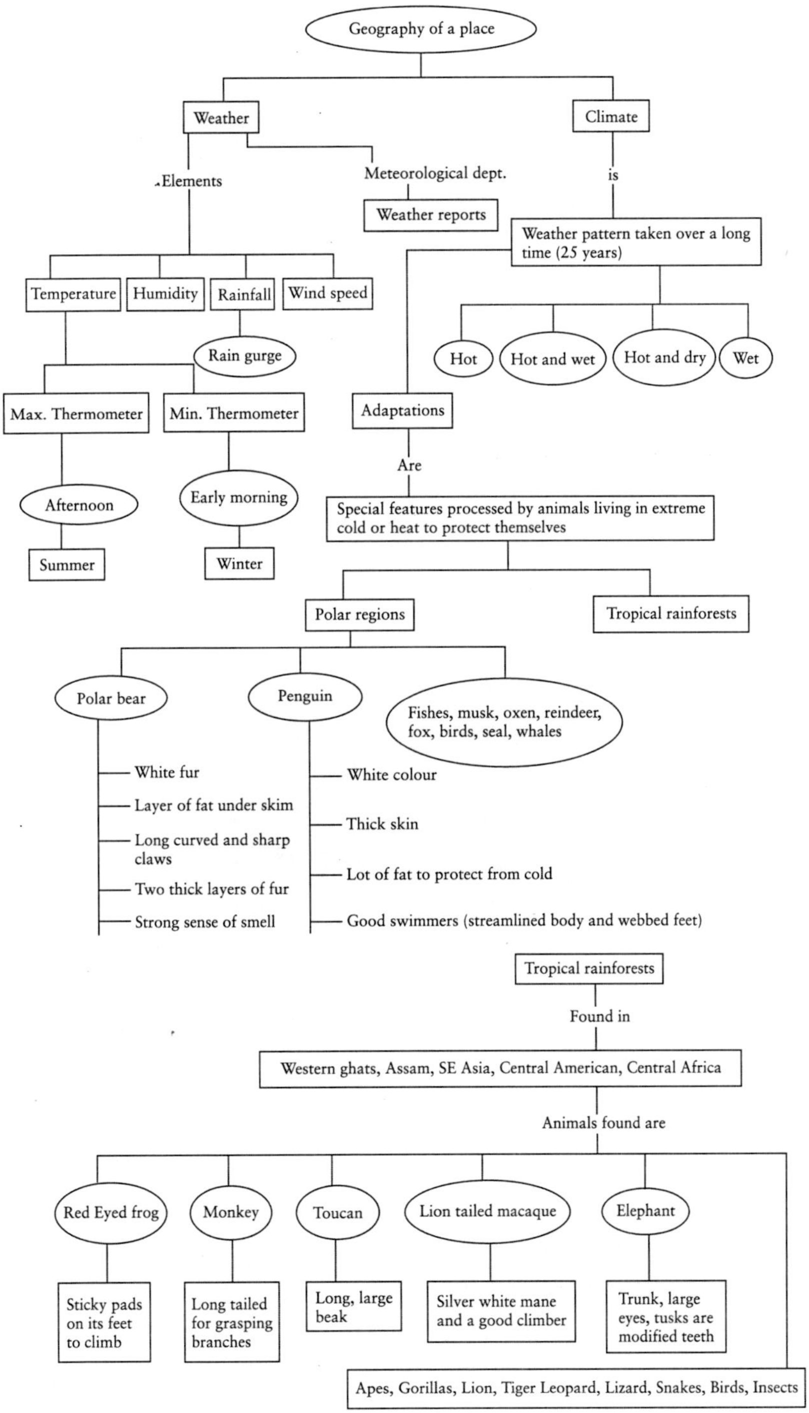

WORKSHEET I

1. What is the type of human settlement given above?

___

___

2. What are the advantages/disadvantages of such a settlement?

___

___

3. Identify the type of settlement

___

___

4. What are the developments that should be introduced to the rural areas?

___

___

5. Differentiate between the following:
   - Temporary and permanent settlement
   - Urban and rural settlements
   - Compact and scattered settlements

___

___

___

WORKSHEET II

1. Have you ever changed your place of living (towards urban), what are the reasons for it?

____

____

2. In Indian society, women earn through producing goods in their homes (making bamboo baskets, broom sticks, agarbatti, beedi), picking and recycling rubbish to support their family income. But their hard work is paid in meagre amount which does not allow them to improve their standard of life. The gender discrimination in terms of payment is also in practice. As a responsible citizen, what is your role in improving the situation?

____

____

3. Gradually in cities and towns transportation becoming unmanageable due to increasing number of cars and private vehicles. Do you think, using public transport system may solve the problem? Discuss in groups and make your suggestions.

____

____

4. The life conditions of unorganised labours (construction, waste collection etc.) in urban and metropolitan area are very miserable. They are deprived of permanent and quality accommodation due to geographical instability and they are unable to receive general government facilities like goods on subsidized cost and remain out-of-coverage of basic health, education and development services. Discuss this problem in your group, and work out some strategy to address it?

____

____

5. The extreme pollution by direct flow of industrial and domestic sewage through cannels and drains, dumping of non-biodegradable waste into river and rapid development works related to construction of roads and bridges by human activities causes threat to other

animals and birds habitation as well as their extinction. The following data is of Okhla Bird Sanctuary located in Yamuna river basin at Delhi. The following table gives the details of bird census of this year (2010) with respect to 2009.

Name of the Bird	Number of migratory birds observed in 2010	Number of migratory birds observed in 2009
Bar-headed geese	112	212
Gadwal	72	302
Northern Shoveler	484	854
Northern pintail	172	272
Common coot	231	355
Mixed flock of brown-headed and black-headed gull	345	877
Eurasian widegeon	15	18
Grey leg geese	411	416
Eurasian spoonbills	6	16
Common teal	78	184
Common pochard	28	320
Tufted pochard	4	236
Greater flamingos (local bird)	20 (tracked later)	Large numbers

Discuss in your class how to regulate human activities, so that sustainable environment can be achieved.

____

____

____

____

WORKSHEET III

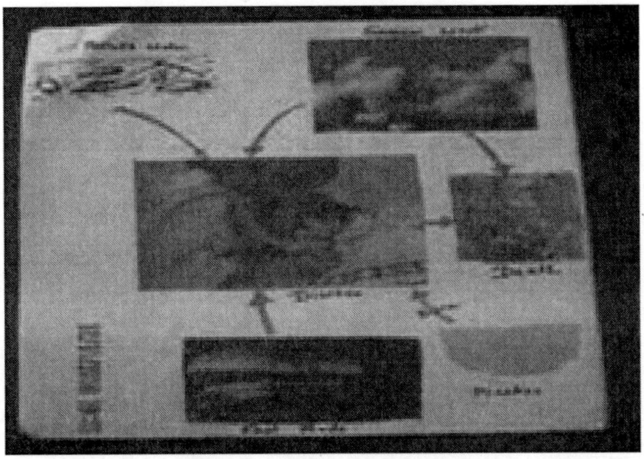

Answer the following:

(1) What are the factors responsible for unhealthy nature of human health (List any 4)?

(2) How do waterlogged areas near your house affect the health of people around you?

(3) What are the precautions that you take during monsoon season to prevent yourself from getting diseases like fever?

(4) List any two community activities that one can do to create a healthy environment around you?

(5) There is a belief in our religious practice where, polluting rivers (putting things in river, taking bath, immersing ganesh statue in river) had been done for a long. In recent times rivers becoming major source of drinking water for urban and rural areas this practice become more dangerous. How to overcome this problem without hurting religious sentiments.

(6) "Where hunger rules, peace cannot prevail"? "In India, agriculture neither intellectually satisfying, nor economically rewarding". Comment.

Conclusion

There is a felt need for educational reform that extends beyond the boundaries of individual school subjects and which requires the attention of teachers, educational administrators, planners and curriculum agencies. It is particularly important for national officials to be sensitive towards achieving a high standard of physical, social and cognitive development (Somerset and Eckholm, 1990, p. 18). In environmental education also we can see that there is a need for educational reforms that require the attention of teachers and administrators.

It was observed that in the present situation, there is a lacuna where Environmental Education is introduced in school system. It gives emphasis on environmental aspect but not the developmental aspect. If it is only the environment that is given importance, it is unilateral. Hence there is a need to incorporate social, political and economic aspects which should be considered together within the existing curriculum. It is in the whims of teachers to develop a positive attitude towards ESD and also to integrate ESD meaningfully into the existing curriculum. The prevailing teaching methods are not appropriate for transacting ESD in order to alter the knowledge on sustainable development. So, there is a need to integrate ESD along with appropriate pedagogical techniques for attaining knowledge, skills and values related to ESD.

Since ESD is a subject for creating awareness, necessary skills and values, so that the child can take his/her place responsibly in the society for sustainable development of the future, the pedagogical methods to be followed should be different. The pedagogical situations should be created in such a manner in order to make the child sensitive to the world around him and create meanings from the surroundings and from his own experiences. ESD should be incorporated in the entire curriculum starting from pre-schooling to higher education, which should be transacted in a meaningful manner using appropriate pedagogical techniques. Looking into the researches' conducted in the past, which were more concerned with creating environmental awareness and studying environmental attitude, and the trend in the world's concern which is focused on sustainable development, it was intended to research upon ESD. This study attempts to develop an intervention programme by integrating ESD in the Science and Social Science subjects of VII standard NCERT textbooks. Hence, the book is an attempt on how to integrate ESD into the school curriculum. The book will help teachers and teacher educators in designing curriculum as well as in transacting it in an integrated manner.

Bibliography

Al-bashaireh, Z. (2007). The effect of an environmental education program based on a systemic approach at Mu'tah University. Paper presented in 4th International conference on environmental education: Environmental education towards a sustainable future—Partners for the Decade of Education for sustainable development, 24-28 November 2007, CEE, Ahmedabad.

Andrew, S. (2007). Human knowledge and deep intelligence: Transition to connectedness. Paper presented in International conference of All India Association for Educational Research (AIAER) on Education for sustainable development, September 14-16th 2007, Adipur, Kachchh, Gujarat.

Anjali, P. and Chaman, S. (2007). Our festivals—Celebration for us and curse for the environment. Paper presented in 4th International conference on environmental education: Environmental education towards a sustainable future—Partners for the Decade of Education for sustainable development, 24-28 November 2007, CEE, Ahmedabad.

Annakodi, R. (2008). Environmental awareness among the high school students of Coimbatore. Seminar proceedings of recent Trends in Environmental education. RIE, NCERT, Mysore.

Apedoe, X.S. (2008). Engaging students in inquiry: tales from an undergraduate geology laboratory-based course. Science Education, 92(4), Wiley Blackwell, pp. 631-63.

Asha, R. (2008). Awareness of teacher educators about environment for protecting human health and quality of life. Seminar proceedings of recent Trends in Environmental education. RIE, NCERT, Mysore.

Atkinson, R. (2007). Bringing practical environment and development education materials into the schools of transition countries. Paper presented in 4th International conference on environmental education: Environmental education towards a sustainable future-Partners for the Decade of Education for sustainable development, 24-28 November 2007, CEE, Ahmedabad.

Bacha, J.E. (2006). Generating Positive and Lasting Change through Language Learning: ESD in Second Language Education, Paper presented at the 10th APEID International Conference Learning Together for Tomorrow: Education for Sustainable Development 6-8 December 2006, Bangkok, Thailand.

Baharul, I. (2007). ICT based Environment Education Project: A modernization context for the education of minorities. Paper presented in 4th International conference on environmental education: Environmental education towards a sustainable future-Partners for the Decade of Education for sustainable development, 24-28 November 2007, CEE, Ahmedabad.

Baker, C.S. (2002). Vulnerability and assets in urban poverty: Bringing together participatory methods and a sustainable livelihoods framework. Ph.D., University of Toronto (Canada), 2002, in Dissertation Abstracts International, 63(12), June 2003, p. 4473-A.

Baska, J.V., Bass, G., Ries, R., Poland, D. and Avery, L.A. (1998). A National Study of Science Curriculum Effectiveness with High Ability Students. *Gifted Child Quarterly*; 42(4), pp. 200-11, New Delhi: Sage Publications.

Beck, D.E. and Cowan, C.C. (1996). Spiral dynamics: Mastering values, leadership and change. Oxford: Blackwell.

Behra, B. (2007). Plea for sustainable learning through Vygotsky's approach of costructivism. Paper presented in International conference of All India Association for Educational Research (AIAER) on Education for sustainable development, September 14-16th 2007, Adipur, Kachchh, Gujarat.

Bell, S. and Morse, S. (2007). Problem Structuring Methods: Theorizing the Benefits of Deconstructing Sustainable Development Projects, *The Journal of the Operational Research Society*, 58(5), Special Issue: *Problem Structuring Methods* II (May, 2007), pp. 576-87, Published by: Palgrave Macmillan Journals on behalf of the Operational Research Society, retrieved from http://www.jstor.org/stable/4622736 on 04/03/2011.

Bhattacharya, G.C. (2007). On preparing sensitized teachers of environmental education for a sustainable future. Paper presented in 4th International conference on environmental education: Environmental education towards a sustainable future-Partners for the Decade of Education for sustainable development, 24-28 November 2007, CEE, Ahmedabad.

Binkley, H.B. (2003). Frequency of use of constructivist teaching strategies and its effect on academic performance, student social behavior in relationship to class size. Ph.D., University of Central Florida, in Dissertation Abstracts International, 64(2), August 2003, p. 348-A.

Bishnu, B.H. (2007). Comparative study of different models of Informal Environmental education in Nepal. Paper presented in 4th International conference on environmental education: Environmental education towards a sustainable future-Partners for the Decade of Education for sustainable development, 24-28 November 2007, CEE, Ahmedabad.

Borg, R.W. (1981). Experimental, Quasi-Experimental and single subject research. Applying Educational Research: A practical guide for teachers. p. 197, New York: Longman.

Brundtland Commission (1987), Retrieved on 05-09-2007, http://en.wikipedia.org/wiki/Brundtland_Commission

Buch, M.B. (Ed.) (1988-92). Fifth Survey of Research in Education (1988-1992). New Delhi: NCERT.

Buch, M.B. (Ed.) (1991). Fourth Survey of Research in Education (1983-1988). New Delhi: NCERT.

Buch, M.B. (Ed.) (1986). Third Survey of Research in Education (1978-1983). New Delhi: NCERT

Burningham, K. and Thrush, D. (2001). Rainforests are a long way from here: the environmental concerns of disadvantaged groups, summary of findings. York: Joseph Rowntree Foundation.

Chhokar, K.B., Pandya, M. and Raghunathan, M. (2004). What is Sustainable Development? Understanding Environment, p. 270, New Delhi: Sage Publications.

Chung Ko, A.C. and Lee, J.C. (2003). Teachers' Perceptions of Teaching Environmental Issues within the Science Curriculum: A Hong Kong Perspective. *Journal of Science Education and Technology*, Vol. 12, No. 3 (Sep., 2003), pp. 187-204: Springer, retrieved from http://www.jstor.org/stable/40188766 on 04/03/2011

Church, C. and Elster, J. (2002). Thinking locally, acting nationally: Lessons for national policy from work on local sustainability. York: Joseph Rowntree Foundation.

Cohen, S. (2001). States of denial: Knowing about atrocities and suffering. Oxford: Blackwell.

Constantina, S. and Christos, G. (2007). Interpretation as a disciplinary Interface in Sustainable education. Paper presented in 4th International conference on environmental education: Environmental education towards a sustainable future-Partners for the Decade of Education for sustainable development, 24-28 November 2007, CEE, Ahmedabad.

Cook-Greuter, S. (1999). Postautonomous ego development: A study of its nature and measurement. Ph.D thesis. Cambridge, MA: Harvard University.

Corvalan, C.F., Kjellstrom, T. and Smith, K.R. (1999). Health, Environment and Sustainable Development: Identifying Links and Indicators to Promote Action. Epidemiology. 10(5) Published by: Lippincott Williams & Wilkins, retrieved from http://www.jstor.org/stable/3703362 on 04/03/2011, pp. 656-60.

CUSAT (2010). Recommendations of The three-day international conference on climate change and environment (ICCCE, 2010). Cochin University for Science and Technology (CUSAT), 24-26 October 2010, *Science Reporter*, January 2011, pp. 52-54.

Dash, D., Mishra, B. and Satapathy, M.K. (2008). Education for Sustainable development. A study of attitude of secondary school teachers. *Indian Educational Review*, 44(1), January 2008, New Delhi: NCERT, pp. 97-123.

Dass, P.M. and Deal, D.V. (2007). Environmental education through community action project. *School Science Review*, 88(325), pp. 51-55.

David, K. (2007). Climate capabilities and ESD. Paper presented in 4th International conference on environmental education: Environmental education towards a sustainable future-Partners for the Decade of Education for sustainable development, 24-28 November 2007, CEE, Ahmedabad.

Declaration of the United Nations Conference on the Human Environment (1972), Retrieved on 05-09-2007, http://www.unep.org/Documents.Multilingual/Default.asp?DocumentID=97&ArticleID=1503

Deopuria, R.P. (1984). A comparative study of teaching science through Environmental and Traditional approach in schools of Madhya Pradesh. Ph.D. Edu., Jabalpur University, Fourth survey of research in education (1983-1988), Vol. I, M.B. Buch, NCERT, New Delhi.

Dharmani, S. (2007). Structure and placing ESD in the curriculum. Paper presented in International conference of All India Association for Educational Research (AIAER) on Education for sustainable development, September 14-16th, 2007, Adipur, Kachchh, Gujarat.

Dimitriou, Christidou and Hatzinikita (2007). Pupil's ideas about reducing air pollution. Paper presented in 4th International Conference on Environmental Education, Environmental Education towards a sustainable future—Partners for the decade of Education for sustainable development, CEE, Ahmedabad, India, 24-28th November 2007.

Dinah, M.P. and Cecily, A.R. (2001). Sustainable Development: The Ethics Support the Economics, *Journal of Business Ethics*. 32(2), Published by: Springer, retrieved from http://www.jstor.org/stable/25074564 on 04/03/2011, pp. 157-68.

Ding, G.K.C. and Shen, L.Y. (2010). Assessing sustainability performance of built projects: a building process approach, *International Journal of Sustainable Development*, 13(4).

Dixit, S. (2006). Children are Environment ambassadors. *The Hindu Newspaper*, 1st December, 2006, p. 3.

Driver, R. and Oldham, V. (1986). A Constructivist Approach to Curriculum Development. *Studies in Science Education*, pp. 13, 10-22.

Driver, R., Asoko, H., Leach, J., Mortimer, E., and Scott, P. (1994). Constructing scientific knowledge in the classroom. *Educational Research*, 23(7), pp. 5-12.

Dunphy, D., Griffiths, A. and Benn, S. (2003). Organizational change for corporate sustainability. London: Routledge.

Efrat, E., Zmira, M., Michal, Z., Dalia, D., Nicos, V., and Agapy, V. (2007). Multinational EE learning through On-line discussion groups and hands—on inquiries in the topic of Bio-invasions in the Mediterranean sea—A case study. Paper presented in 4th International conference on environmental education: Environmental education towards a sustainable future-Partners for the Decade of Education for sustainable development, 24-28 November 2007, CEE, Ahmedabad.

Facione, P.A. (1990). Executive Summary "The Delphi Report", Critical Thinking: A statement of Expert Consensus for Purposes of Educational Assessment and Instruction. The California Academic Press.

Fadeeva, Z. and Mochizuki, Y. (2010). Roles of Regional centres of expertise on ESD, lessons learnt in the first half of UNDESD, *Journal of Education for Sustainable Development*, 4(1).

Fien, J. (2004). A decade of commitment: Lessons learnt from Rio to Johannesburg. in UNECO ed., Educating for a sustainable future: commitments and partnerships (proceedings of the High level International Conference on Education for Sustainable Development at the World Summit on Sustainable Development, Johannesburg, 2-3 September 2002, Barcelona: UNESCO, pp. 75-135.

Fien, J. and Maclean, R. (2000). Teacher Education for Sustainability. II. Two Teacher Education Projects from Asia and the Pacific. *Journal of Science Education and Technology*, 9(1), Published by: Springer retrieved on 04-03-2011 from http://www.jstor.org/stable/40188539, pp. 37-48.

Fosnot, C.T. (1996). *Constructivism: Theory, Perspectives and Practice*. New York: Teacher's College, Columbia University.

Furst, E.J. (1948). Relationship between tests of intelligence, tests of critical thinking and of knowledge. Retrieved on 24-7-11 from http://www.jstor.org/pss/27529195

Garret, H.E. (1967). *Statistics in Psychology and Education*. Bombay: Vakils.

Glasser, H. (2010). An early look at building a social learning for sustainability community of practice, RCE Grand Rapids' Flagship project. *Journal of Education for Sustainable Development*. March 2010, Vol. 4, No. 1.

Hartungi, R. (2010). Evaluation of SD projects: Participatory approach. *International Journal of Sustainable Development*, 13(4).

Holden, E. and Linnerud, K. (2010). Environmental attitudes and household consumption: and ambiguous relationship, *International Journal of Sustainable Development*, 13(3), 2010.

Howland, D. and Becker, M.L. (2002). GLOBE: The Science behind Launching an International Environmental Education Program. *Journal of Science Education and Technology*, 11(3), Published by: Springer, retrieved on 24-7-11 from http://www.jstor.org/stable/40186543 on 04-03-2011 pp. 199-210.

Hunter, A.B., Laursen, S.L. and Seymour, E. (2007). Becoming a scientist: The role of undergraduate research in students' cognitive, personal and professional development. *Science Education*, January 2007, 9(1), Wiley Blackwell, pp. 36-74.

Indira Gandhi, (1988), World Conservation Strategy for India.

Indu and Suryalatha. (2008). Environmental awareness among student teachers. Seminar proceedings of recent Trends in Environmental education. RIE, NCERT, Mysore.

Iyengar, S. (2007). Education for sustainable development, Paper presented in International conference of All India Association for Educational Research (AIAER) on Education for sustainable development, September 14-16th 2007, Adipur, Kachchh, Gujarat.

Jackson, M.G. (2001). Effective Environmental education needs ' New Science'. *Indian Educational Review*, 37(2), pp. 22-38.

Jackson, M.G. (2001). Environmental Education in India what has been achieved? *Indian Educational Review*, 37(1), New Delhi: NCERT, pp. 20-30.

Joshi B.P. (1981). Development of science education for upper Primary classes based on the Environmental approach. SIE, Rajasthan, Fourth survey of research in education (1983-1988), Vol. I, M.B. Buch, New Delhi: NCERT.

Jubilee, P. and Manjula, R. (2008). Environmental awareness and attitude of secondary school teachers of Maldives. Seminar proceedings of recent Trends in Environmental education. RIE, NCERT, Mysore.

Judith, B. (2003). *Teaching and Learning Science, A Guide to Recent Research and its Applications*. London, New York: Continuum.

Kalton, G. (1983). *Introduction to Survey Sampling*. Newbury Park, CA: Sage.

Kartikeya, S.B. (2010). International forum for sustainable Asia and the Pacific. *Journal of Education for Sustainable Development*, 4(1).

Kartikeya, S.V. (2000). Strategies in Environmental Education—Experiences from India. International Meeting of Experts in Environmental Education, Organized by Xunta de Galicia in collaboration with UNESCO, Santiago de Compostela, Spain, November, 20-24.

Kaul, L. (1984). *Methodology of Educational Research*. New Delhi: Vikas Publications.

Kerlinger, F.N. (1983). *Foundations of Behavioral Research*. New Delhi: Surjeet Publications.

Kholia, B.S., Joshi, R., Lachungpa, U. and Das, P.S. (2010). International year of Biodiversity-revisiting curricula for conservation. *Current Science*, 99(12), p. 1637.

Kollmuss, A. and Agyeman, J. (2002). Mind the gap: Why do people act environmentally and what are the barriers to pro-environmental behaviours. *Environmental Education Research*, 8(3), pp. 239–60.

Kumar, A. (2003). *Environmental Challenges of the 21st Century*. New Delhi: APH Publishing Corporation.

Kumar, S. and Ram, B. (2006). Awareness of Environmental education among students. MERI, *Journal of Education*, Vol. I, No. II, New Delhi: Management Education and Research Institute.

Lakshmi, G.B. and Sailaja, V.V. (2008). A study of Environmental attitude of women prospective teachers in relation with attitude towards science, Seminar proceedings of recent Trends in Environmental education. RIE, NCERT, Mysore.

Macnaghten, P., White, G.R., Jacobs, M. and Wynne, B. (1995). Public Perceptions and Sustainability in Lancashire. Lancaster: Lancashire County Council.

Maiteny, P.T. (2002). Mind in the gap: Summary of research exploring 'inner' influences on pro-sustainability learning and behaviour. *Environmental Education Research*, 8(3), pp. 299-306.

Marie, D.T. (2002). Relationship of constructivist learning environment to student attitudes and achievement in high school mathematics and science. Ph.D thesis, the University of Nebraska-Lincoln, 2002, in *Dissertation Abstracts International*, 63(7), p. 2455-A.

Maruyaa, H. (2008). Education to enrich social capital for sustainable development: A case study from Turkey. *Indian Educational Review*. 44(1), New Delhi: NCERT, pp. 32-45.

McCurdy, L.E., Roberts, J., Rogers, B., Love, R., Etzel, R., Paulson, J., Witherspoon, N.O., and Dearry, A. (2004). *Incorporating Environmental Health into Pediatric Medical and Nursing Education, Environmental Health Perspectives*, 112(17), Published by: Brogan & Partners retrieved from http://www.jstor.org/stable/3435912 on 04-03-2011, pp. 1755-60.

McDonald, S. and Songer, N.B. (2008). Enacting Classroom inquiry: Theorizing Teachers' conceptions of science teaching, *Science Education*, 92(6), Wiley Blackwell, pp. 973-93.

Mitchell, B. (1994). Sustainable Development at the Village Level in Bali, Indonesia. *Human Ecology*. 22(2), Published by Springer, retrieved on 4th March 2011 from http://www.jstor.org/stable/4603123, pp. 189-211.

Mohd Nor, S. and Assanarkutty, S.J. (2007). The need for a New approach in Environmental education. Paper presented in 4th International conference on environmental education: Environmental education towards a sustainable future-Partners for the Decade of Education for sustainable development, 24-28 November 2007, CEE, Ahmedabad.

Mortensen, L.L. (2000). Teacher Education for Sustainability, Global Change Education: The Scientific Foundation for Sustainability. *Journal of Science Education and Technology*, 9(1), published by: Springer retrieved from http://www.jstor.org/stable/40188538 on 04-03-2011, pp. 27-36.

Munjanganja, L.E. (2010). Introduction, in Roland Dubois and Koontee Balgobin, Gabriel S. Konayuma, Modesto Sylvester Gomani, John Simiyu, Joy Kasandi Kelemba, Matthews Lebogang Phiri, (eds.), *Integrating Sustainable Development in Technical and Vocational Education and Training, Six Case Studies from Southern and Eastern Africa*, UNESCO-UNEVOC International Centre for Technical and Vocational Education and Training, Bonn, Germany, retrieved on 5-4-2011 from www.unesco.org/unevoc

Murtezan, I., Alajdin, A. and Mili, S. (2007). Environmental Education for Sustainability in Macedonian High Schools: An analysis of the new curriculum content. Paper presented in 4th International conference on environmental education: Environmental education towards a sustainable future-Partners for the Decade of Education for sustainable development, 24-28 November 2007, CEE, Ahmedabad.

Nakum, P. and Patel, R. (2007). Structuring ESD in curriculum design at Higher Education level. Paper presented in International conference of All India Association for Educational Research (AIAER) on Education for sustainable development, September 14-16th 2007, Adipur, Gujarat.

Nasrin, (2007). *Education, Environment and Society*. pp. 5-6, New Delhi: APH Publishing Corporation.

Natassia, G. and Beckmann, J.F. (2010). You Need to Know: There Is a Causal Relationship between Structural Knowledge and Control Performance in Complex Problem Solving Tasks. *Intelligence*. 38(3), pp. 345-52.

National Council of Educational Research and Training (2000). National Curriculum Framework for School Education. New Delhi: NCERT.

National Council of Educational Research and Training (2005), National Curriculum Framework 2005, New Delhi: NCERT.

NCERT, Annual Report (2001-2002), New Delhi: NCERT.

NCERT, *Textbook of Science*, (2008), VII standard, New Delhi: NCERT.

Olli, E., Grendstad, G. and Wollebaek, D. (2001). Correlates of environmental behaviors: Bringing back social context. *Environment and Behaviour*, 33(3), pp. 181-208.

Padmini, (2007). Environmental awareness for sustainable development—A study. Paper presented in International conference of All India Association for Educational Research (AIAER) on Education for sustainable development, September 14-16th 2007, Adipur, Kachchh, Gujarat.

Pai (1981). *Fourth Survey of Research in Education* (1983-1988). Vol. I, M.B. Buch, New Delhi: NCERT, pp. 712-13.

Palmer, J.A. (1998). *Environmental Education in the 21st Century: Theory, Practice, Progress and Promise*, New York: Routledge.

Pande, S. (2007). *Environmental Awareness Among Rural and Urban Children: A Comparative Study*. University News, 45(05), pp. 11-14.

Pandey, R., Tyagi, M. and Goel, K. (2008). Learner centered education for sustainable development in Preschool education. *MERI Journal of Education*, III(1), New Delhi: Management Education and Research Institute.

Pandya, M. (2000). Teacher Education for environmental education in India. Paper presented at the third UNESCO/Japan seminar on EE in Asian-Pacific region, Tokyo, Japan, March 2000, Retrieved on 9-02-09, from http://www.greenteacher.org/images/EE%20Papers/Teacher%20Education%20for%20Environmental%20Education%20in%20India.pdf

Pandya, M. (2004). Continuing Professional Development in EE, Some examples of course designs, Paper presented at the eighth UNESCO/Japan seminar on EE in Asian-Pacific region, Tokyo, Japan, September 13-15, 2004, Retrieved on 9.02.09, from http://www.greenteacher.org/images/EE%20Papers/Continuing%20Professional%20Development%20in%20EE%20Some%20Examples%20of%20Course%20Designs.pdf

Patel, R. (2007). Education for sustainable development—A curriculum design at school level. Paper presented in International conference of All India Association for Educational Research (AIAER) on Education for sustainable development, September 14-16th 2007, Adipur, Kachchh, Gujarat.

Paul, R., Binker, A.J.A., Douglas, M. and Ken, A. (1989). *Critical Thinking Handbook: High School, a guide for redesigning Instruction*. Center for critical thinking and Moral critique.

Pellicer, E.G. (2007). Methodology for constructing critical thinking among young children to address air quality issues in the local context. Paper presented in 4th International conference on environmental education: Environmental education towards a sustainable future-Partners for the Decade of Education for sustainable development, 24-28 November 2007, CEE, Ahmedabad.

Prahalad, S. (2007). Ecovillage Design Education (EDE): The Gaia way for ethical and sustainable communities. Paper presented in 4th International conference on environmental education: Environmental education towards a sustainable future-Partners for the Decade of Education for sustainable development, 24-28 November 2007, CEE, Ahmedabad.

Preethi, N. (1999). Damming Evidence, *The Hindu*, 19th September 1999, retrieved on 9-02-09, from http://www.greenteacher.org/images/EE%20Papers/Damming%20Evidence.pdf

Rajeswari, (2008). A study of Environmental awareness among adolescent students. Seminar proceedings of recent Trends in Environmental Education. RIE, NCERT, Mysore.

Raven, J., Raven, J.C., and Court, J.H. (1998). *Standard Progressive Matrices 1998 Edition-Introducing the Parallel and Plus Versions*, Oxford, UK: Oxford Psychologists Press.

Raven, J.C. (1958). Standard Progressive Matrices. Oxford, UK: Oxford Psychologists Press.

Ravikiran, R. (2008). Awareness and attitude of Elementary school teachers towards Education for sustainable development in East Godavari District (A.P). *Dissertation of Master of Education*, RIE, University of Mysore, Mysore.

Rio Declaration (1992). Agenda 21-Chapter 36: Promoting Education, Public Awareness and Training, Retrieved on 05-09-2007, http://habitat.igc.org/agenda21/a21-36.htm

Robertson, G.P., Broome, J.C., Elizabeth, A., Chornesky, Frankenberger, J.R., Johnson, P., Lipson, M., Miranowski, J.A., Owens, E.D., Pimentel, D. and Thrupp, L.A. (2004). *Rethinking the Vision for Environmental Research in US Agriculture, BioScience*, 54(1), Published by: University of California Press on behalf of the American Institute of Biological Sciences, retrieved on 04-03-2011 from http://www.jstor.org/stable/1314586, pp. 61-65.

Rogers, M.A.P. and Abell, S.K. (2008). The design, enactment, and experience of Inquiry-based instruction in undergraduate science education: A case study. *Science Education*, 92(4), Wiley Blackwell, pp. 591-607.

Roland, D., Balgobin, K., Konayuma, G.S., Gomani, M.S., Simiyu, J., Kelemba, J.K. and Phiri, M.L. (2010). Integrating sustainable development in Technical and Vocational Education and training, Six Case Studies from Southern and Eastern Africa, UNESCO-UNEVOC International Centre for Technical and Vocational Education and Training, Bonn, Germany, retrieved on 5-4-2011 from www.unesco.org/unevoc

Samarapungavan, A., Mantzicopoulos, P., and Patrick, H. (2008). Learning science through inquiry in Kindergarten. *Science Education*, 92(5). Wiley Blackwell.

Santi, S., Troy, H. and Saysomdeth, D. (2007). Community outreach: Using radio for biodiversity conservation in Lao People's Democratic Republic. Paper presented in 4th International conference on environmental education: Environmental education towards a sustainable future-Partners for the Decade of Education for sustainable development, 24-28 November 2007, CEE, Ahmedabad.

Schack, G.D. (1993). Effect of a creative problem-solving curriculum on students of varying ability levels, *Gifted child quarterly*, 37(1), New Delhi: Sage Publications, pp. 32-38.

Seokhee, C. (2010). The Role of IQ in the Use of Cognitive Strategies to Learn Information from a Map. *Learning and Individual Differences*. 20(6), pp. 694-98.

Seokhee, C. and Chia-Yi, L. (2011). Influence of Family Processes, Motivation, and Beliefs about Intelligence on Creative Problem-solving of Scientifically Talented Individuals. *Roeper Review*, 33(1), pp. 46-58.

Shabatat, A., Mohammad, A., Merza, A. and Nizam, H. (2009). The Direct and Indirect Effects of Environmental Factors on Nurturing Intellectual Giftedness. *International Journal of Special Education*, 24(3), pp. 121-31.

Shamim, A. (2007). Institutionalising climate change education in the secondary school curriculum of Southwest Bangladesh. Paper presented in 4th International conference on environmental education: Environmental education towards a sustainable future-Partners for the Decade of Education for Sustainable Development, 24-28 November 2007, CEE, Ahmedabad.

Shankar, T. (2007). *Methods of Teaching Environmental Education*, New Delhi: Crescent Publishing Corporation, pp. 140-41.

Sharma, P. and Goel, G. (2010). Nuclear power for energy production and hazardous waste regulation in India, *Current Science*, 99(8).

Silby, D. and Kagawa, F. (2010). Runaway climate change as challenge to the 'closing circle' of ESD. *Journal of Education for Sustainable Development*. 4(1), pp. 37-50.

Smith, V.C. and Jones, W.E. (1959). *Science for Modern Living*. New York: J.B. Lippincott Company.

Solomon, J. (1994). The Rise and Fall of Constructivism. *Studies in Science Education*, pp. 23, 1-19.

Somerset, A. and Ekholm, M. (1990). "Different information requirements for different levels of decision-making", in K.N. Ross and L. Mählck, L. (eds.). (1990). *Planning the quality of education: The collection and use of data for informed decision-making*. Paris: United Nations Educational, Scientific and Cultural Organization/Oxford: Pergamon Press.

Sridevi, K.V. (2004). Effectiveness of Constructivist approach on students Achievement in Science, Scientific attitude and Perception of Nature of Science at Secondary level, Ph.D. thesis, University of Mysore, R.I.E, NCERT, Mysore.

Stern, P.C. (2000). Toward a coherent theory of environmentally significant behavior. *Journal of Social Issues*, 56(3), pp. 407-424.

Subramaniam and Prabha (2008). Status of environmental awareness among high school students from Coimbatore district. Seminar proceedings of recent Trends in Environmental education. RIE, NCERT, Mysore.

Suda, I. (2002). Glocalizing an environmental conflict: Thai Press and Pak Mun Dam. Ph.D., The University of Iowa, 2000, in *Dissertation Abstracts International*, 63(12), p. 4135.

A. Sunitha, S.K. (2007). Audio-visual media tools for community based disaster risk management. Paper presented in 4th International conference on environmental education: Environmental education towards a sustainable future-Partners for the Decade of Education for sustainable development, 24-28 November 2007, CEE, Ahmedabad.

Suresh, S. and Kadhiravan, S. (2007). Influence of personality on the Environmental Awareness ability of college students. *Journal of Community Guidance and Research*, 24(1), pp. 58-69. Sustainable Development: Learning and Perspectives from India, retrieved on 20th March 2009 from; http://www.envfor.nic.in/divisions/ic/wssd/doc4/consul_book_persp.pdf

Tapas, C.R., and Sunanda, B. (2007). Scope of climate change education in Bangladesh. Paper presented in 4th International conference on environmental education: Environmental education towards a sustainable future-Partners for the Decade of Education for sustainable development, 24-28 November 2007, CEE, Ahmedabad.

Tasaki, T., Kameyama, Y., Hashimoto, S., and Moriguchi, Y., Harasawa, H. (2010). A survey of National Sustainable development indicators. *International Journal of Sustainable Development*, 13(4).

Taylor, A.R., Jones, M.G., Broadwell, B., Oppewal, T. (2008). Creativity, inquiry or accountability? Scientists' and teachers' perception of science education. *Science Education*, 92(6), Wiley Blackwell, pp. 1058-75.

The Johannesburg World Summit on Sustainable Development (WSSD, 2002). Retrieved on 21-05-2008, from http://www.iisd.ca/wssd/background.html and http://www.fao.org/wssd/

Thompson, M., Ellis, R. and Wildavsky, A. (1990). *Cultural Theory*. Oxford: Westview Press.

Torbert, W.R., Cook-Greuter, S., Fisher, D., Foldy, E., Gauthier, A., Keeley, J., et al. (2004). *Action inquiry: The secret of timely and transforming leadership*. San Francisco, CA: Berrett-Koehler.

UNECE Strategy for Education for Sustainable Development (CEP/AC.13/2005/3/Rev.1), High-level Meeting of Environment and Education Ministries, Vilnius 2005.

UNESCO (1992). Earth Summit. retrieved on 21-05-08 from http://www.earthcharterinaction.org/content/pages/Read-the-Charter.html

UNESCO (1997). Educating for a Sustainable Future: A Transdisciplinary Vision for Concerted Action. paragraph 89. Retrieved on 05.02.2008, from http://www.unesco.org/education/tlsf/TLSF/theme_a/mod01/uncom01t05s01.htm

UNESCO (2000). United Nations General Assembly, "United Nations Millennium Declaration," Resolution 55/2, United Nations A/RES/55/2, 18 September 2000, page x.

UNESCO (2004). United Nations Decade of Education for sustainable development: Draft International Implementation Scheme 2005-2014. Paris: UNESCO.

UNESCO (2005a). United Nations Decade of Education for sustainable development: Draft International Implementation Scheme 2005-2014 (January 2005 edition). Paris: UNESCO.

UNESCO (2005b). United Nations Decade of Education for sustainable development 2005-2014: Draft International Implementation Scheme (September 2005 final edition). Paris: UNESCO, retrieved from http://unesdoc.org/images/0014/001403/140372e.pdf

UNESCO-UNEVOC (2004), International Centre for Technical and Vocational Education and Training. 2004c. Orienting Technical and Vocational Education and Training for Sustainable Development. A Discussion Paper. Bonn: UNESCOUNEVOC.

United Nations Decade for Education for Sustainable Development (UNDESD), (2002), retrieved on 21-05-2008 from http://209.85.175.104/search?q=cache:71IoxHM4Vm0J:www.unece.org/env/esd/events.reg/UNESCO.JAN06.doc+UNDESD&hl=en&ct=clnk&cd=2&gl=in

United Nations General Assembly resolution 57/254 of 20 December 2002.

United Nations General Assembly resolution A/RES/55/2 of 18 September 2000.

United Nations(1989), Convention on the Rights of the Child.

Veliappan, Raja, W.D. and Sadananthan, M. (2008). Higher secondary students' awareness about environmental pollution. Seminar proceedings of recent Trends in Environmental education. RIE, NCERT, Mysore.

York and Frank, R. (2002). The ecological sustainability of human societies: An empirical analysis of environmental impact theories. Ph.D. thesis, Washington State University, 2002 in Dissertation Abstracts International, 63(7), p. 2716-A.